Multiple *q* and Investment in Japan

Kazumi Asako · Jun-ichi Nakamura ·
Konomi Tonogi

Multiple *q* and Investment in Japan

DBJ

Springer

Kazumi Asako
Rissho University
Tokyo, Japan

Jun-ichi Nakamura
Research Institute of Capital Formation
Development Bank of Japan
Tokyo, Japan

Konomi Tonogi
Rissho University
Tokyo, Japan

ISBN 978-981-15-2980-1 ISBN 978-981-15-2981-8 (eBook)
https://doi.org/10.1007/978-981-15-2981-8

This Springer imprint is published by the registered company Springer Nature Singapore Pte Ltd.
The registered company address is: 152 Beach Road, #21-01/04 Gateway East, Singapore 189721, Singapore

Acknowledgements

In writing the present book, we have received various types of support from many individuals either directly, through valuable comments that helped improve our research, or indirectly, through joint work in the early stages of previous projects that eventually led to the present outcome. In alphabetical order, these individuals include, among others, Profs. Koichi Ando, Mototsugu Fukushige, Toru Inoue, Morio Kuninori, Hideaki Murase, Keiichi Shima, and Akiyuki Tonogi. We would also like to thank the editorial committee at the Research Institute of Capital Formation, Development Bank of Japan for offering us the opportunity to publish this book as well as the members of the peer review committee and participants in the review conference, who provided valuable advice in the intermediate and final stages of writing this book. Any remaining errors are the authors' own. The content and opinions presented in this book are solely attributable to the authors and are unrelated to any organizations with which the authors are affiliated.

Finally, we wish to acknowledge the receipt of grants from the Japan Society for the Promotion of Science, Grant-in-Aid for Scientific Research [S] (2006–10), [A] (2010–12), and [B] (2013–16) and the 2015 Joint Use and Research Center Project of the Institute of Economic Research, Hitotsubashi University.

Contents

About the Authors

Kazumi Asako is Professor of Economics at the Faculty of Economics, Rissho University in Tokyo. He graduated from the University of Tokyo with BA in 1974 and Yale University with Ph.D. in Economics in 1979. Besides having been affiliated at the University of Tsukuba, Yokohama National University, Hitotsubashi University and Rissho University, he was also visiting researcher at Bank of Japan, Ministry of Finance, Economic Planning Agency and Japan Development Bank. His major interests in economics topics have expanded to macroeconomics and environmental economics. Professor Asako has published a number of articles in Japanese and English journals including *Econometrica, Journal of Monetary Economics*, and *Journal of Environmental Economics and Management.* He has also written and edited many academic books including *Studies on the Japanese Business Cycle.* He is also well known as the co-author of introductory textbooks on macroeconomics, statistics for economics, Japanese economy and one written for high school students.

Jun-ichi Nakamura is General Manager of the Research Institute of Capital Formation at the Development Bank of Japan (DBJ). He earned a BA from Keio University in 1989 and an MA in Economics from the University of Tokyo in 1995. He joined DBJ in 1989 and has enjoyed a long career as an economist at the Economic and Industrial Research Department (1999–2004) and Research Institute of Capital Formation (2006–11 and 14–present). From 2011 to 2014, he was also Associate Professor at the Institute of Economic Research of Hitotsubashi University. With research interests covering capital investment and corporate finance, he has published a number of articles in Japanese and English journals, including *World Economy*. He also contributed to SpringerBriefs in DBJ's Economics Research Series with his earlier work "Japanese Firms During the Lost Two Decades: The Recovery of Zombie Firms and Entrenchment of Reputable Firms."

Konomi Tonogi is Associate Professor at the Faculty of Economics, Rissho University. Prior to this, she was an Associate Professor at the Faculty of Economics, Kanagawa University. She graduated from Chuo University with BA in

2002 and received her Ph.D. in Economics from Hitotsubashi University in 2015. Her research interests focus on firm value and investment dynamics, productivity and intangible assets, business cycles, and macroeconomic policy. Her research has been published in academic journals including *Journal of Income and Wealth*, *Journal of Knowledge Management, Economics and Information Technology* and *International Productivity Monitor*. She is a member of the Japanese Economic Association and the Japan Society of Monetary Economics.

Chapter 1
Survey of the Literature

Abstract In this chapter, we review the development of capital investment research over the past few decades from both theoretical and empirical points of view. We emphasize its development in Japan, but we do not limit our focus to Japan. The starting point for this field of study is that Tobin's q theory has not lived up to expectations in terms of empirical studies even though it is profoundly rooted in the microeconomic foundations of firms. To overcome this issue, many theoretical models, accompanied by new empirical findings, have been proposed; these models do not, however, overwrite all former discussions. Following an introductory discussion in Sect. 1.1, Sect. 1.2 describes a variety of studies on the development of post q theory, and Sect. 1.3 summarizes the current understanding based on accumulated investment research. This research is based on the presumption that all capital goods are homogeneous and can be aggregated as a single capital good. We emphasize the heterogeneity of capital goods and the non-linearity of adjustment costs in investment, which constitute the central theme of this book.

Keywords Investment function · Tobin's q · Investment adjustment cost · Investment irreversibility · Heterogeneity of capital goods · Multiple q

1.1 Introduction

The standard approach to corporate investment behavior is the so-called q theory, or q model, in which the investment rate is a linear function of only the "q" ratio, which is the firm's market value as measured by its capital goods. Based on the introductory discussion by Tobin's (1969), q theory was established with a neoclassical microfoundation alongside investment adjustment costs. As is well known, however, the explanatory power of straightforwardly applying the theory to actual investment data proved to be almost uniformly unsatisfactory. Nonetheless, owing to its theoretical

The central motivation for and development of this chapter relies largely on Asako, Tonogi, and Nakamura (2014) and Asako, Nakamura, and Tonogi (2016). The content of and opinions in this chapter are solely attributable to the authors and are unrelated to any organizations with which the authors are affiliated.

K. Asako et al., *Multiple q and Investment in Japan*,
https://doi.org/10.1007/978-981-15-2981-8_1

robustness, q theory's importance as a benchmark for investment analysis remains unchanged.

Many research projects have been conducted to examine the poor empirical applicability of q theory and to attempt to modify and improve the theory. Discussions are still ongoing and fit broadly into two categories. The first includes studies that rethink the theoretical assumptions of q theory, and the second includes attempts to improve the empirical analysis in terms of dataset selection and more refined analytical techniques. Studies in the former category examine the real-world validity of assumptions such as a single capital good (or multiple homogeneous capital goods), the quadratic adjustment cost function, and perfect capital markets, and they attempt to explain the broader reality. The latter strand of research includes the search for estimation methods that can overcome measurement error in the q ratio; analyses based on panels of time series data by place of business, company, or industry; and the stricter treatment of "negative investments," such as sales and retirements of facilities.[1]

As touched on above, it almost goes without saying that the literature on the investment behavior of firms is abundant, and it extends to a variety of theoretical and empirical problems. Pursuing all of these problems at once is too far-fetched. Thus, our focus in this book is limited to the following point taken from the findings of novel research that emerged beginning in the second half of the 1980s. Specifically, the clarification of two types of heterogeneity—namely, differences in investment behavior across different capital goods and differences in investment behavior when newly acquiring equipment (positive investment) versus selling or retiring equipment (negative investment)—has emerged as one of the major problems remaining for empirical research.[2]

The capital stock that firms actually possess is composed of many different types of capital goods, such as buildings and machinery. That each type of capital good follows a different investment pattern, such as the building cycle or Kuznets swing and the Juglar cycle of investment in machines, has been well known for a long time. However, in almost all cases, the standard investment models and empirical research, as represented by q theory, assume that all capital goods are homogeneous. Moreover, the distinction between positive and negative heterogeneity has been almost entirely neglected in investment analysis, in contrast with employment analysis, in which job creation and job destruction do not cancel each other out and are treated separately.

It can be said that the main reason for continuing to use this simplification despite the poor performance of empirical analyses is data constraints. Paradoxically, the use of data at the place-of-business level as part of the recent trend toward giving importance to micro data has, in some respects, spurred on this problem. For example, in the case of listed companies in Japan, detailed statements of tangible fixed assets

[1] See Asako et al. (2016) for more information on these discussion points. For a general reference, comprehensive overviews of the developments in investment research in recent years are already provided by, for example, Caballero (1999), Hayashi (2000), and Bond and Van Reenen (2007). Furthermore, reviews of the Japanese literature are provided by Suzuki (2001) and Miyagawa (2005).

[2] We also examine heterogeneity in the acquisition mode of capital in Chap. 6.

are disclosed according to goods, but no such detailed statements exist for goods at the place of business level. Similarly, studies using data from other countries that focus on the heterogeneity of capital goods fundamentally use data at the firm or industry level. Furthermore, with regards to gross investment flows, a problem arises when negative investment takes the form of the close of a place of business; specifically, this becomes missing data at the place-of-business level.[3]

Thus, this book utilizes detailed data on the tangible fixed assets of Japanese firms that have been accumulated over many years by the Development Bank of Japan and by other institutions for listed and non-listed firms, respectively. Sometimes the data are used as they stand, and sometimes they are used after statistical transformations. We perform a variety of empirical analyses by augmenting the standard q model to create a Multiple q framework, or the "Multiple q model," which incorporates heterogeneity in multiple capital goods.

The Multiple q model was first theoretically proposed by Wildasin (1984), and it was then applied to empirical analyses by Asako, Kuninori, Inoue, and Murase (1989, 1997). Based on these previous studies, our Multiple q model adds an additional device, namely, differences in positive or negative investment behavior, and cases in which convex adjustment costs, which are a prerequisite for the q model, are not necessarily appropriate. After an abnormal upsurge in investment in land and buildings during the bubble-economy period, Japanese firms that underwent the process of eliminating their excess capacity (negative investment) after the bubble collapsed became a good source of data for analyzing heterogeneity across types of capital goods and differences in positive or negative investment. At the same time, the results of this analysis are not simply of academic interest but could also become important basic data for considering the revival of Japanese companies in the future.

1.2 The Development of Post *q* Theory

1.2.1 q Theory and the Failure of Empirical Research

Under this investment theory, which has been called Tobin's q theory ever since it was proposed by Tobin (1969), q is defined as the ratio of the firm's market value—that is, the cost of purchasing the firm in its entirety—to the total cost of replacing the capital stock held by that firm. This ratio is observable in actual data and is called the "average q." If $q > 1$, then capital investment is being carried out because real investment is evaluated in the market more highly than its cost, or in short, real investment is more advantageous than holding equities, as Tobin (1969) points out. According to the microeconomic foundations of neo-classical firm theory, the average q must be replaced by the marginal q, which is the imputed price of capital

[3] As Suzuki and Honda (2014) point out, the place of business is the actual decision maker regarding capital investment and employment in only a few cases. Thus, when focusing on the decision making of firms, it is considered appropriate to use data on firms.

measured in investment goods and is defined as the ratio of the marginal enterprise value gained from implementing one unit of investment to the replacement cost of the marginal unit of capital stock. This revision is not complete, however, as it lacks a mechanism for determining the volume of investment. One possible solution is to use the adjustment cost of investment.

In fact, as studies such as those by Lucas (1967), Gould (1968), and Uzawa (1969) show, the optimal behavior of competitive firms should incorporate the adjustment cost of investment, and the flow investment is uniquely determined at the level at which an investment's total marginal cost is equal to the imputed price of the capital. As an extension to this result, Lucas and Prescott (1971), Mussa (1977), Nickell (1978), and Abel (1980) obtain an investment function with a one-to-one correspondence to the marginal q by solving the firms' dynamic optimization problem. Further, Yoshikawa (1980) and Hayashi (1982) identify the conditions under which the average q corresponds to the marginal q.[4] This condition theoretically rationalizes estimating the investment function using the average q instead of the marginal q, which is difficult to observe directly.

In this way, a neoclassical micro foundation was superimposed on Tobin's ideas to establish "q theory." This q theory, as Asako and Kuninori (1989) indicate, includes special cases, such as the acceleration principle that has long been used for capital stock adjustment theory and the so-called Jorgensen model that is based on the concept of the user cost of capital, and, thus, it was appealing as a unified theory.

Furthermore, q theory was expected to become a powerful analytical tool for empirical researchers. Specifically, q theory led to the conclusion that, like marginal q, average q was a sufficient statistic for investment volume. In other words, variables other than q are redundant in investment functions, providing no additional statistical explanatory power. Further, if we assume that the adjustment cost function is a quadratic function of the investment rate, the theoretically adequate investment function is extremely simple and easy to estimate as well, as the investment rate is a linear function obtained only from the average q.

However, in contrast to these theoretical conjectures, q theory's limited explanatory power with regards to actual data was a fundamental problem.[5] Asako and Kuninori (1989) summarize its problems in the following ways:

(1) The explanatory power of q, which should be a sufficient statistic, is not all that high (i.e., the coefficient on q is not significant, or even if it is significant, the coefficient is extremely small)[6];

---

[4]The conditions are as follows. The production and adjustment cost functions are linearly homogeneous, the product market is perfectly competitive, and firms take the factor of production's price and discount rate as exogenous.

[5]Even in studies that competitively compare the performances of various investment models (i.e., so-called "horse races"), the results have generally shown that the q type model cannot win against the acceleration or Jorgensen type models (either model, fundamentally, is merely a special case of q theory).

[6]In the linear investment function, the q coefficient equals the reciprocal of the slope of the tangent of the quadratic adjustment cost function. In other words, an extremely small q coefficient signifies

(2) When variables other than q, such as the cash flow, value of output, or operating ratio, are added to the list of explanatory variables, these variables become significant and, in some instances, decrease the explanatory power of q itself[7];
(3) Major serial correlation is observed in the residual term, and lagged q becomes significant as an explanatory variable.

Thus, since the second half of the 1980s, a primary focus of investment function research has been either investigating the cause of these problems or trying to solve them, and various ideas have been proposed and executed. If we were to group these attempts, disregarding any time series or anterior-posterior relations, we might consider the following four categories: (i) the search for a better q, (ii) re-examinations of the estimation equation, (iii) the appearance of various new theories, and, relatedly, (iv) the deep plowing of micro data. The findings within each category are summarized below.[8]

1.2.2 The Search for a Better q

This category of studies primarily aims to improve the average q itself. First, it includes research into a tax-adjusted q that explicitly considers the effects of aspects of the tax system, such as corporate taxes, investment tax credits, and the corporate tax-saving effects of recording depreciation and amortization expenses, on firm value and investment costs. In the United States, the investment environment changed substantially in the 1980s following the introduction of and amendments to the Reagan tax system. To some extent, tax adjustments to the average q improve the empirical performance of q theory for the period when the tax system greatly changed, but they do not provide a far-reaching solution to the issues with the average q. This method is also limited in terms of considering the effects of the tax system, as, for example, it unavoidably assumes static expectations on the future tax system.

Second, fundamental problems with employing the average q as a proxy for the marginal q became the focus over time, and the idea that directly estimating the marginal q using separate, observable variables might be a more productive method

an extremely large adjustment cost (i.e., a very slow adjustment speed). Schaller (1990) surveys the empirical research using data on the United States and points out that the estimated q coefficients are roughly in the range of 0.003–0.01.

[7]In addition, some studies, such as that of Ogawa and Kitasaka (1998), point out that the value of land assets held and land prices have significantly positive effects on investment. This phenomenon is specific to Japanese firms in the period prior to the collapse of the bubble economy, which occurred against the backdrop of banks' using land as collateral for financing.

[8]Erickson and Whited (2000) also mention three possible reasons for the empirical problems surrounding q theory: q theory's assumption that only the management's expectations of future profits determine investments, the econometric assumptions for deriving the linear investment function that use the average q, and the measurement error with the use of average q as a proxy for the marginal q.

gained support (below, this method is called the marginal q approach). Here, a fundamental problem emphasized was that the theoretical assumptions used to justify using the average q—namely, the first order or degree one homogeneity of both the production and adjustment cost functions and perfect competition in the product market—were not well established. Another problem was a distortion that was impossible to ignore in stock prices that were indispensable for the measurement of enterprise value, which is the numerator of the average q.[9]

However, given the starting point that the marginal q cannot be directly observed, a corresponding trade-off is necessary to estimate the marginal q. In other words, entrepreneurs' expectations of the marginal revenue of capital and the discount rate over an unlimited period in the future must be specified, and, thus, strong assumptions must be made. Typically, researchers assume that the stochastic process that generates future profit and discount rates is stable, and entrepreneurs' expectations are estimated using the vector autoregression (VAR) model based on actual values. This method has been widely used, as, for example, by Abel and Blanchard (1986) and Otaki and Suzuki (1986).[10]

For example, Ogawa and Kitasaka (1995) use this method to calculate the marginal q by industry in Japan from 1970 to 1990, and they compare the results to the average q. They hypothesize that if the marginal q is appropriately measured, the deviation of the average q from the marginal q reflects monopolistic rents based on imperfect competition or a stock-price bubble. They conclude that the deviation of the average q from the marginal q is non-stationary and that, because this deviation is not completely explained away by monopolistic rents, the average q contains bubble and fad elements. Further, Ogawa and Kitasaka (1998) focus on the same period and compare the performance of the investment function utilizing the average q based

[9]A major assumption of the q theory framework is that stock prices correctly reflect the market value of capital stock, as so-called fundamentals (the present discounted value of future cash flows). In reality, however, even if stock prices regress to the fundamentals on average, they can be extremely volatile in the short run and can contain substantial noise. Furthermore, divergences from the fundamentals are not unusual over the long run, as in the case of a bubble economy. In recent years, research toward proposing an improved method of computing the average q that focuses on the distortions produced by stock prices has been persistently carried out. For example, Cummins, Hassett, and Oliner (2006) estimate firm value using the present discounted value of analysts' predictions of firms' future earnings, and the significance of the average q in the linear investment function improves. Moreover, even among firms thought to be facing liquidity constraints, their results indicate that the cash flow variable is no longer significant. In addition, Philippon (2009) uses arbitrage relations between stocks and debt and the Black-Scholes-Merton model and proposes estimating firm value and the average q from bond market information and, similarly, shows improvements in empirical performance.

Tobin (1969)'s original intention is considered to formulate the argument from Chap. 12 of Keynes' General Theory. In other words, it tacitly assumes that the numerator of q is not a fundamental but rather reflects "a state of long-term expectation" that moves easily. Thus, reportedly, although Tobin himself quickly realized that his own theory can be interpreted within a neo-classical framework, he had a negative view of this interpretation.

[10]Estimates of the marginal q constructed using this method are frequently called "fundamental q," following Gilchrist and Himmelberg (1995).

on data by industry in Japan to that of the investment function utilizing the marginal q, and they find the latter to be the winner.[11]

However, in the results for the investment function utilizing the marginal q, the coefficient on q remains small; in contrast, the explanatory power of cash flow and land assets is high. Thus, as in studies on other countries, it is not the case in Japan that the problems facing the use of the average q in the investment function have been fully conquered. Whited (1998) summarizes that no drastic improvements have been made by the marginal q approach in overall performance or in resolving the problems, compared to the average q.

1.2.3 Re-examining the Estimation Equation

Regardless of the various efforts to improve q, once we simply accept that cash flow has strong explanatory power for investment, it is natural to interpret this finding as evidence that imperfections in capital markets, such as liquidity constraints, have some sort of effect on investment. Thus, keeping in mind the credit crunch in the United States at the beginning of the 1990s and, in stark contrast, the close relations between firms and banks in Japan, researchers have rapidly attempted to investigate the effects of capital market imperfections, as suggested by this investment-cash flow sensitivity.[12] However, this method is susceptible to various technical problems in estimating the investment function based on q theory (e.g., measurement error in q; the identification of simultaneous equations; and the preconditions of q theory, such as perfect competition). These criticisms have resulted in more opportunities to rigorously re-examine the specifications of the investment function to be estimated.

The first issue to be examined was the problem of simultaneity. Specifically, because q and investment are both determined simultaneously as endogenous variables, bias may arise in the ordinary least squares (OLS) estimator, which, in turn, generates the spurious explanatory power of cash flow. Hayashi and Inoue (1991) show that if the simultaneity problem is controlled using the instrumental variable

[11]Moreover, Ogawa and Kitasaka (1998) add a non-fundamentals variable calculated from the difference between the average q and the marginal q to the investment function explanatory variables and analyze the effect of the bubble economy on investment levels. In their estimates, after controlling for various effects on investment, such as the effects of land assets being used as collateral, they find that the coefficient on the non-fundamentals is significantly negative. In contrast, Chirinko and Schaller (2001) use aggregate data from the major firms in Japan between 1966 and 1991 to carry out various analyses on the existence of a bubble economy and its effects on investment and, as part of a series of research, conduct a test similar to that of Ogawa and Kitasaka (however, they do not consider land assets), finding the opposite conclusion that the bubble economy pushed up investment.

[12]Hubbard (1998) surveys and summarizes its typical results and criticisms. Furthermore, Erickson and Whited (2000) apply measurement error corrections and robust estimators with regard to measurement error and show that even among firms experiencing financial constraints, the explanatory power of cash flows practically disappears.

method, the significance of cash flow declines. However, the estimated coefficient on q remains small even if it is significant.

Furthermore, the ad hoc adding of variables other than q, including but not limited to cash flows, to the list of explanatory variables lacks a theoretical foundation. Based on this notion, Hubbard and Kashyap (1992) and Whited (1992) add a borrowing constraint to the q theory optimization problem. Then they formulate an Euler equation assuming that the undetermined Lagrangean multiplier regarding the borrowing constraint is a function of variables such as land assets and future earnings. By estimating this Euler equation they attempt to verify the imperfection of the capital market in a way theoretically justifiable.

Among the first-order conditions of the dynamic optimization problem for investment, the Euler equation expresses the dynamic conditions that the imputed price of capital must satisfy over time. Substituting out from this expression the imputed price or the marginal q term using the first-order condition, one can estimate the resultant investment function. This idea (the Euler equation approach) was originated by Abel (1980), but it came to be widely used as a result of the debate regarding the imperfection of the capital market. The greatest benefit of using this approach for empirical research is that the value of q is not required for estimation, and all of the surrounding issues that render the average q distinct from the marginal q become irrelevant.[13]

However, it is difficult to say that this Euler equation approach has achieved sufficient success in a practical sense. Specifically, as Whited (1998) points out, in many cases, the verification of the over-identification constraint of the generalized method of moments (GMM), which is the typical estimation method, is dismissed, suggesting the possibility that the formulation is misspecified. Additionally, Oliner, Rudebusch, and Sichel (1995) use aggregate data for capital goods in the United States to carry out a competitive comparison of predicted performance and find that the Euler equation approach is inferior to traditional models, such as the acceleration principle, and to the q model.

Furthermore, Oliner, Rudebusch, and Sichel (1996) also point out that, from the perspective of the Lucas critique, the estimation value of the structural parameter in the Euler equation that ought to be stable is, in fact, unstable. As with the marginal q approach, studies occasionally show an improvement in explanatory power by imposing the imperfection of the capital market. However, even if these studies are robust, it seems reasonable to believe that they have only succeeded in eliminating some of the problems facing q theory.

[13]However, as this estimator focuses only on the first-order necessary condition and does not use any information on the transversality condition, which is the sufficient condition for the existence of an optimal solution, the efficiency of the estimator is considered to be inferior in theory (Hayashi, 2000). Studies have also noted the disadvantage that the Euler equation never holds under the situation that results in a boundary solution, such as the "zero investment" solution described later.

1.2.4 The Appearance of New Theories

As described above, attempts to improve q theory while maintaining its fundamental framework have been largely unsuccessful. In this context, the literature began to question the validity of the convex adjustment cost from its foundations, and the volume of research aiming to develop a new theory gradually began to increase. Specifically, a model of lumpy and intermittent or infrequent investment behavior has gathered attention, only to be explained through the inclusion of fixed costs in the investment adjustment cost function and investment irreversibility.

If we assume that the optimal capital stock level with regards to given expected earnings is uniquely determined, a gap from the optimal level is generated by an exogenous change to expected earnings. At this time, in standard q theory, convex adjustment costs are built into the model. Under these convex adjustment costs (typically, the quadratic function of the adjustment volume or the adjustment rate), as the adjustment width grows, the additional adjustment costs increase at a faster rate. Thus, when a newly generated gap is large, it is not adjusted all at once, and the adjustment of the leftover portion occurs when the new gap is small. However, such "leveling" or "smoothing" action in the adjustment process contradicts the severity of investment fluctuations that are known empirically to occur in practice from analyses of business cycles.

Lumpy and intermittent or infrequent investments indicate that a period in which no investments are made (inaction) continues for a while and then a large-scale investment is made all at once. In other words, even if capital stock diverges somewhat from the optimal level, it does not immediately bring about active behavior, and when the gap exceeds the threshold value, the adjustment is made all at once (the so-called (s, S) policy or bang-bang policy). As is also clear intuitively, a typical case in which this type of behavior is rational is one in which fixed costs are incurred in each round of adjustment.

Alternatively, a model that considers the influence of investment irreversibility has attracted attention as another mechanism for selecting action or no investments despite capital stock that deviates from the optimal level. Investment irreversibility refers to the nature of capital stock that, once it is installed, is difficult to convert to other purposes and once an investment is made, it cannot be reversed. Arrow (1968) previously pointed out the importance of this property, but it once again became the focus of attention when the movement searching for an alternative to q theory became active after the second half of the 1980s, as it can be used for analyzing the controlling influence that uncertainty has on investment. As a result, a body of research on this topic accumulated by the first half of the 1990s.[14]

[14]In theoretical studies on the effects of uncertainty on capital investment, Hartman (1972) and Abel (1983) first conclude that "uncertainty promotes investment" in the case of firms in perfect competition with linear homogeneous neoclassical production functions. However, a problem arose in that the suppressing aspect of uncertainty might be stronger for actual firms. This issue became the starting point for a series of analyses that incorporated investment irreversibility. Their main findings are summarized by Dixit and Pindyck (1994). Ultimately, theoretically speaking, depending

Typically, investment opportunities resulting in uncertain investment earnings with determinate costs are assumed to (i) be completely irreversible (i.e., the investment amount is a completely sunk cost or the amount recovered from a negative investment is zero) and (ii) have a monopoly over investment opportunities. This type of opportunity is sometimes called a *real* option, in contrast to an option agreement in the financial market, because the possession of such an investment opportunity can be interpreted as a call option that has no expiration date and, thus, can be exercised at the time that is most advantageous for investment earnings. Then, the hurdle (the threshold value of q) to execute the investment is increased by the additional cost associated with giving up the option (i.e., the opportunity cost). Thus, as uncertainty increases, the value of the call option rises, and the probability that the firm holds back from executing the investment also increases.

However, the phenomenon that a firm whose capital stock has diverged from the optimal level holds back from adjustment behavior (by selecting inaction or zero investment) can be explained only by investment irreversibility regardless of the presence or absence of uncertainty. Moreover, even with regards to irreversibility, it is not necessary to assume complete irreversibility, as described above. Instead, it is acceptable to consider whether the sales value of capital goods falls below their purchase value (partial irreversibility or costly reversibility) or whether the convex adjustment costs are asymmetrical owing to a kink at the boundary of the point at which the investment rate equals zero (i.e., whether the curve has different left-hand and right-hand side derivatives at this point).[15]

Abel and Eberly (1994) consider an investment model under conditions of uncertainty into which they incorporate both partial irreversibility and traditional convex adjustment costs, and they show that investment becomes a monotonically non-decreasing function of the marginal q over three areas separated by two threshold values, q_H and q_L. Then, they find that a positive investment is optimal for $q > q_H$, a negative investment is optimal for $q < q_L$, and zero investment is optimal for $q_H \geq q \geq q_L$. Furthermore, in the instant that q exceeds the threshold value, the investment rate jumps from zero (when neither fixed costs nor irreversibility are present) to the level suggested by convex adjustment costs, which can be explained as one type of lumpy adjustment behavior.

Although Abel and Eberly (1994) claim to have succeeded in "unifying" q theory with the fixed costs and irreversibility model, this claim has been criticized. Caballero and Leahy (1996) and Caballero (1999) point out that the fixed costs in Abel and Eberly's model are "flow fixed costs" dependent on the length of the adjustment period rather than "stock fixed costs" that are independent of time span. It turns out that, upon introducing stock fixed costs, the monotonicity of the q investment

---

on the prior assumptions, both "promotion" and "suppression" are possible, but, empirically, it can be said that at the current point in time, the rough consensus is that uncertainty's suppressing effect on investment is stronger. Surveys of the research in this field have been provided by Suzuki (2001) and Nakamura (2003).

[15]However, as we will see in Chap. 4, in a model of investment irreversibility that does not include fixed costs and has asymmetrical adjustment costs, no discontinuity exists in the relation between investment and q, and lumpy adjustment behavior does not appear.

function is no longer established. Indeed, to explain adjustment behavior with stock fixed costs, a framework that goes beyond q theory is ultimately required.

Although the differences in the definitions of fixed costs and lumpiness are theoretically important, in empirical analysis, which assumes a discrete time model, identifying both is difficult to begin with, and, thus, in the discussion below, we use Abel and Eberly's (1994) definitions when referring to "fixed costs" and "lumpiness."[16]

1.2.5 Deep Plowing of Micro Data

In empirical research on investment, the preparation and publication of individual data not only at the level of the overall firm but also at the level of the place of business has played a major role in the process of identifying a framework that empirically has a certain level of fit with reality. From the second half of the 1980s to the 1990s, as represented by the Longitudinal Research Database (LRD) of the United States Census Bureau, original public statistics data at the level of the place of business, which previously could only be used in an aggregate form, were edited and integrated, and a trend of providing long-term follow-up individual data for research purposes became widespread. Previously, long-term follow-up individual data were only provided at the firm level (usually for listed firms), so this development was a major breakthrough for empirical researchers. As a result, many studies took place over a wide range of fields, such as employment and production, utilizing the characteristics of data at the individual place-of-business level.

If we consider capital investment at the place-of-business level, we see that a series of studies demonstrates the wide range of lumpy and intermittent/infrequent investment behavior. Doms and Dunne (1998) find many cases of circumstantial evidence for lumpy and intermittent/infrequent investment behavior. For example, the individual data on manufacturing places of business in the United States between 1972 and 1988 collected in the LRD indicates that more than half of them had experienced a large-scale investment (investment spike) with a capital increase rate of 37% or more in one year. Furthermore, from a comparison at the place-of-business level, they find that the smaller the scale of the place of business is, the more pronounced the lumpiness and intermittency are, and they argue that this result suggests a background of indivisible capital.

Additionally, in a development in empirical research that advanced a step forward from simple data observations, Caballero, Engel, and Haltiwanger (1995) focus on the distribution of the gaps between the optimal level of capital stock at each place

[16]The argument of the lumpiness of capital stock adjustments on the macro level is completely different one from that developed here. For example, if idiosyncratic demand shocks are uniformly distributed among firms, the lumpy nature of the capital stock adjustment at the individual firm level disappears on the macro level through aggregation. On the contrary, even if the capital stock is adjusted in a smooth manner according to the convex adjustment costs at the individual firm level, lumpiness on the macro level can be observed by the strategic complementarity in individual investments or by a kind of "herd behavior" among corporate managers.

of business and their actual levels to clarify the relationship between micro-level lumpiness and intermittency and macro-level changes to investment. In addition, Caballero and Engel (1999) model this idea into a more formal shape and verify the existence of lumpiness and intermittency through the investment function aggregated at the industry level.[17]

In another study on lumpy and intermittent or infrequent investment behavior, Cooper, Haltiwanger, and Power (1999) theoretically show that the probability that a large-scale investment is carried out increases in conjunction with the length of time that has lapsed since the last large-scale investment, and this finding is supported by micro data.[18]

1.3 The Point Reached by Investment Research on Single Capital

In this section, we review the point reached by investment research thus far within the framework of single or homogeneous capital including both q theory and following augmented theories. After categorizing this development from a unified view as the differences in the formulation of the investment adjustment cost function, we discuss limitations of single or homogeneous capital premise evident from the results of an empirical analysis that uses the augmented theories.

1.3.1 A Comparison of Models with Alternative Adjustment Costs

As described in the last section, a new theoretical framework was developed owing to the dissatisfaction with the empirical performance of q theory, and, utilizing the opportunity provided by access to data at the place-of-business level, capital investment research in general made major progress both theoretically and empirically from the second half of the 1980s through the first half of the 2000s. Building on this progress, Cooper and Haltiwanger (2006) consider a comprehensive adjustment cost

[17] Ikeda and Nishioka (2006) carry out the same verification using data by industry in Japan.

[18] Studies that carry out the same verification using data for listed companies in Japan include those of Shima (2005) and Miyagawa and Tanaka (2009). In initial studies of lumpy and intermittent or infrequent investment behavior, such as those by Doms and Dunne (1998) and Caballero et al. (1995), many researchers stress that inaction or zero investment and lumpy adjustment behavior or large-scale investment are a series of phenomena. However, as is noted in the previous subsection, counterarguments insist that both can theoretically be discussed as independent phenomena, and, furthermore, that both does not occur at the same time empirically. For example, in the comments by Michael Woodford on Caballero et al. (1995), Woodford points out that the data presented in the study cannot be said to be evidence of lumpiness but rather is consistent with an "intermittently continuous adjustment model" through a combination of convex adjustment costs and irreversibility.

function that encompasses q theory alongside a new theoretical framework and try to compare each theory by estimating their parameters. This study provides a benchmark to confirm the achievements made by investment research and its remaining problems. Below, the main points under discussion are reconfirmed by referring to the framework of this thesis.

After observing the business environment (say, productivity shock A) at the start of each period, firms' owner-managers solve the problem of dynamic optimization to maximize firm value, which is the present discounted value of net cash flows up to the infinite future, and make investment decisions. Excluding capital depreciation and the adjustment costs of investment, the gross profit function of a firm is symbolically written as

$$\Pi(A, K) = AK^{\alpha}, \tag{1.1}$$

where the parameter $\alpha > 0$ expresses technological characteristics or market control. When $\alpha = 1$, this function is consistent with the assumptions of standard q theory with perfect competition and constant returns to scale. Furthermore, let the price or the replacement cost of capital goods be p and assume that capital accumulates according to

$$K' = (1 - \delta)K + I, \tag{1.2}$$

where K' denotes capital stock at the beginning of the next period (or the end of the current period), K is capital stock at the beginning of the current period, δ is the capital depreciation rate, and I is capital investment in the current period. Equations (1.1) and (1.2) implicitly assume that investment in the current period contributes to production and profit only from the following period.[19] Additionally, unless it is specifically mentioned otherwise, the sales value of a negative investment is equal to p, whereas the cash outflow from a capital investment (the purchase of capital goods) and the cash inflow from a negative investment are both expressed by $p\big(K' - (1 - \delta)K\big)$.

Within the above basic framework, we present five alternative models, Model 1 to Model 5, in the following discussion. These models vary in terms of the investment adjustment cost type incorporated in the model: no adjustment costs, convex adjustment costs, non-convex adjustment costs incorporating opportunity cost-type

[19]This assumption that investment during a period becomes productive capacity at the end of the period is called an "end-of-period model" following Tonogi, Nakamura, and Asako (2010). The alternative assumption that all investment during a period becomes productive capacity at the beginning of that period and contributes to production in the current period is called a "beginning-of-period model." Basically, the two models have no essential differences in theoretical terms, but it is necessary to select the appropriate model for empirical analysis according to the characteristics of the data and the objectives of the analysis. As such, we use an end-of-period model to explain the theoretical framework in this section, whereas we use the alternative beginning-of-period model in the theoretical model in Chap. 2 and in the empirical analyses thereinafter.

fixed costs, non-convex adjustment costs incorporating only capital proportionate fixed costs, and investment irreversibility.

Model 1: No Adjustment Costs

When the maximization problem for firm value V is solved using dynamic programming, the Bellman equation for optimality is given as

$$V(A, K) = \max_{K'}\left[AK^{\alpha} - p\left(K' - (1-\delta)K\right) + \beta E_{A'|A}\left\{V\left(A', K'\right)\right\}\right], \quad (1.3)$$

where β is the discount factor and $E_{A'|A}\{\cdot\}$ is the expected value operator based on the forecasted productivity shock in the next period given current period information. Here, investment adjustment costs are not considered, but because this framework is a discrete time model, the investment amount can be identified ex post by a reverse operation from Eq. (1.2). This framework without any adjustment costs is called Model 1 when mentioned below.

Model 2: Convex Adjustment Costs

In standard q theory, the convex adjustment cost function $C\left(K', K\right)$ is generally supposed to be homogeneous of degree one with respect to the outstanding capital stock at the end and at the beginning of current period, represented by K' and K, respectively, which implies that $C\left(K', K\right) = C\left(K'/K, 1\right)K$. We further assume here that the adjustment costs take a quadratic form with $\gamma > 0$, as follows:

$$C\left(K', K\right) = \frac{\gamma}{2}\left(\frac{K' - (1-\delta)K}{K}\right)^2 K. \quad (1.4)$$

The coefficient parameter γ controls the size of the adjustment costs of investment, and, as is shown below, plays an important role in terms of characterizing the investment function according to Tobin's q theory. When Eq. (1.2) is substituted into Eq. (1.4), it is immediate that the adjustment cost is a function of the investment rate I/K in addition to the outstanding capital stock K.

The Bellman Eq. (1.3) can now be rewritten as

$$V(A, K) = \max_{K'}\left[AK^{\alpha} - \frac{\gamma}{2}\left(\frac{K' - (1-\delta)K}{K}\right)^2 K - p\left(K' - (1-\delta)K\right) + \beta E_{A'|A}\left\{V\left(A', K'\right)\right\}\right] \quad (1.5)$$

from which, as the first-order condition with regards to K' or $V_{K'} = 0$,[20] we obtain the investment function

[20] A subscript to a function expresses as usual its partial derivative.

$$\frac{I}{K} = \frac{1}{\gamma}\left[\beta E_{A'|A}\left\{V_{K'}\left(A', K'\right)\right\} - p\right]$$
$$= \frac{1}{\gamma} E_{A'|A}[(q-1)p], \tag{1.6}$$

where $V_{K'}\left(A', K'\right)$ is the imputed price of capital or the marginal firm value expected at the beginning of the next period by adding one unit of capital and $q = \beta V_{K'}/p$ is Tobin's marginal q, as it is the ratio of the current discounted value of the imputed price of capital $\beta V_{K'}$ to the replacement cost of capital p. Equation (1.6) is a familiar investment function that is linear in q.[21]

Further, if $\alpha = 1$, the value function V is linear homogeneous with regards to K, and, thus,

$$E_{A'|A}\{V_{K'}\} = E_{A'|A}\left\{\frac{V}{K'}\right\} \tag{1.7}$$

is established, and the marginal $q = \beta V_{K'}/p$ implicit in Eq. (1.6) can be replaced by the average $q = \beta V/pK'$. This framework with the standard convex investment adjustment cost is called Model 2.

Model 3 and Model 4: Fixed Adjustment Costs

To explain lumpy and intermittent or infrequent investment, it is necessary to incorporate non-convex adjustment costs into the fixed costs with regards to the investment rate or to assume investment irreversibility. Recall, as was pointed out in Sect. 1.2.4, that lumpiness does not follow from investment irreversibility alone.

If non-convex adjustment costs are introduced, the Bellman equation can be written as follows:

$$V(A, K) = \max\left\{V^i(A, K), V^a(A, K)\right\}, \tag{1.8}$$

where the superscripts i and a stand, respectively, for inaction and action, and

$$V^i(A, K) = AK^\alpha + \beta E_{A'|A}\left[V\left(A', (1-\delta)K\right)\right], \tag{1.9a}$$

$$V^a(A, K) = \max_{K'}\left[\mu A K^\alpha - FK - p\left(K' - (1-\delta)K\right) + \beta E_{A'|A}\left\{V\left(A', K'\right)\right\}\right], \tag{1.9b}$$

where we introduce parameters $0 \le \mu \le 1$ and $F \ge 0$. whose meanings are explaind below. Framework (1.8) and (1.9) as a whole indicates that when a firm compares its value V^i under zero investment (inaction) to its value V^a under either positive or

[21]Here, q is the "expected q" at the beginning of the next period, as we use the end-of-period model for the accumulation of capital. See Chap. 2 for a detailed discussion on the end-of-period model in comparison with the beginning-of-period model.

negative investment (action), it selects the larger of the two. When zero investment is selected, there are no changes to cash flow resulting from the purchase or sale of capital goods and adjustment costs. However, when either positive or negative investment is selected, we assume that two types of fixed costs are typically generated.

The first type of these costs comes from the assumption that operations are suspended temporarily owing to the implementation of investment ($1 - \mu$, corresponds to the period in which operations are suspended). For this type of fixed cost, that is, for non-convex adjustment costs incorporating opportunity cost-type fixed costs, if μ is a constant, then when business conditions are better (i.e., productivity A is higher), it serves as a stronger control factor. We call this framework Model 3. The second type is based on the assumption of pure fixed costs, FK, in proportion to only the scale of the capital stock K. We call this framework Model 4.

Model 5: Investment Irreversibility

Finally, Model 5 assumes investment irreversibility, which is generally incorporated into the model in the form of the sales value of capital goods p_s falling below their purchase value p_b. For example, we can consider the following Bellman equation:

$$V(A, K) = \max\left\{V^b(A, K), V^s(A, K), V^i(A, K)\right\}, \tag{1.10a}$$

where

$$V^b(A, K) = \max_{K'}\left[AK^\alpha - p_b\left(K' - (1-\delta)K\right) + \beta E_{A'|A}\left\{V\left(A', K'\right)\right\}\right], \tag{1.10b}$$

$$V^s(A, K) = \max_{K'}\left[AK^\alpha - p_s\left(K' - (1-\delta)K\right) + \beta E_{A'|A}\left\{V\left(A', K'\right)\right\}\right], \tag{1.10c}$$

$$V^i(A, K) = AK^\alpha + \beta E_{A'|A}\left[V\left(A', (1-\delta)K\right)\right] \tag{1.10d}$$

with $p_s/p_b \leq 1$. The superscripts b, s, and i now stand, respectively, for buying or positive investments, selling or negative investments, and inaction or no investment.

Cooper and Haltiwanger (2006) essentially perform a comparative assessment of the five alternative models, Model 1 to Model 5. Rather than directly estimating the underlying investment function, they use the following method. Namely, in the first step, using data on investment at the place-of-business level collected in the LRD described in Sect. 1.2.5, they choose four statistics thought to best show the investment behaviors in the LRD. Specifically, they choose the occurrence rates of positive and negative investment spikes (an absolute value of the investment rate of 20% or more), the serial correlation of investment, and the correlation between productivity shocks and investment. Then, they carry out a comparative competition using a simulation to examine to what extent the above five models can reproduce these four statistics. As a result, although the models can fit some of the four statistics (e.g., the non-convex adjustment cost models (Models 3 and 4) fit with the occurrence rate of a positive investment spike and the investment irreversibility model (Model 5) fits with the occurrence rate of a negative investment spike and the serial correlation of investment), they confirm that none of these models can sufficiently explain all of the statistics independently.

Thus, in the second step, they estimate the parameters $(\gamma, \mu, F, p_s/p_b)$ of the following Bellman equation that encompasses all of the models (excluding Model 1, with no adjustment costs) based on the same LRD data set[22]:

$$V(A, K) = \max\left\{V^b(A, K), V^s(A, K), V^i(A, K)\right\}, \tag{1.11a}$$

where for $0 \le \mu \le 1, F \ge 0, p_s/p_b \le 1$ and

$$\begin{aligned} V^b(A, K) = \max_{K'} \Bigg[\mu A K^\alpha - FK - \frac{\gamma}{2}\left(\frac{K' - (1-\delta)K}{K}\right)^2 K \\ - p_b\left(K' - (1-\delta)K\right) + \beta E_{A'|A}\left\{V\left(A', K'\right)\right\}\Bigg], \end{aligned} \tag{1.11b}$$

$$\begin{aligned} V^s(A, K) = \max_{K'} \Bigg[\mu A K^\alpha - FK - \frac{\gamma}{2}\left(\frac{K' - (1-\delta)K}{K}\right)^2 K \\ - p_s\left(K' - (1-\delta)K\right) + \beta E_{A'|A}\left\{V\left(A', K'\right)\right\}\Bigg], \end{aligned} \tag{1.11c}$$

$$V^i(A, K) = AK^\alpha + \beta E_{A'|A}\left[V\left(A', (1-\delta)K\right)\right]. \tag{1.11d}$$

Specifically, with regards to the four statistics (moments) used in the first step, the simulated method of moments (SMM) is used to select the parameter value that results in the smallest divergence between the actual data and the simulated moment. As a result, they find that all parameters are estimated significantly and that the fit worsens if any of the single models are excluded. In other words, the results suggest that combining the various types of models that have been proposed since q theory is the only way to achieve explanatory power commensurate to the actual data.[23] Cooper and Haltiwanger (2006) gives an interpretation that their findings probably reflect the fact that each type of capital has unique adjustment process. They conclude

---

[22]In actuality, they estimate the opportunity cost type and the capital proportional fixed cost type of non-convex type adjustment costs separately. Namely, when estimating μ, they set $F = 0$, and when estimating F, they set $\mu = 1$.

[23]Uchida, Takeda, and Shirai (2012) apply the same method to data on Japan's automotive-parts industry. In their provisional estimates, none of the parameters for any of the adjustment cost types are significant, which passively supports a model without adjustment costs.

therefore as long as data for each capital good cannot be obtained, only a hybrid-type model should be empirically successful.

1.3.2 Non-linear Adjustment Costs and the Heterogeneity of Capital

Owing to the increasing complexity of investment theories since q theory and the spread of structural estimations, empirical research aiming to explicitly estimate the investment function is not being carried out as actively as before. However, it is not the case that the investment function has lost its importance as an analytical tool that enables an intuitive argument.

If fixed investment adjustment costs and investment irreversibility exist, then, theoretically, investment behavior should be unresponsive to changes to the earnings environment within a constant range. This notion is also empirically supported by analyses of micro data and is accepted as a new stylized fact. In this case, as shown in Fig. 1.2, an N-shaped non-linear investment function can be obtained that has a non-responsive section in the region around $q = 1$,[24] which is in clear contrast to the linear investment function derived from the standard q theory with a quadratic adjustment cost function, which is typically drawn as in Fig. 1.1. In Fig. 1.2, a hypothetical point-symmetry shape is drawn around the origin, and the slopes of (a) and (c) and the position and width of the area of (b) depend on and are changed by the adjustment cost parameters. In an extreme example, if we assume that the collectible cash amount is zero with a negative investment, the slope of (a) is zero, and it is absorbed in (b), as shown in Fig. 1.3.

In the estimation of the non-linear investment function, the formulation of adjustment costs by Barnett and Sakellaris (1998) that simplifies the model of Abel and Eberly (1994) is widely known for its convenience and has been frequently used for empirical analysis, including by Suzuki (2001) and Suzuki and Honda (2014). Empirical findings on the concrete shape of this non-linearity are not necessarily consistent, and much empirical research, including studies by Barnett and Sakellaris (1998) and Honda and Suzuki (2000), has observed an S-shaped investment function similar to a logistic curve that indicates the existence of a non-response range with regards to q at both ends of the distribution of q,[25] as is shown in Fig. 1.4.

[24] As is argued in the previous section, for a combination of investment irreversibility and convex adjustment costs, the continuity of the function is maintained despite the shape of the investment function, as in Fig. 1.2 with the kink. In contrast, for a combination of fixed adjustment costs and convex adjustment costs that is to be discussed in the case of the Multiple q model, in the instant that the zero investment area is exceeded, the investment rate jumps from zero, and the function becomes discontinuous, as is seen in Fig. 4.1 in Chap. 4.

[25] The S-shaped form consists of the part in which the investment rate becomes convex for q, as in the section from (a) to (b) in Fig. 1.4, and the part that is concave, as in the section from (b) to (c) in the same figure. However, in Barnett and Sakellaris (1998), the convex part is not necessarily observed clearly.

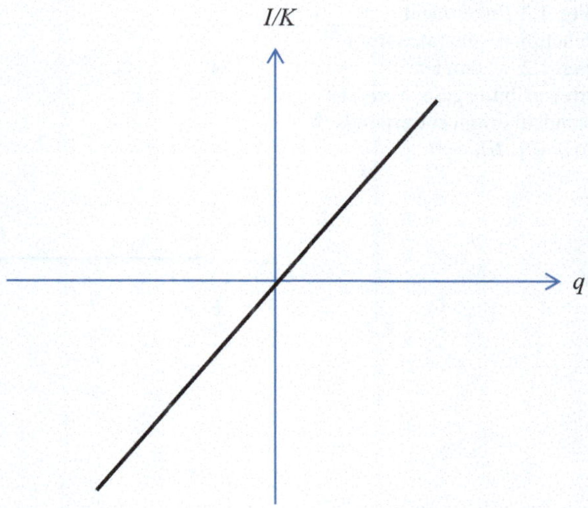

Fig. 1.1 Linear investment function derived from q theory. *Note* The standard origin corresponds to $q = 1$, $I/K = 0$

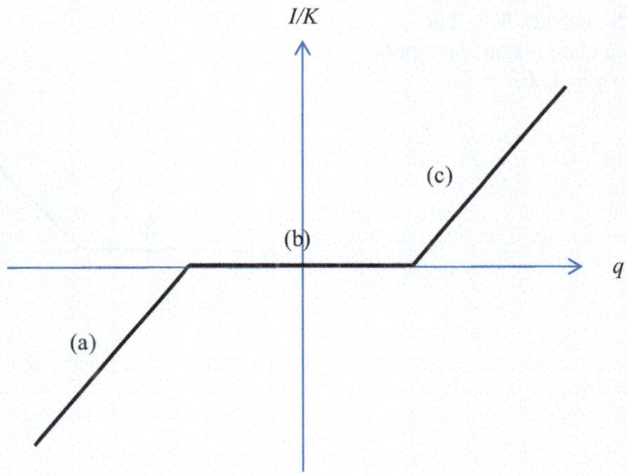

Fig. 1.2 Non-linear investment function with an insensitive section to q (N-shaped). *Note* The standard origin corresponds to $q = 1$, $I/K = 0$

This finding can be considered to indicate the removal of part (a) in the non-linear investment function suggesting investment irreversibility, as in Fig. 1.2, and the addition of part (c).

Regarding this result, a debate remains as to whether the non-existence of part (a) in Fig. 1.2 can be considered evidence of complete irreversibility, as in Fig. 1.3, or if it simply reflects the lack of negative investment data[26] and does not contradict investment irreversibility. On one hand, the concave portion with regards

[26]Theoretically, capital investment should be defined as the amount of new acquisitions of capital goods minus the amount sold or retired, but because the amount of sold or retired is difficult to obtain and unreliable, empirical research frequently uses the amount of new acquisitions as a proxy variable. Moreover, negative investment at the firm level is considered to frequently occur in the form of an abolition of a place of business. However, individual data at the place-of-business level

Fig. 1.3 Investment function degenerated from Fig. 1.2: a complete irreversibility case. *Note* The standard origin corresponds to $q = 1, I/K = 0$

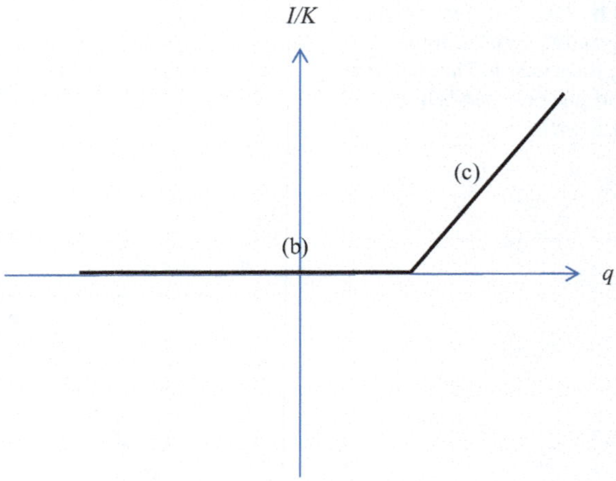

Fig. 1.4 Logistic-type investment function (S-shaped). *Note* The standard origin corresponds to $q = 1, I/K = 0$

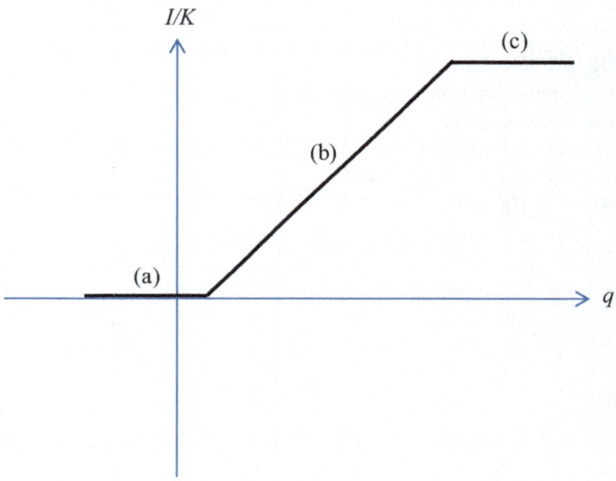

to q, as reflected by the section from (b) to (c) in Fig. 1.4, requires an explanation that goes beyond the framework of investment irreversibility. For example, from a theoretical perspective, one possibility is that the portion suggests the existence of prohibitive adjustment costs with regards to an enormous investment. However, from an empirical perspective, we may consider that if the average q is used as a proxy for q, then an explanation for this finding is that stock prices are influenced by a bubble economy, as in Bond and Cummins (2000). If the dispersion of the average q to the upper side is indeed large, then the slope of the investment function is flat. However, an S-shaped investment function has been widely observed even in studies that do not use the average q.

---

typically omits such cases from the sample, and, thus, these cases are not recognized as negative investments.

The problem, as identified by Eberly (1997), who estimates a model that encompasses an adjustment cost function of multiple classifications at the same time, is that investment functions made up of only the convex part have been observed. Namely, these observations reflect investment behavior that become more responsive to q when q is higher. As a cause of mixing the convex and concave parts with regards to q, Abel and Eberly (2002) consider the heterogeneity of capital goods.

That is to say, upon allowing different threshold values of q for the upper limits of the non-responsive areas for different classifications of capital goods, an increase in q in the area where q is low results not only in an intensive margin that increases investment in capital goods that have already responded to q but also in an extensive margin such that capital goods that up to that time have been non-responsive to q become responsive. However, in an area of sufficiently high q, all capital goods exceed the threshold value, and only the intensive margin is relevant. At this time, if the threshold value follows a normal distribution, the aggregated investment function with regards to q has an S-shaped form that is convex if q is low and concave if q is high. According to Eberly (1997), the reason that she strongly observes the convex part in her data and Barnett and Sakellaris (1998) strongly observe the concave part in their data is that the former uses a balanced panel of listed firms and the latter uses a non-balanced panel that includes small and medium sized firms and that, in many cases, the data of the latter study correspond to an area of relatively high q.

1.3.3 Toward Estimation of the Investment Function According to Capital Goods

Since at least the study of Wildasin (1984), who extended q theory to cases of multiple goods, the importance of explicitly analyzing the heterogeneity of capital goods has been understood. Today, when trends in new research have tried to overcome the limitations of q theory in a world of single capital goods and have brought about certain level of results, it is extremely interesting that, once again, awareness of the heterogeneity of capital goods has been raised. However, even during the interim period, some sporadic empirical research focused on the heterogeneity of capital goods. Here, we introduce some examples of studies other than those on the Multiple q model, which are described starting in the next chapter.

Chirinko (1993) uses data at the firm level in the United States and attempts to verify whether the poor empirical performance of the conventional q model that assumes a single capital good is due to a misspecification of the homogeneity of capital goods or to measurement error in q. He explicitly considers the heterogeneity of capital goods, in a way which differs slightly from Wildasin (1984) with regards to the parameters of adjustment costs, dismisses the null hypothesis of homogeneity, and obtains the finding that the parameters that indicate the size of the adjustment costs are higher for structures than for machinery and appliances. Moreover, he dismisses the measurement error hypothesis. Similarly, after a series of empirical analyses in the United States using macro data, including studies of the q model, Oliner et al. (1995) confirm that the precision of estimates and forecasts for structures is inferior to those for machinery and appliances, and they indicate that the reason for this result may be that structures are composed of more diverse contents.

As a reason for the low explanatory power of the q model, Goolsbee and Gross (1997) point out that the heterogeneity of capital is an important problem but is not discussed very frequently. For example, when a firm buys a certain type of capital and sells a different type of capital with the same value, if the heterogeneity of capital is not recognized, the balance of the investment amount is considered to be zero. However, the adjustment costs are not zero. Thus, using a unique data set consisting of 16 types of capital goods in the airline industry in the United States, they measure the shape of the investment function. The result suggests an N-shaped investment function, as in Fig. 1.2, and the non-responsive area is clearly longer in the positive direction. Moreover, whether positive or negative, the investment function is linear in the responsive area, suggesting a standard quadratic adjustment cost function. However, the non-linearity of these different capital goods disappears when estimating the investment function in a standard q model setting with an aggregation at the firm level. Further, the slope of aggregate investment function is underestimated compared to that observed in the responsive area of non-linear investment function of each type of capital.

Bontempi, Boca, Franzosi, Galeotti, and Rota (2004) use panel data on Italian, non-listed, medium-to-small firms and estimate the linear investment function with GMM separately according to capital goods ("structures" and "machinery and appliances") using the marginal q approach. Their results for the investment function of machinery and appliances are consistent with the q theory that assumes a traditional quadratic adjustment cost function, and they are significant and pass the over-identification test. In contrast, in their results for structures, the coefficient is not significant and suggests a misspecification.

Conversely, Boca, Galeotti, and Rota (2008) use the same data and estimate the investment function in the form of allowing non-linearity in marginal q, including for machinery and appliances. Specifically, they adopt a piecewise linear function and statistically verify the validity of the formulation for no kink (that is, a normal linear investment function), two kink points, and four kink points, and they find that the model with four kink points is basically supported. Moreover, they use this formulation to estimate the kink points and slopes of each portion for structures and for machinery and appliances. For values of q below a certain threshold in either category of capital, they confirm that the curve follows an S-shape (Fig. 1.4) rather than an N-shape (Fig. 1.2). Thus, as far as this S-shape appears by the mechanism of the extensive and intensive margins described by Abel and Eberly (2002), it indicates that unobservable heterogeneity remains within each category of capital.

Goolsbee and Gross (1997), Bontempi et al. (2004), and Boca et al. (2008) all possess micro data by the category of capital goods not only in terms of net capital investment but also of new acquisitions and of sales and retirements separately. Thus, in addition to the net investment function, they further attempt to estimate the gross investment function for new acquisitions only and for sales and retirements only.

They are similar in that their estimation results for new acquisitions only roughly conform with the net investment function, whereas, in contrast, a correlation with q is hardly observed for sales and retirements. Abel and Eberly (2002), who do not consider the heterogeneity of capital goods, also estimate the investment function for new acquisitions only and for sales and retirements only and find that q has no significant effect for the latter. However, q has a negative and significant effect on the probability of implementing sales and retirements, indicating that fixed adjustment costs exist for negative investments.

If we consider the relative frequency and magnitude of new acquisitions and sales and retirements (the former is usually overwhelmingly more frequent and of larger scale), it is natural that the same trends are seen between the results of the net investment function (i.e., the usual definition of capital investment) and those of the investment function for new acquisitions only. However, with regards to sale and retirement behavior, despite the fact that this behavior is clearly different from new acquisitions behavior, little usable data is available and many points still require elucidation. Together with the category of capital goods, the exploration of the heterogeneity in terms of positive and negative investments is one of the most important problems remaining for the empirical analysis of investment.

1.4 Concluding Remarks

In this chapter, we briefly looked back at the development of capital investment research over the past few decades from both theoretical and empirical points of view, focusing on its development in Japan but considering studies from other areas as well.

The tipping point of capital investment research is that q theory, a theory rooted in neoclassical microeconomic foundations that had been considered the culmination of investment theory in unifying traditional investment functions, did not live up to expectations in terms of empirical studies. To overcome this issue, the investment model has been developed in a variety of ways, and new empirical findings have been obtained from micro data at the place-of-business level, and research has accumulated at a remarkable speed.

However, these developments have not overwritten all former discussions. The convex investment adjustment cost function assumed by q theory still coexists with new theories that are an essential element in describing investment behavior such as lumpy, intermittent investment. We have not emphasized this fact so far, but one reason for this coexistence includes differences in the level of aggregation with respect to the investment entity. For example, recent dynamic stochastic general equilibrium macroeconomic models often incorporate the investment model proposed by Christiano, Eichenbaum, and Evans (2005) (CEE), which is considered to be highly consistent with aggregate data and is employed as a standard. This function type imposes a penalty on changes in the investment level consistent with the convex adjustment cost, and further it can explain the influences of past investment levels (one of the anomalies regarding q theory). In other words, it implies stickier investment behavior than q theory does, in contrast to the theory of lumpy, intermittent investment. According to Eberly, Rebelo, and Vincent (2011), the CEE model possesses relatively high explanatory power with regards to the investment behavior of large companies because, as Doms and Dunne (1998) suggest, aggregation may have leveled lumpy, intermittent investment behavior on the place-of-business level.[27]

In the remainder of this book, after developing the theoretical discussion of the Multiple q model in Chap. 2, we perform empirical analyses from Chap. 3 onwards. Namely, Chap. 3 presents our investment data for firms that are classified into five categories of capital goods. We discuss why and how we construct each firm's capital stock data with three different methods depending on the evaluation of capital disinvestment through sales and retirements. In Chap. 4, we first estimate firm's investment function for each capital good within the Multiple q framework, and we test the homogeneity of capital goods. Then, we analyze the possibility of departure from the linear investment function by introducing fixed costs in adjusting investments, which provides a clue to lumpy investment. In Chaps. 5 and 6, we update the sample periods and extend the Multiple q model to incorporate firm-size-dependent heterogeneity of capital goods and acquisition-mode-dependent heterogeneity of capital goods, respectively.

References

Abel, A. B. (1980). Empirical investment equations: An integrative framework. In K. Brunner & A. H. Meltzer (Eds.), *On the state of macroeconomics, vol. 12 of the Carnegie-Rochester conference series* (pp. 39–91). Elsevier.

Abel, A. B. (1983). Optimal investment under uncertainty. *American Economic Review, 73,* 228–233.

Abel, A. B., & Blanchard, O. J. (1986). The present value of profits and cyclical movements in investment. *Econometrica, 54,* 249–273.

Abel, A. B., & Eberly, J. C. (1994). A unified model of investment under uncertainty. *American Economic Review, 84,* 1369–1384.

Abel, A. B., & Eberly, J. C. (2002). Investment and q with fixed costs: An empirical analysis. In *Mimeographed.* Northwestern University.

Arrow, K. J. (1968). Optimal capital policy with irreversible investment. In J. N. Wolfe (Ed.), *Value, capital, and growth, essays in honor of sir John Hicks* (pp. 1–19). Edinburgh University Press.

Asako, K., & M. Kuninori (1989). Capital investment theory and empirical research in Japan. In H. Uzawa (Ed.), *Japanese economy: The trajectory of accumulation and growth* (pp. 151–182). University of Tokyo Press. (In Japanese).

Asako, K., Kuninori, M., Inoue, T., & Murase, H. (1989). Land evaluation and measurement of Tobin's q theory / Estimation of Multiple q. *Economics Today, 10*(3). (In Japanese).

[27]Interestingly, they describe another very practical backdrop, as follows. When a senior manager (with the authority to make a final decision on an investment project) assesses the investment budget of each division, they tend to set the previous year's budget as a starting line. If this is the case, the larger the divergence from the previous year is, the lower the probability of budget approval is. Such behavioral traits in decision making process apparently result in the sticky nature of investment.

Asako, K., Kuninori, M., Inoue, T., & Murase, H. (1997). Capital investment and land investment: 1977–1994. In K. Asako & M. Otaki (Eds.), *Dynamics of modern macroeconomics* (pp. 323–349). University of Tokyo Press. (In Japanese).
Asako, K., Nakamura, J., & Tonogi, K. (2016). The development of investment research and Multiple *q* in Japan. *International Journal of Finance and Accounting, 5*(5A), 1–29.
Asako, K., Tonogi, K., & Nakamura, J. (2014). Frontier of investment research—elucidation of heterogeneity and Multiple *q* model. In A. Horiuchi, M. Hanazaki, & J. Nakamura (Eds.), *The Japanese economy: Financial development and corporate behavior in a changing environment* (pp. 153–208). University of Tokyo Press. (In Japanese).
Barnett, S., & Sakellaris, P. (1998). Non–linear response of firm investment to ***Q***: Testing a model of convex and non-convex adjustment costs. *Journal of Monetary Economics, 42,* 261–288.
Boca, A. D., Galeotti, M., & Rota, P. (2008). Non-convexities in the adjustment of different capital inputs: A firm level investigation. *European Economic Review, 52,* 315–337.
Bond, S. D., & Cummins, J. G. (2000). The stock market and investment in the new economy: Some tangible facts and intangible fictions. *Brookings Papers on Economic Activity, 2000*(1), 61–124.
Bond, S., & Van Reenen, J. (2007). Microeconometric models of investment and employment. In J. J. Heckman & E. E. Leamer (Eds.), *Handbook of econometrics* (pp. 4417–4498). North Holland.
Bontempi, E., Boca, A. D., Franzosi, A., Galeotti, M., & Rota, P. (2004). Capital heterogeneity: Does it matter? Fundamental *Q* and investment on a panel of Italian firms. *RAND Journal of Economics, 35,* 674–690.
Caballero, R. J. (1999). Aggregate investment. In J. B. Taylor & M. Woodford (Eds.), *Handbook of macroeconomics* (pp. 813–862). North Holland.
Caballero, R. J., & Engel, E. (1999). Explaining investment dynamics in U.S. manufacturing: A generalized (*S, s*) approach. *Econometrica, 67,* 783–826.
Caballero, R. J., Engel, E., & Haltiwanger, J. C. (1995). Plant–level adjustment and aggregate investment dynamics. *Brookings Papers on Economic Activity, 1995*(2), 1–54.
Caballero, R. J., & Leahy, J. (1996). *Fixed costs: The demise of marginal q*. NBER Working Paper, No. 5508.
Chirinko, R. S. (1993). Multiple capital inputs, *Q*, and investment spending. *Journal of Economic Dynamics and Control, 17,* 907–928.
Chirinko, R. S., & Schaller, H. (2001). Business fixed investment and 'Bubbles': The Japanese case. *American Economic Review, 91,* 663–680.
Christiano, L. J., Eichenbaum, M., & Evans, C. L. (2005). Nominal rigidities and the dynamic effects of a shock to monetary policy. *Journal of Political Economy, 113,* 1–45.
Cooper, R., & Haltiwanger, J. C. (2006). On the nature of capital adjustment costs. *Review of Economic Studies, 73,* 611–633.
Cooper, R., Haltiwanger, J., & Power, L. (1999). Machine replacement and the business cycle: Lumps and bumps. *American Economic Review, 89*(4), 921–946.
Cummins, J. G., Hassett, K. A., & Oliner, S. D. (2006). Investment behavior, observable expectations, and internal funds. *American Economic Review, 96,* 796–810.
Dixit, A., & Pindyck, R. (1994). *Investment under Uncertainty*. Princeton University Press.
Doms, M., & Dunne, T. (1998). Capital adjustment patterns in manufacturing plants. *Review of Economic Dynamics, 1,* 409–429.
Eberly, J. C. (1997). International evidence on investment and fundamentals. *European Economic Review, 41,* 1055–1078.
Eberly, J. C., Rebelo, S., & Vincent, N. (2011). What explains the lagged investment effect? *Journal of Monetary Economics, 59,* 370–380.
Erickson, T., & Whited, T. (2000). Measurement error and the relationship between investment and *q*. *Journal of Political Economy, 108,* 1027–1057.
Gilchrist, S., & Himmelberg, C. (1995). The role of cash flow in reduced-form investment equations. *Journal of Monetary Economics, 36,* 541–572.
Goolsbee, A., & Gross, D. (1997). *Estimating adjustment costs with data on heterogeneous capital goods*. NBER Working Paper, No. 6342.

Gould, J. P. (1968). Adjustment costs in the theory of investment of the firm. *Review of Economic Studies, 35,* 47–56.

Hartman, R. (1972). The effects of price and cost uncertainty on investment. *Journal of Economic Theory, 5,* 258–266.

Hayashi, F. (1982). Tobin's marginal and average *q*: A neoclassical interpretation. *Econometrica, 50,* 213–224.

Hayashi, F. (2000). The cost of capital, *Q*, and the theory of investment demand. In L. Lau (Ed.), *Econometrics vol. 2 econometrics and the cost of capital* (pp. 55–83). MIT Press.

Hayashi, F., & Inoue, T. (1991). The relation between firm growth and *Q* with multiple capital goods: Theory and evidence from panel data on Japanese firms. *Econometrica, 59,* 731–753.

Honda, Y., & Suzuki, K. (2000). Estimation of the investment thresholds of large Japanese manufacturers. *Japanese Economic Review, 51,* 473–491.

Hubbard, R. G. (1998). Capital-market imperfections and investment. *Journal of Economic Literature, 36,* 193–225.

Hubbard, R. G., & Kashyap, A. K. (1992). Internal net worth and the investment process: An application to U.S. agriculture. *Journal of Political Economy, 100,* 506–534.

Ikeda, D., & Nishioka, S. (2006). *Intermittent capital investment (lumpy investment): Analysis based on the generalized (S, s) model.* Bank of Japan Working Paper Series, No. 06-J-15. (In Japanese).

Lucas, R. E. (1967). Adjustment costs and the theory of supply. *Journal of Political Economy, 75,* 321–334.

Lucas, R. E., & Prescott, E. (1971). Investment under uncertainty. *Econometrica, 39,* 659–682.

Miyagawa, T. (2005). *The economics of long-term stagnation –globalization and the transformation of industrial structure*. University of Tokyo Press. (In Japanese).

Miyagawa, T., & Tanaka, K. (2009). Corporate investment behavior in the Japanese economy. K. Fukao (Ed.), *Japanese economy and economic policy in the bubble/deflationary period vol. 1: Macro economy and industrial structure* (pp. 87–128). Keio University Press Inc. (In Japanese).

Mussa, M. (1977). External and internal adjustment costs and the theory of aggregate and firm investment. *Economica, 44,* 163–178.

Nakamura, Y. (2003). *Theory of investment behavior*. Toyo Keizai Inc. (In Japanese).

Nickell, S. (1978). *The investment decisions of firms*. Cambridge University Press.

Ogawa, K., & Kitasaka, S. (1995). Corporate evaluation and capital investment in the asset market. In Y. Honda (Ed.), *Japanese economy* (pp. 23–47). Yuhikaku. (In Japanese).

Ogawa, K., & Kitasaka, S. (1998). *The asset market and economic fluctuations–empirical analysis of the modern Japanese economy*. Nikkei Inc. (In Japanese).

Oliner, S. D., Rudebusch, G. D., & Sichel, D. (1995). New and old models of business investment: A comparison of forecasting performance. *Journal of Money, Credit and Banking, 27,* 806–826.

Oliner, S. D., Rudebusch, G. D., & Sichel, D. (1996). The Lucas critique revisited assessing the stability of empirical Euler equations for investment. *Journal of Econometrics, 70,* 291–316.

Otaki, M., & Suzuki, K. (1986). Tobin's *q* theory and fluctuations in profit rate-discount rate. *Kokumin Keizai, 152,* 23–39. (In Japanese).

Philippon, T. (2009). The bond market's *q*. *Quarterly Journal of Economics, 124,* 1011–1056.

Schaller, H. (1990). A re-examination of the *Q* theory of investment using U.S. firm data. *Journal of Applied Econometrics, 5,* 309–325.

Shima, K. (2005). Lumps in equipment investment of Japanese firms: A hazard analysis. *The Electric Economic Review, 54,* 1–17. (In Japanese).

Suzuki, K. (2001). *Capital investment and money market: Information asymmetry and uncertainty*. University of Tokyo Press. (In Japanese).

Suzuki, K., & Honda, Y. (2014). Nonlinear capital investment functions: The piecewise linear function approach. In A. Horiuchi, M. Hanazaki, & J. Nakamura (Eds.), *The Japanese economy: Financial development and corporate behavior in a changing environment* (pp. 209–239). University of Tokyo Press. (In Japanese).

Tobin, J. (1969). A general equilibrium approach to monetary theory. *Journal of Money, Credit, and Banking, 1,* 15–29.

Tonogi, K., Nakamura, J., & Asako, K. (2010). Estimation of Multiple q models of investment: Investment behavior over heterogeneous capital goods during the period of excess capacity reduction. *Economics Today*, *31*(2). (In Japanese).

Uchida, I., Takeda, Y., & Shirai, D. (2012). *Technology and capital adjustment costs: Micro evidence of automobile electronics in the auto-parts suppliers*. RIETI Discussion Paper Series, 12-E-001.

Uzawa, H. (1969). Time preference and the Penrose effect in a two-class model of economic growth. *Journal of Political Economy, 77,* 628–652.

Whited, T. M. (1992). Debt, liquidity constraints, and corporate investment: Evidence from panel data. *Journal of Finance, 47,* 1425–1460.

Whited, T. M. (1998). Why do investment Euler equations fail? *Journal of Business and Economic Statistics, 16,* 479–488.

Wildasin, D. E. (1984). The q theory of investment with many capital goods. *American Economic Review, 74,* 203–210.

Yoshikawa, H. (1980). On the 'q' theory of investment. *American Economic Review, 70,* 739–743.

Chapter 2
Augmentations to Multiple q Theory

Abstract In Sect. 2.1, we augment the q theory of investment for a single capital good to a framework that includes multiple categories of capital goods that have their own investment adjustment costs. The resulting Multiple q model establishes, under a set of assumptions that includes linear marginal adjustment costs, an estimable relationship between the investment rate of each capital good and the Total q, which is simply equivalent to the standard Single q evaluated in the stock market. In Sect. 2.2, we review the empirical research on the Multiple q model.

Keywords Heterogeneity of capital goods · Multiple q model · Single q · Partial q · Total q · Beginning-of-period model

In this chapter, we attempt to estimate the investment function in the Multiple q framework (hereinafter, Multiple q model) first introduced by Wildasin (1984) and developed and applied by Asako, Kuninori, Inoue, and Murase (1989, 1997). Following Asako et al. (1989, 1997), a series of estimations were conducted on the investment function of the Multiple q model framework using data on Japanese listed firms by, among others, Tonogi, Nakamura, and Asako (2010), Asako and Tonogi (2010), and Asako, Nakamura, and Tonogi (2016).

2.1 The Multiple q Model

Wildasin (1984) was the first to attempt to extend Tobin's standard q theory by relaxing the assumption of homogeneous capital goods, followed by Asako et al. (1989). Wildasin (1984) shows that, in the multiple goods model, a monotonic one-to-one relationship between the simple total investment amount and the q ratio no longer holds but that q can be expressed as a linear combination of the investment amount for each of the multiple capital goods.

The content of and opinions in this chapter are solely attributable to the authors and are unrelated to any organizations with which the authors are affiliated.

K. Asako et al., *Multiple q and Investment in Japan*,
https://doi.org/10.1007/978-981-15-2981-8_2

Asako et al. (1989) refer to the multiple goods theory in Wildasin (1984) as "Multiple q theory," and they call the conventional q theory that assumes homogeneous capital goods the "Single q theory." They systematically show that Multiple q theory can be regarded as a generalization of Single q theory by introducing new concepts, such as the "Partial q," which corresponds to the q ratio for each capital good, and the "Total q," which represents their integration. They also establish the fundamental methodology for the empirical analysis, including a statistical test for whether the heterogeneity of capital goods, an assumption of Multiple q theory, is valid.

Tonogi et al. (2010) note that although the correspondence with theory is unclear in the continuous time model, empirical analyses using financial data require specifying the timing of capital investment at the beginning or the end of the fiscal period (in other words, specifying whether capital investment in the current fiscal period contributes to production in the same fiscal period), and they derive two kinds of investment functions based on discrete-time models corresponding to each of these two assumptions. They also test data for Japanese listed firms and confirm that the "beginning-of-period model" is generally a better fit than the "end-of-period model" is. Using the beginning-of-period model, Asako and Tonogi (2010) reconstruct concepts, such as the Partial q and Total q developed for the continuous-time model by Asako et al. (1989, 1997), for the context of the discrete-time model. Moreover, they consider expanding the Multiple q model to ease the assumption of a smooth, convex adjustment cost function.

In the beginning-of-period model, a firm's owner–manager makes investment decisions in each period based on information about the business environment observed at the beginning of the period (represented by productivity shock A) and immediately carries out the selected investment. Newly installed capital stock contributes to production fully during the current period, and capital depreciation in a period occurs at the end of the period. The model includes n types of capital goods. The physical depreciation rate of the j-th capital good is denoted by $\delta_j (j = 1, 2, \ldots, n)$, the capital stock at the end of the previous period after depreciation is denoted by $(1 - \delta_j)K_j$, the capital investment at the beginning of the current period is denoted by I_j, and the capital stock after the investment is denoted by $K_j^{'}$. Then, we obtain

$$I_j = K_j^{'} - (1 - \delta_j)K_j, \tag{2.1}$$

and the net investment rate Z_j after capital depreciation is written as

$$Z_j \equiv \frac{I_j}{(1 - \delta_j)K_j^{'}}, \tag{2.2}$$

which can take any value in the range of $Z_j \leq 1/(1 - \delta_j)$, including negative values.

When investing, the firm has to incur adjustment costs in addition to the purchase costs of capital goods. We assume that the adjustment costs for each capital good are separable and can be expressed as a quadratic function of the investment rate Z_j of the relevant capital good, as follows:

$$C\left(K_1', \ \cdots, \ K_n', K_1, \ \cdots, \ K_n\right) = \sum_{j=1}^{n} \frac{\gamma_j}{2}(Z_j - a_j)^2(1-\delta_j)K_j' \tag{2.3}$$

The parameter $\gamma_j > 0$ represents the size of the adjustment cost (strength of friction) for each capital good, and a_j is the parameter corresponding to the investment rate for which the adjustment cost takes its minimum value.[1] The more the investment rate Z_j deviates from a_j, the greater is the rate of increase of the adjustment cost. Generally, it is natural for a_j, which is the benchmark, to be zero, as is implicitly assumed in the single capital good model in Eq. (1.4) developed in Chap. 1, or to be in the neighborhood of the capital depreciation rate, δ_j. However, in this chapter, this value is empirically estimated.

The firm's production function, which extends the gross profit function in Eq. (1.1) of Chap. 1 to an economy with multiple capital goods, is assumed to take a Cobb–Douglas form:

$$F\left(A, K_1', K_2', \ldots, K_n'\right) = AK_1'^{\alpha_1} K_2'^{\alpha_2} \cdots K_n'^{\alpha_n}, \text{ with} \sum_{i=1}^{n} \alpha_j = 1, \tag{2.4}$$

where the α_j's are nonnegative constants. Note that, instead of the gross profit in Eq. (1.1), which is a function of the capital stock before capital investment in the current period, Eq. (2.4) implies that production is a function of the capital stocks, including capital investment in the current period. In other words, all current investments are supposed to become productive immediately at the beginning of the current period. In contrast, current investment is assumed to only become productive at the end of the current period in the theoretical framework developed in Chap. 1, implying that the production function in Eq. (2.4) is a prerequisite for the beginning-of-period framework.

Then, the Bellman equation of the dynamic optimization problem for the maximization of firm value V in each period is expressed as follows:

$$\begin{aligned} &V(A, K_1, \ K_2, \ \ldots, \ K_n) \\ &\quad = \max_{K_j'} \left[AK_1'K_2' \cdots K_n' - \sum_{j=1}^{n} \frac{\gamma_j}{2}(Z_j - a_j)^2(1-\delta_j)K_j' \right. \\ &\qquad \left. - \sum_{j=1}^{n} p_j\left(K_j' - (1-\delta_j)K_j\right) + \beta E_{A'|A}\left\{V\left(A', \ K_1', \ K_2', \ldots, \ K_n'\right)\right\} \right]. \end{aligned} \tag{2.5}$$

Here, p_j is the price of capital good j relative to the product price, which is the numeraire; β is the discount factor; and $E_{A'|A}\{\cdot\}$ is the expected value operator

[1] As with Z_j, a_j can take any value in the range of $a_j \leq 1/(1-\delta_j)$, including a negative value.

based on the forecasted productivity shock in the next period, which is based on information in the current period. As both the production function and the investment adjustment cost function are homogeneous of degree one, the value function V is also homogeneous of degree one for stocks of n types of capital.

The first-order maximization condition for enterprise value can be expressed by partially differentiating Eq. (2.5) with regards to K_j, as follows

$$\frac{\partial V(A, K_1, K_2, \ldots, K_n)}{\partial K_j} = (1-\delta_j)\gamma_j(Z_j - a_j) + (1-\delta_j)p_j. \tag{2.6}$$

However, from Euler's theorem on homogeneous functions,

$$\sum_{i=1}^{n} \frac{1}{(1-\delta_j)} \frac{\partial V(A, K_1, K_2, \ldots, K_n)}{\partial K_j}(1-\delta_j)K_j = V(A, K_1, K_2, \ldots, K_n), \tag{2.7}$$

must hold as a mathematical identity. Thus, from Eqs. (2.6) and (2.7),

$$\sum_{j=1}^{n} \gamma_j(Z_j - a_j)(1-\delta_j)K_j + \sum_{j=1}^{n} p_j(1-\delta_j)K_j = V(A, K_1, K_2, \ldots, K_n), \tag{2.8}$$

follows immediately.

By dividing both sides of Eq. (2.8) by the volume sum of all capital goods adjusted for depreciation, $\sum_{j=1}^{n}(1-\delta_j)K_j$, and rearranging the result, we therefore obtain the following relationship, which can be understood as the investment function of the Multiple q model:

$$(q-1)P = \sum\nolimits_{j=1}^{n} \gamma_j Z_j s_j - \sum\nolimits_{j=1}^{n} \gamma_j a_j s_j. \tag{2.9}$$

Here, three newly defined variables or indices are introduced. The first is the q ratio, which represents the average q as literally the ratio of the firm value V to its replacement costs aggregated as a value sum over n kinds of capital goods adjusted for depreciation, as follows:

$$q = \frac{V}{\sum_{j=1}^{n}(1-\delta_j)K_j}. \tag{2.10}$$

Second, the price of capital P is the implicit deflator of the aggregated capital stock:

$$P = \frac{\sum_{j=1}^{n} p_j(1-\delta_j)K_j}{\sum_{j=1}^{n}(1-\delta_j)K_j} = \sum_{j=1}^{n} p_j s_j. \tag{2.11}$$

Third, s_j is the composition ratio of each capital good type in the aggregated capital stock:[2,3]

$$s_j = \frac{(1-\delta_j)K_j}{\sum_{j=1}^{n}(1-\delta_j)K_j}. \tag{2.12}$$

In our Multiple q model investment function, once we focus on the j-th capital good, three of the relevant non-parametric terms or variables that appear in Eq. (2.9), namely $(q-1)P$, $Z_j s_j$, and s_j, are all observable as data; thus, in accordance with Eq. (2.9), we can obtain estimates of γ_j and $\gamma_j a_j$ by linearly regressing the term $(q-1)P$ on the variables $Z_j s_j$ and s_j, which are the coefficient parameters of the adjustment cost function.

When Eqs. (2.7) and (2.10)–(2.12) are fully incorporated, the right-hand side of Eq. (2.9) is transformed into

$$\begin{aligned}(q-1)P &= \frac{V}{\sum_{j=1}^{n}(1-\delta_j)K_j} - P \\ &= \sum_{j=1}^{n}\left(\frac{1}{(1-\delta_j)}\frac{\partial V(A, K_1, K_2, \ldots, K_n)}{\partial K_j}\cdot s_j\right) - P \\ &= \sum_{j=1}^{n}\left(\frac{1}{(1-\delta_j)}\frac{\partial V(A, K_1, K_2, \ldots, K_n)}{\partial K_j} - p_j\right)s_j. \end{aligned} \tag{2.13}$$

Then, it is clear that $(q-1)P$ is equal to the weighted average of the marginal efficiency of each capital good in excess of its replacement cost with a weight of s_j.

Asako et al. (1989, 1997) call the marginal profitability of each capital good divided by the capital-good purchase price, that is,

$$q_j \equiv \frac{\partial V(A, K_1, K_2, \ldots, K_n)/\partial K_j}{(1-\delta_j)p_j}, \tag{2.14}$$

the "Partial q" of that capital good, and they call the standard average q the "Total q" in the sense that it reflects the notion of q that covers all capital goods. From

[2]Here, by setting the constraint that the two adjustment-cost function parameters, γ_j and $\gamma_j a_j$, are equal for all capital goods, Eq. (2.9) can be reduced to the standard investment function (i.e., the Single q model, in which the investment rate is a linear function of the average q) based on the assumption of single capital goods.

[3]When the end-of-period model is applied instead of the beginning-of-period model, the left-hand side of Eq. (2.9) should be replaced by the conditional expectations of the end-of-period values forecasted based on the information as of the beginning of the period. In addition, Eqs. (2.10)–(2.12) are replaced by those without capital depreciation because capital investment in the current period is not assumed to become productive during the current period in the end-of-period model. Namely, mathematically, these equations should be replaced by equations with $\delta_j = 0$. See Tonogi et al. (2010) for more details.

Eqs. (2.13) and (2.14), it is understood that the relationship between the Total q and the Partial q is

$$(q-1)P = \sum_{j=1}^{n} (q_j - 1) p_j s_j, \tag{2.15}$$

which, after substituting out Eq. (2.11) and dividing both sides by P, reduces to

$$q = \sum_{j=1}^{n} q_j \left(\frac{p_j s_j}{p} \right). \tag{2.16}$$

Once the Partial q in Eq. (2.14) is substituted into Eq. (2.6), we obtain the relationship between the Partial q and the investment rate Z_j defined in Eq. (2.2) as

$$q_j = \frac{\gamma_j}{p_j} (Z_j - a_j) + 1, \tag{2.17}$$

from which we can derive

$$Z_j = a_j + \frac{1}{\gamma_j} p_j (q_j - 1). \tag{2.18}$$

Thus, the investment rate of each capital good is expressed as a linear function of the corresponding Partial q.

In passing, we note that by properly introducing a new aggregate adjustment cost parameter γ and aggregate investment capital ratios Z and a over n types of capital goods as, respectively, $\gamma = \sum \gamma_j$, $Z = \sum (\gamma_j / \gamma) Z_j s_j$, and $a = \sum (\gamma_j / \gamma) a_j s_j$, we obtain, in parallel with Eqs. (2.17) and (2.18), the following two equations:

$$q = \frac{\gamma}{P} (Z - a) + 1, \tag{2.19}$$

$$Z = a + \frac{1}{\gamma} P (q - 1). \tag{2.20}$$

The aggregate investment capital ratios Z and the parameter a are doubly weighted averages over n types of capital goods, reflecting both the volume ratios of capital goods and the ratios of the relevant adjustment costs of investment. Because of the inherent linearity in the underlying individual investment functions for the n types of capital goods, Eqs. (2.19) and (2.20) indicate that these linear relations are retained if the corresponding parameters and variables are properly weighted at the same time. This result establishes the aggregation of the Multiple q model through the Total q.

2.2 Review of the Empirical Research on the Multiple q Model

As explained, Asako et al. (1989, 1997), Tonogi et al. (2010), and Asako and Tonogi (2010) estimate the Multiple q investment function assuming a smooth, convex investment adjustment cost function and making use of listed firm data and the average q based on equity price information. We briefly review the main results obtained from these analyses.

Asako et al. (1989, 1997) analyze the manufacturing industry and obtain estimates from two types of capital goods, land and capital stock other than land, as in the analysis of Chap. 5 of this book. The calculation of capital stock other than land follows the method of Hayashi and Inoue (1991). Stocks and gross investment series for multiple capital goods considering differences in the price-change and capital depreciation rates for five types of capital assets, including buildings, structures, and machinery, are constructed and then totaled together with inventory. Asako et al. (1989, 1997) focus on land within the set of capital goods and carry out the analysis using two capital goods because, at that time, active investments were being made in land in Japan alongside the rapid increase in equity and land prices. Thus, it was thought that treating land as a capital good (i.e., a quasi-fixed production factor) that incurs a unique adjustment cost at the time of investment might improve the goodness of fit of the q model.

For this reason, great care is taken in constructing the land data, with the precise calculations considering such elements as differences in the rates of increase of land values according to the purpose of use and location. Using cross-sectional data from each year, the validity of the following three models is tested:

- **Model A (Single q that does not include land)**:
  Investment in land has no adjustment cost and, thus, the Partial q of land is always equal to one.
- **Model B (Single q that includes land)**:
  Land is homogeneous with other capital goods and can be incorporated as is.
- **Model C (Multiple q)**:
  Investments in land incur different adjustment costs from investments in buildings, machinery, and equipment; land and other capital goods have different Partial q values.

Asako et al. (1989), analyze fiscal year 1977 to fiscal year 1987 to show that, within the Single q framework, cases in which land is included in capital stock are more compatible with q theory than are cases in which it is not included. In addition, the results of the Multiple q model show clear differences in the estimated values of the adjustment cost parameter for land and that for capital stock other than land, indicating that the Single q model is not suitable. However, in some years, the Partial Q corresponding to $p_j(q_j - 1)$ in Eq. (2.18) obtained from the estimation results of the Multiple q model is negative. Moreover, although the estimated Partial Q values of capital stock other than land are somewhat consistent with the trend in the investment rate, the results for land remain puzzling in terms of their consistency with the theory. For example, the investment rate for land is consistently positive even in years in which a negative Partial Q is obtained. Asako et al. (1989) argue that the Partial Q for land is negative (q_j is less than one) because of a bubble in land prices and an excessively high price of land as a capital good.

Asako et al. (1997) extend the analysis period up to fiscal year 1994 in sequence with their previous study and try to answer the questions left unanswered by Asako et al. (1989) by making modifications. For example, they exclude the increase in the value of land due to increased real land prices from land investment by individual firms, and they use the concept of gross investment rather than that of net investment for capital goods other than land. As a result, whereas Asako et al. (1989) find several years in which the Partial Q of capital goods other than land is negative, Asako et al. (1997) find that this value is positive in every year and has a stable and positive correlation with the gross investment rate, as is consistent with the theory. However, the Partial Q of land, which Asako et al. (1989) find to be positive for several years, is negative every year in Asako et al. (1997), and this result is once again inconsistent with the gross investment rate of land. Although land is a production factor with its own unique adjustment costs, according to their interpretation, this result may be caused by a bubble in land prices and the overestimation of its contribution as a production factor.

Subsequently, Tonogi et al. (2010) and Asako and Tonogi (2010) analyze the Multiple q model based on unbalanced panel data from approximately 2,500 listed firms, including the non-manufacturing industry, covering fiscal year 1982 to fiscal year 2004 (divided into four periods for each business cycle phase). After subdividing capital goods other than land into four categories (i.e., buildings and structures; machinery and equipment; vessels and vehicles; and tools, furniture, and fixtures), they create a time series for gross investment and capital stock using three data construction methods that differ with regard to the evaluation of sold or retired amounts for existing facilities. They also add the cash flow and interest-bearing debt ratios as additional control variables, and they estimate the Multiple q investment function.

First, Tonogi et al. (2010) reject the null hypothesis that the parameters related to the adjustment costs of the five types of capital goods, including land are all equal, for all four sample periods. Based on this result, Asako and Tonogi (2010) consider the possibility of partial homogeneity and test the homogeneity between "certain capital goods" and the "other four capital goods that are regarded (tentatively) as homogeneous." They also conduct a pairwise test in which any two of the capital goods are homogeneous. As a result, they confirm that although partial homogeneity is not rejected in some cases, these combinations are not uniform depending on the sample period and the data construction method for gross investment and capital stock, and they conclude that the Multiple q model should be used based on the assumption that these five capital goods are fundamentally heterogeneous.

However, even for the Multiple q model, concerning the goodness of fit of the investment function, the significance and robustness of the parameters of the adjustment cost function are not high. Even in cases with relatively high explanatory power, such as those in which the sold or retired amounts of existing facilities are considered to be uniformly equal to zero, the cash flow and interest-bearing debt ratios, which should be inherently redundant in the framework of q theory, are estimated to have significant effects. Thus, factors remain that cannot be explained by simply considering the heterogeneity of capital goods and maintaining the same convex-type adjustment cost framework. Based on this result, Asako and Tonogi (2010) and Asako et al. (2016) ease the constraint of a smooth, convex adjustment cost function and attempt to estimate the non-linear Multiple q investment function, some of which is discussed more in detail in Chap. 4.

The parameter of the adjustment cost function is often estimated to have an insignificant effect, perhaps owing to the influence of additional control variables. Asako and Tonogi's (2010) estimates of Partial q also substantially differ depending on the analysis period and the data construction method. In these results, the estimates of the land Partial q are comparatively stable, and, regardless of the data construction method, they are significantly positive in the estimation periods leading up to a bubble economy (i.e., 1982–86 and 1987–91) and significantly negative in the estimation periods after the collapse of a bubble economy (i.e., 1992–97 and 1998–2004).

2.3 Concluding Remarks

In this chapter, based on the standard q theory of investment for a single capital good developed in Chap. 1, we first augmented the standard q theory of investment for a single capital good to a framework with multiple categories of capital goods that have their own investment adjustment costs, which we call the Multiple q framework. Even so, we saw that, if each of the marginal adjustment costs of multiple heterogeneous capital goods is given as a linear function of the investment rate of each capital good, we obtain a relationship between Total q (which is simply equivalent to the standard Single q evaluated in the stock market) and a linear combination of the marginal adjustment costs of each capital good. This relationship is interpreted as the investment function within the framework of the Multiple q model and is, in an empirical analysis, an estimable relationship between the investment rate of each capital good and Total q. Second, we discussed the definitions and usage of and the relationship between Partial q, Total q, Single q, and Multiple q. We also discussed to a certain extent the conditions under which we can obtain linear marginal adjustment costs with respect to each investment rate in the heterogeneous capital stocks.

In Sect. 2.2, we reviewed the empirical research pursued on the basis of heterogeneous capital goods. We noted a series of estimations conducted within the framework of the Multiple q model using data on Japanese firms, from which the chapters of the present book stem.

References

Asako, K., Kuninori, M., Inoue, T., & Murase, H. (1989). Land evaluation and measurement of Tobin's *q* theory / Estimation of Multiple *q*, *Economics Today*, *10*(3). (In Japanese).

Asako, K., Kuninori, M., Inoue, T., & Murase, H. (1997). Capital investment and land investment: 1977–1994. In K. Asako and M. Otaki (Eds.), *Dynamics of modern macroeconomics* (pp. 323–349). University of Tokyo Press. (In Japanese).

Asako, K., Nakamura, J., & Tonogi, K. (2016). The development of investment research and Multiple *q* in Japan. *International Journal of Finance and Accounting, 5*(5A), 1–29.

Asako, K., & Tonogi, K. (2010). Heterogeneity of capital stock and Multiple *q*. *The Economic Review, 61,* 325–341. (In Japanese).

Hayashi, F., & Inoue, T. (1991). The relation between firm growth and *Q* with multiple capital goods: theory and evidence from panel data on Japanese firms. *Econometrica, 59,* 731–753.

Tonogi, K., Nakamura, J., & Asako, K. (2010). Estimation of Multiple *q* models of investment: investment behavior over heterogeneous capital goods during the period of excess capacity reduction, *Economics Today*, *31*(2). (In Japanese).

Wildasin, D. E. (1984). The *q* theory of investment with many capital goods. *American Economic Review, 74,* 203–210.

Chapter 3
Construction and Summary Statistics of the Data

Abstract In this chapter, we discuss the data that we use in most of the empirical work throughout this study. Some are based on established datasets, whereas others have to be constructed from raw data using additional assumptions, as published data do not exist or cannot be accessed. The most crucial missing data are that on disinvestments of capital stock through sales and retirements, which heavily affect the evolution of capital stock. In Sect. 3.1, we introduce and compare three methods for constructing disinvestment data for each category of capital goods. In Sect. 3.2, we examine the summary statistics of the constructed data and related statistics in preparation for the full-fledged empirical analyses to come in the subsequent chapters.

Keywords Heterogeneity of capital goods · Disinvestment · Sales and retirements · Proportional method · Book-Value method · Zero method · Total q

As we touched on in the previous chapter, Asako, Kuninori, Inoue, and Murase (1989) and, in a follow-on study, Asako, Kuninori, Inoue, and Murase (1997) test the validity of the Multiple q model by analyzing data from fiscal year 1977 through fiscal year 1994, regarding land as a capital good distinct from other capital goods. Although these two studies are successful in utilizing the Multiple q model to show that the land price in Japan was too high during the bubble economy in the latter half of the 1980s, they conclude that empirical research on a much longer data set or an entirely different data set is necessary to further ascertain the usefulness and validity of the Multiple q model.

However, to extend the analyses of Asako et al. (1989, 1997) to the present day, we must obtain updated market valuation data for each of land held nationwide by firms, which is an almost impossible task, as we must start by mining a huge amount of raw, unrecorded data. Thus, in this study, in which our main purpose is to focus on the heterogeneity of multiple capital goods in general rather than focusing on land as a special capital good distinct from other capital goods, we apply and check the usefulness of the Multiple q model rather directly and simplistically. Motivated by the concern that the Japanese economy faces a general overcapacity of capital stock,

The content of and opinions in this chapter are solely attributable to the authors and are unrelated to any organizations with which the authors are affiliated.

K. Asako et al., *Multiple q and Investment in Japan*,
https://doi.org/10.1007/978-981-15-2981-8_3

which was accumulated when the Japanese asset bubble reached its full scale in the late 1980s, we utilize data on this more-than-two-decade overcapacity adjustment process to systematically examine the investment functions of heterogeneous capital goods.

As such, we do not pursue the precision of the firm land ownership data, and we employ another data set, which we will explain later. We expect this analysis to yield interesting results with respect to elucidating the actual state of the Japanese economy in the transitional days up to the middle of the 2000s and to developing empirical analysis methods for heterogeneous capital investment. In the Multiple q model analyses to be developed in the next chapter, depreciable fixed assets are subdivided into four other categories as well as land. These categories are "buildings and structures," "machinery and equipment," "vessels and vehicles," and "tools, furniture, and fixtures."

3.1 Three Methods to Construct Capital Investment Data

Two types of data series naturally arise when capital investment and capital stock statistics are collected. One is "progress-based," in which an investment is acknowledged at the time of capitalization as construction work in progress, and the other is "installation-based," in which an investment is acknowledged when it starts to operate within a production capacity. The latter installation-based concept is consistent with Tobin's q theory. Thus, in the empirical analyses in Chap. 4 and later chapters, capital investment value is essentially defined as the difference between the new acquisition value of capital goods, excluding construction in progress, and the residual market value of capital goods sold or retired. However, no observable data for the residual market value of capital goods sold or retired exist to be deducted, and limited data is usable for estimation. For these reasons, prior research in Japan adopts the following three alternative methods.

The first is a method in which the book value of the sold or retired amount (reversely calculated from the accounting identity) is multiplied by the market-to-book ratio. This method is hereinafter referred to as the Proportional method. The second is a method in which the book value of the sold or retired amount (reversely calculated from the accounting identity) is used as is. This method is hereinafter referred to as the Book-Value method. The third method considers accurate calculation to be impossible owing to data constraints, and, because sold or retired capital is small relative to the total investment amount, uniformly sets the value of this capital equal to zero. This method is hereinafter referred to as the Zero method. Another interpretation of the Zero method is to consider the amount of sold or retired capital as a fixed percentage of existing equipment and include this value in depreciation. Under this interpretation, it is impossible to keep track of non-periodic or large-scale sales and retirements.

The time series data for capital investment and capital stock certainly differ depending on the residual market value of the sold or retired capital goods set by these three different methods. The three methods can be mutually compared and contrasted as follows. Estimation results using capital investment data obtained through the Zero method reflect only the new acquisition behavior of capital goods. However, when we use data obtained through the other two methods, the sale and retirement behaviors of capital goods are also analyzed explicitly as negative investments or intended capital decumulations.

In the following discussion, we provide an overview of the three methods. The prior studies that serve as the foundation of this overview, with the exception of Asako et al. (1989, 1997), aggregate the investment amounts and stock data for each capital good following a properly set method and then estimate the investment function within the Single q framework. However, what we compare and examine in detail in the following sections is the construction method for the investment data for each capital good, which pertains to depreciable fixed assets. For the methods used to prepare the data regarding the capital investment amount for land, refer to Tonogi, Nakamura, and Asako (2010).

3.1.1 Proportional Method

The Proportional method takes advantage of the theoretical relationship in which, under set conditions, the value obtained by multiplying the residual book value of the sold or retired asset by the market-to-book ratio (the ratio of the nominal capital stock calculated using the perpetual inventory method to the book value of the corresponding assets) is equal to the residual market value of the sold or retired asset. This method is adopted by Asako et al. (1989) and Hayashi and Inoue (1991). Here, we obtain [1]

$$\begin{aligned}
&\text{(nominal capital investment in the current period)}\\
&\quad = \text{(increase in the asset during the current period)}\\
&\qquad - \text{(the residual book value of the sold or retired asset during the current period)}\\
&\qquad \times \text{(market-to-book ratio).} \qquad (3.1)
\end{aligned}$$

Additionally, as no data directly correspond to financial statements, we can indirectly calculate, based on the accounting identity, the residual book value of the sold or retired asset during the current period using the following equation:

$$\begin{aligned}
&\text{(residual book value of the sold or retired asset during the current period)}\\
&\quad = \text{(increase in the asset during the current period)}\\
&\qquad - \text{(difference in the asset's book value at the beginning and the end of the period)}\\
&\qquad + \text{(depreciation amount of the asset in the current period).} \qquad (3.2)
\end{aligned}$$

[1] Throughout Sect. 3.1, "the asset" refers to the asset corresponding to the capital stock under analysis.

3.1.2 *Book-Value Method*

The Book-Value method directly uses the book value as the residual market value of the sold or retired asset. It is adopted by Suzuki (2001). As with the Proportional method, the residual book value of the sold or retired asset is indirectly calculated from the accounting identity. In other words, in the Book-Value method, the nominal capital investment amount for the current period is calculated as follows:

$$\begin{aligned}&(\text{nominal capital investment in the current period})\\&\quad = (\text{increase in the asset during the current period})\\&\qquad - (\text{residual book value of the sold or retired asset during the current period}).\end{aligned} \tag{3.3}$$

3.1.3 *Zero Method*

The Zero method presupposes that the residual market value of the sold or retired asset is zero (i.e., it is disregarded in the practical sense). This method is adopted by Hori, Saito, and Ando (2006), among others. Hori et al. (2006) point out the difficulty of adequately estimating the residual market value of the sold or retired asset owing to restrictions on data and argue that sold or retired assets constitute a sufficiently small proportion of nominal capital investments that the Zero method can be adopted. In the Zero method, by definition, the nominal capital investment in each period is never negative, and the actual capital stock does not decrease for any reason other than depreciation. The formula to calculate the nominal capital investment in the current period using the Zero method removes all terms other than the first one on the right side of Eqs. (3.1) and (3.3) to obtain

$$\begin{aligned}&(\text{nominal capital investment in the current period})\\&\quad = (\text{increase in the asset during the current period}).\end{aligned} \tag{3.4}$$

3.2 Data Overview

The listed company financial data used for the analyses in this study are taken from the Corporate Financial Databank compiled by Development Bank of Japan (DBJ), which records the individual financial results of all companies listed on the First and Second Sections of the Tokyo, Osaka, and Nagoya Stock Exchanges. Because the fiscal calendars differ depending on the company, we regard the financial results of companies whose fiscal year-ends fall between April of the current year through

March of the following year as data for that fiscal year. The panel that we analyze is unbalanced because it includes data of delisted and newly listed companies. We construct each company's capital stock data using the perpetual inventory method and set the benchmark year as follows: fiscal year (FY) 1977 is used for companies that existed before FY 1977, and the year in which data are first recorded in the Corporate Finance Databank is used for companies listed after FY 1977.

FY 1977 is set as the start of the period given that the main focus in Chap. 4 is investment behavior after the mid-1990s. In addition, data constraints prior to FY 1976 would inevitably generate serious discontinuities in the time series (estimation work is necessary due to the lack of disclosure requirements around depreciation expenses for capital goods and accumulated depreciation). For the estimated values in the benchmark year, we use the book value as the market value. For details on other data sources and construction methods, refer to Tonogi et al. (2010).

3.2.1 Capital Stock and Capital Investment

We calculate the capital stock and capital investment data using each of the three methods detailed in the previous section for each of the following categories of capital goods: buildings and structures; machinery and equipment; vessels and vehicles; tools, furniture, and fixtures; and land.[2] Below, we compare the trends in fiscal year (FY) 1978 and FY 2004 for each method using mean values that exclude data in the top and bottom 0.5% for each fiscal year. This exclusion eliminates the impacts of exceptional events, such as the reclassification of assets held by huge privatized businesses and abnormal decreases in capital stocks due to the conversion of a business into a holding company.

We first observe the trend in the sum of real capital stock for all capital goods, including land (Fig. 3.1). The Proportional and Book-Value methods shift to follow decreasing trends over time, with peaks in FY 1998 and FY 2000, respectively, whereas the Zero method continues to increase even after the mid-1990s. The chronological changes are generally similar for the Proportional and Book-Value methods, but the data levels are always higher for the Book-Value method. These differences are attributable to differences in the assumptions around sales and retirements of capital goods. However, differences stemming from disparities among the three methods, including the Zero method, are quite limited in terms of the composition of capital good.

---

[2]Excluding "noncurrent assets for rent" and "other depreciable assets," which are not subject to analysis, six types of depreciable fixed assets are recorded in the detailed data on fixed tangible assets within the Corporate Financial Databank, as follows: "buildings," "structures," "machinery and equipment," "vessels (including aircraft)," "vehicles," and "tools, furniture, and fixtures." Of these, buildings and structures are treated as one capital good as the two categories have highly correlated investment rates, and vessels and vehicles are treated as one good, as many companies do not own vessels.

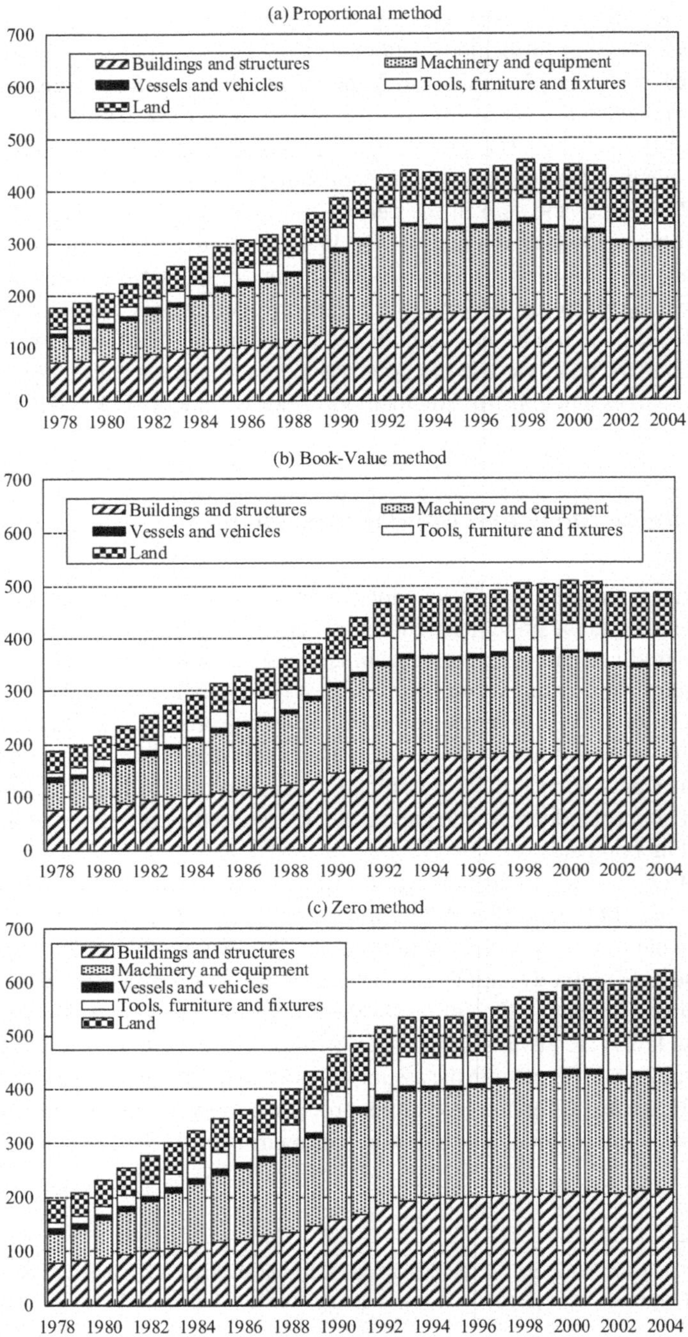

Fig. 3.1 Trends and composition of real capital stock (mean value in 100 million yen)

Next, we look at the investment rate or the investment capital stock ratio by capital good (Fig. 3.2), and we observe the following general relationship between the three alternative methods for all capital goods in regard to the level of the investment rate:

$$\text{Proportional Method} < \text{Book-Value Method} < \text{ZeroMethod}$$

For tools, furniture, and fixtures, the deviation range is relatively small, and the trends over time are similar. However, the deviation range for land and that for vessels and vehicles are wide, and the trends over time clearly differ. Machinery and equipment falls in the middle.

If we observe this figure in more detail, the investment rate of land has relatively similar levels and trends for the Proportional and Book-Value methods and is negative from FY 2001 onwards. As in prior studies, both the Proportional and Book-Value methods use the last-in, first out (LIFO) assumption to evaluate the sold or retired value of land. However, Hori et al. (2006), who adopt the Zero method, do not consider land as a subject for analysis. Here, we assume that under the Zero method, the sold or retired value of land is zero, as in the case of other depreciable fixed assets. The investment rate for vessels and vehicles, in contrast, is relatively similar for the Book-Value and Zero methods. Only the data using the Proportional method is negative from FY 1997 onwards.

Additionally, although this result is not shown, if the median value of the investment rate is used instead of the mean, its trend is similar to that of the Zero method for any capital good, and, thus, we can verify that deviations such as those described above are mainly generated by (negative) outliers.

3.2.2 *Observation of Total q Data*

We follow prior studies based on the Multiple q model, such as those of Asako et al. (1989, 1997), and we estimate the investment function by regarding land as a capital good that entails an adjustment cost unique to its investment. We do not assume any adjustment costs for assets other than depreciable fixed assets and land, which are inclusively categorized as capital stock. The assets other than capital stock include inventories, intangible assets, financial assets, and so forth. Then, the Total q consistent with the Multiple q investment function given by Eqs. (2.9) in Chap. 2 can be expressed as follows:

$$\frac{\text{(firm value)} - \text{(market value of portfolio assets excluding capital stock)}}{\text{(replacement cost of capital stock)}}.$$

Because we adopt the beginning-of-period model, these numerical values are all measured at the beginning of the period, that is, they do not include new investment or disinvestment during the period.

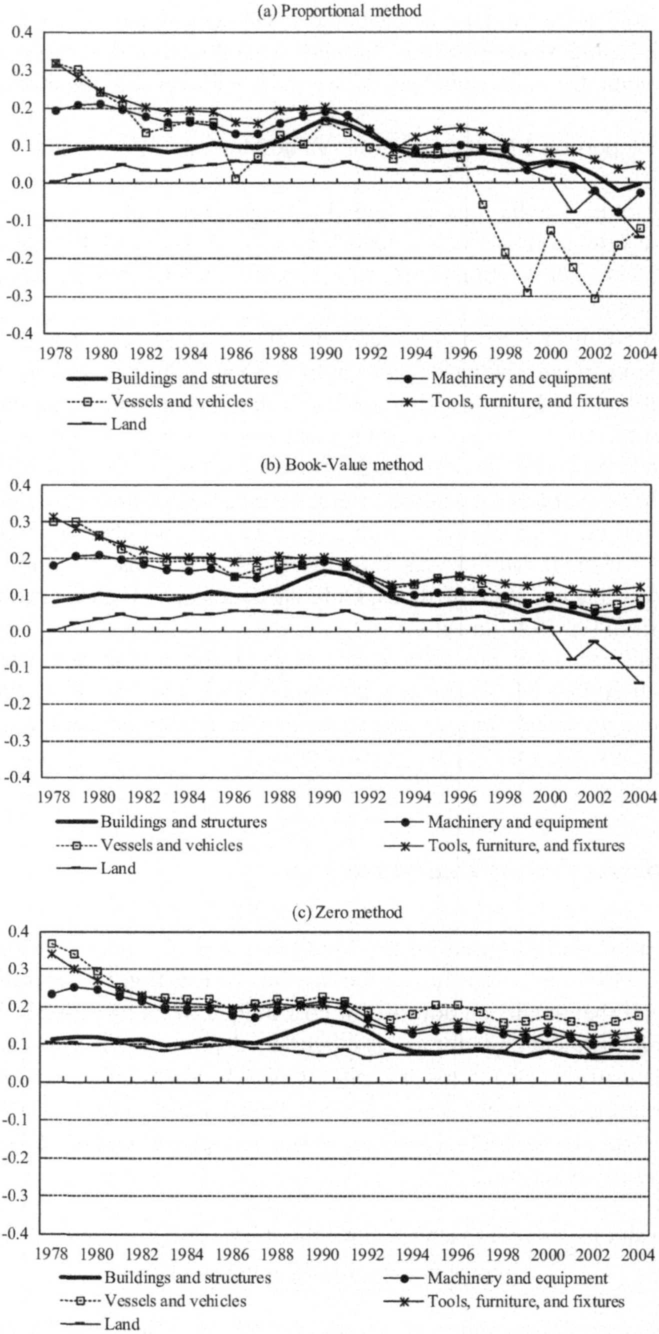

Fig. 3.2 Investment rate by capital good (mean value)

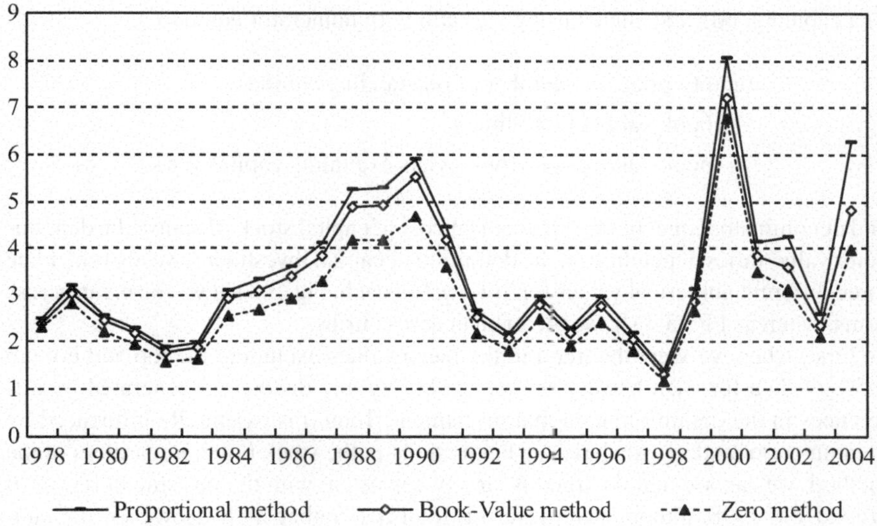

Fig. 3.3 Total q (mean value)

In what follows, we assume that the market price of the claim rights (equity and debt) to the company correctly reflects the firm value and that the market price of liabilities and portfolio assets excluding capital stock is equal to the book value. As in Figs. 3.3 and 3.4, we observe the trend in the Total q (the average q including land

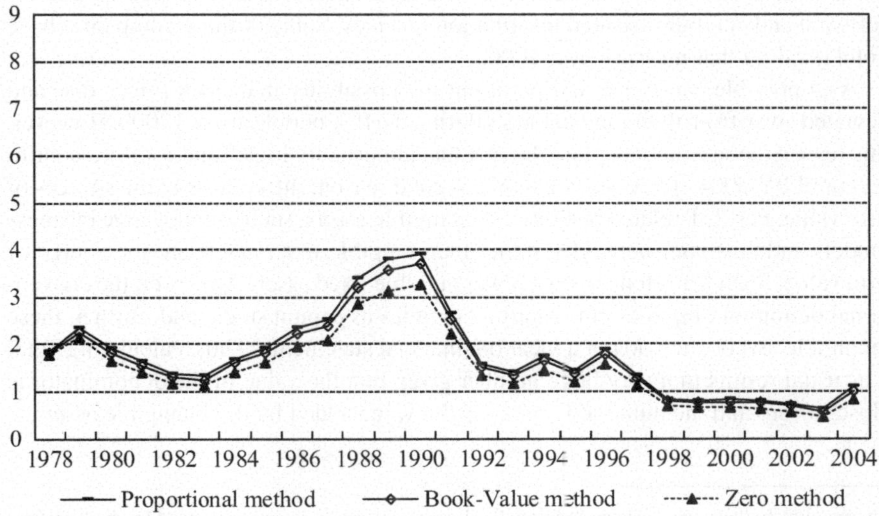

Fig. 3.4 Total q (median value)

as a capital good)[3] calculated using the ratio with numerator equal to

(equity price) × (number of outstanding equities)
+ (book value of liabilities)
− (book value of portfolio assets excluding capital stock)

and denominator equal to the replacement cost of capital stock. Because the denominator value varies depending on the definition of capital investment, we also calculate three different numerical values for Total q. For each, Fig. 3.3 shows the mean across firms, whereas Fig. 3.4 shows the median across firms.

First, when we view the trend in the mean values excluding the top and bottom 0.5% of data for each fiscal year, we see hardly any distinction generated by differences in the definition of capital investment. Total q is essentially influenced by the numerator and, particularly, by fluctuations in the stock price. Regardless of the method, we can see that the trend is largely consistent with the investment rate until around FY 1998, although the level of Total q is rather high. However, the subsequent period shows intense fluctuations with growing volatility, as seen by peak levels exceeding those in the bubble period. The deviation from the investment rate trend is apparent.

In contrast, even though the trend in Total q measured by the median value is similar to that using the mean value until about FY 1998, after which the former Total q value remains low. Thus, we can see the mean value largely increases owing to upper outliers. Looking at the Total q values of individual companies, cases of values over 100 are apparent starting in the late 1990s, particularly among companies in information and communications technology (ICT) and in ICT-related industries, such as software and computer-related information services. Some of these companies have Total q values that measure over 1000.

As a possible cause, we first point out the possibility that stock prices rose and deviated away from their fundamentals during the ICT bubble around 2000. However, this reason alone cannot explain the fact that abnormally high Total q values continued until FY 2004. Thus, we consider a second reason: differences in the sources of firm value. For ICT-related businesses, intangible assets, such as innovative business models and customer networks, rather than tangible fixed assets are the source of firm value. Such firms tend to own fewer tangible fixed assets. However, the conventional definition of q does not regard intangibles as capital stock, and, further, these intangible assets often do not appear on financial statements. Thus, calculating Total q as usual results in a very large number given that the value of the denominator is close to zero and the numerator contains the value added by the intangible assets.

[3] As previously mentioned, when defining Total q, the portion of the assets owned by the company that correspond to the theoretical capital stock is not necessarily self-evident. Hayashi and Inoue (1991) adopt the Proportional method and regard land, depreciable fixed assets, and inventory, as capital stock. In addition, Hori et al. (2006), who adopt the Zero method, regard all owned assets, excluding land and fixed assets for rent, as capital stock.

In such cases, Total q should not be the target of analysis, as it does not carry its inherent meaning as an indicator of capital investment incentives. In the empirical analysis in the next chapter, we pool all data from FY 1998 through FY 2004 and exclude the top and bottom 0.5% (= 1% in total for both ends) of Total q data from the sample. The trend in the mean value of the Total q following this process is very similar to that of the median value.

3.3 Concluding Remarks

In this chapter, we discussed the data we use in most of the empirical work throughout this book. Some data are based on established datasets, such as the Corporate Finance Databank compiled by the DBJ, whereas others must be constructed from raw data based on assumptions, as the published data are inexistent or inaccessible. To handle the missing data on disinvestments of capital stock through sales and retirements, which heavily affect the evolution of the estimated capital stock, we introduce three methods for constructing disinvestment data for each category of capital goods, namely, the Proportional, Book-Value, and Zero methods.

We also examined the summary statistics of the constructed data and related statistics in preparation for the full-fledged empirical analyses to come in the following chapters. The merits and demerits of the three methods are evaluated through the performance of the estimated investment function of the Multiple q model.

References

Asako, K., Kuninori, M., Inoue, T., & Murase, H. (1989). Land evaluation and measurement of Tobin's q theory/estimation of Multiple q. *Economics Today, 10*(3). (In Japanese).

Asako, K., Kuninori, M., Inoue, T., & Murase, H. (1997). Capital investment and land investment: 1977–1994. In K. Asako & M. Otaki (Eds.), *Dynamics of modern macroeconomics* (pp. 323–349). University of Tokyo Press. (In Japanese).

Hayashi, F., & Inoue, T. (1991). The relation between firm growth and Q with multiple capital goods: Theory and evidence from panel data on Japanese firms. *Econometrica, 59*, 731–753.

Hori, K., Saito, M., & Ando, K. (2006). What caused fixed investment to stagnate during the 1990s in Japan? Evidence from panel data of listed companies. *Japanese Economic Review, 57*, 283–306.

Suzuki, K. (2001). *Capital investment and money market: Information asymmetry and uncertainty*. University of Tokyo Press. (In Japanese).

Tonogi, K., Nakamura, J., & Asako, K. (2010). Estimation of Multiple q models of investment: Investment behavior over heterogeneous capital goods during the period of excess capacity reduction. *Economics Today, 31*(2). (In Japanese).

Chapter 4
Investment Behavior of Japanese Firms

Abstract In this chapter, we clarify the sample period and the summary statistics of the three constructed capital stock data sets for listed firms in Sect. 4.1. Then, after discussing the test for the homogeneity of capital goods, we verify in Sect. 4.2 the effectiveness of the Multiple q model by estimating investment functions. We attempt these estimations using the least squares (with fixed effects and random effects model) and instrumental variables methods with a particular focus on system GMM (Generalized Method of Moments). Based on the results of the homogeneity test in Sects. 4.3 and 4.4 expands the theoretical Multiple q model to a non-linear investment function by allowing non-convex, fixed investment adjustment costs. In Sect. 4.5, we estimate the non-linear investment function and discuss the implications of the estimated results. Section 4.6 concludes with several remarks.

Keywords Multiple q model · Heterogeneity of capital goods · Partial homogeneity · Pairwise homogeneity test · Non-linear adjustment cost · Lumpy investment

4.1 Comparison of the Three Methods for Constructing Capital Investment Data

4.1.1 Sample and Estimation Period

Although, following Tonogi, Nakamura, and Asako (2010), we constructed capital stock data of Japanese listed firms using three alternative methods over the period of fiscal years (FY) 1978–2004 in Chap. 3, we exclude data prior to FY 1981 from the analysis, as the set benchmark year still has a large impact for many firms. We divide the period after FY 1982 into the following four periods and estimate the investment function within the Multiple q framework.

The content of and opinions in this chapter are solely attributable to the authors and are unrelated to any organizations with which the authors are affiliated.

K. Asako et al., *Multiple q and Investment in Japan*,
https://doi.org/10.1007/978-981-15-2981-8_4

(1) **1st Period**: FY 1982–1986 (pre-bubble period)
(2) **2nd Period**: FY 1987–1991 (bubble period)
(3) **3rd Period**: FY 1992–1997 (post-bubble collapse period)
(4) **4th Period**: FY 1998–2004 (financial crisis and recovery period)

Because we divide the periods based on changes in the economic situation, the periods do not have uniform lengths. As was described in the previous chapter, the characteristics of each period prominently appear in the trends in the median Total q in Fig. 3.4. In this section, in addition to comparing the performances of the three alternative data construction methods, we examine the process of eliminating overcapacity during the post-collapse phase of the economic bubble (particularly after the mid-1990s) in Japan, which is reflected in the estimation results for the Multiple q investment function in the third and fourth periods.

4.1.2 Comparison of the Three Methods

One reason that the Book-Value and Zero methods are proposed as alternatives to the Proportional method, which initially aimed to maximize the use of the information provided by financial statements, is that the data related to sales and retirements creates problems related to observation error. The data provided by the "Detailed Statement of Property, Plant and Equipment, etc.," which is among the financial statements of listed firms, can easily indicate economically meaningless fluctuations due to arbitrary non-disclosures based on the principle of importance and reclassifications between account items, which can cause missing and abnormal outlier values. For instance, the residual book value of a sold or retired asset in the current period, which is indirectly calculated by equation (3.2):

(increase in the asset during the current period)
− (difference in the asset's book value at the beginning and end of the period)
+ (depreciation amount of the asset in the current period),

can take a negative value. In our data construction, we use a zero value in such cases to calculate the nominal capital investment amount.

The three methods are adopted by the authors of prior studies—studies with varying analytical objectives and varying types of capital goods pertinent for analysis with Tobin's q theory—as each method is considered to be the best fit in some cases. Thus, we cannot argue for the merits or demerits of any method unconditionally, but, as a general principle, there seems to be a trade-off between the intensity of information usage from raw data and the stability of the investment function estimation. In this section, we aim to robustly approach an overall picture of investment behavior, including sale and retirement behavior, by complementing the three methods. Based on whether or not the investment functions estimated using the capital investment and capital stock data constructed by each method (specifically, the parameters of the adjustment cost functions) are statistically significant, the implications for investment behavior can be largely categorized as described below.

Although each of the three methods may or may not lead to statistical significance, both the Proportional and Book-Value methods explicitly assume the presence of sale and retirement behavior, and, thus, we treat them as the same group. Therefore, of the possible eight combinations ($2 \times 2 \times 2$), we discuss four combinations summarized in Table 4.1:

(1) If either or both of the Proportional and Book-Value methods are significant and also the Zero method is significant, then both new acquisition behavior and sale and retirement behavior can be explained within the framework of Tobin's q theory. The superiority of the Proportional or Book-Value method cannot be unconditionally determined.
(2) If either or both of the Proportional and Book-Value methods are significant but the Zero method is not significant, then new acquisition behavior and sale and retirement behavior can be explained within the framework of Tobin's q theory only when they are lumped together. The superiority of the Proportional or Book-Value method is determined by whichever is significant. If both are significant, superiority cannot be unconditionally determined.

Table 4.1 Possible combinations of the significance of estimated parameter and corresponding implication for three methods

	Proportional method	Book-Value method	Zero method	Implication
Case 1	Positive and significant at least for one of two methods		Positive and significant	Both the new acquisition behavior and sale and retirement behavior become explainable within the framework of Tobin's q theory
Case 2	Positive and significant at least for one of two methods		Insignificant or negative	The new acquisition behavior and sale and retirement behavior become explainable within the framework of Tobin's q theory only when they are lumped together as one
Case 3	Insignificant or negative for both of two methods		Positive and significant	Only the new acquisition behavior can be explained within the framework of Tobin's q theory
Case 4	Insignificant or negative for both of two methods		Insignificant or negative	Neither new acquisition behavior nor sale and retirement behavior can be explained within the framework of Tobin's q theory

(3) If neither the Proportional nor the Book-Value method is significant but the Zero method is significant, then new acquisition behavior can be explained within the framework of Tobin's q theory, but sale and retirement behavior is not consistent with the framework of Tobin's q theory.

If none of the three methods is significant, then neither new acquisition behavior nor sale and retirement behavior can be explained within the framework of Tobin's q theory.

4.2 Heterogeneity of Capital Goods

In this section, we estimate the investment function within the framework of the Multiple q model made up of five categories of capital goods: buildings and structures; machinery and equipment; vessels and vehicles; tools, furniture, and fixtures; and land. This estimation has two aims.

The first aim is to verify the limit in terms of the explanatory power of investment functions given the assumption of a continuously convex adjustment cost function by considering the heterogeneity of capital goods at as minute a level as possible. In the estimation of Multiple q investment functions, a rejection of the null hypothesis that the parameters of the adjustment cost function are all equal for each capital good signifies a specification error of the investment functions within the framework of a continuously convex adjustment cost function.

Then, we can regard the limit in terms of the explanatory power of the Multiple q investment functions as that of the framework of a continuously convex adjustment cost function. As Wildasin (1984) shows, under Multiple q theory, the average q is fully explained by the vector of investment amount for each capital good (in other words, it can be expressed as a linear combination that becomes a weighted average). Thus, by adding fundamentally redundant explanatory variables, such as the cash flow and interest-bearing debt ratios, to an investment function within the Multiple q model and verifying whether these variables have significant effects, we can confirm whether the problems encountered during the empirical analysis of the Single q investment function can be attributed solely to the lack of consideration of the heterogeneity of capital goods or if they must also be attributed to other influential factors not covered by Tobin's q theory, as suggested by the fact that the redundant explanatory variables are still significant in the Multiple q model.

The second aim is to verify differences in the investment behavior of Japanese firms by period and type of capital good as well as between new acquisitions and sales and retirements. In pursuing this aim, we cover listed firms across all industries by simplifying the method of land valuation compared to previous studies. In this regard, this analysis is merely the first step in fact-finding. However, we believe it is useful in understanding the reality of the overcapacity elimination process of Japanese firms after the mid-1990s.

4.2.1 Estimation of the Investment Function with the Multiple q Model

Of the investment functions in a Multiple q framework developed in Chap. 2, we use the following equation, which was obtained using the beginning-of-period model, as in Eq. (2.9), as the basic form of the estimating equation:

$$(q-1)P = \sum_{j=1}^{n} \gamma_j \left(\frac{I_j}{(1-\delta_j)K_j^{'}} s_j \right) - \sum_{j=1}^{n} \gamma_j a_j s_j, \tag{4.1}$$

where I_j, $K_j^{'}$, δ_j, and s_j denote, respectively, investment in the j-th good at the beginning of the current period, its capital stock after investment, its depreciation rate, and its composition ratio in the aggregate capital stock defined as in Eq. (2.12). γ_j and a_j are parameters of the investment adjustment cost function that are to be estimated utilizing the regression given by Eq. (4.1). The variables q and P are defined as in Eqs. (2.10) and (2.11), respectively, and they represent the average q or the Total q of the Multiple q model and the implicit deflator of aggregated capital stock.

When we run the regression given by Eq. (4.1), we include as explanatory variables the cash flow and interest-bearing debt ratios (which are inherently redundant according to Tobin's q theory), as well as industry dummies (based on intermediate industrial classifications) and year dummies, both of which are taken from the Corporate Finance Databank compiled by Development Bank of Japan (DBJ). The definitions of cash flows and interest-bearing debt are in accordance with Hori, Saito, and Ando (2006), but unlike their original study, in which total assets are used as the denominator, our study uses the values divided by the capital stock at the end of the current period as the cash flow and interest-bearing debt ratios for estimation.

In the estimation results, if the parameter γ_j of the adjustment cost function is positive and significant, we can say that the investment behavior related to capital good j follows a gradual adjustment process consistent with the smooth, convex adjustment cost function of the beginning-of-period model. The investment rate, a_j, which entails the minimum adjustment cost, can theoretically take any of a positive, zero, and negative value. Consequently, for the estimation parameter $\gamma_j a_j$, which corresponds to the ratio s_j of capital good j (one of the explanatory variables), any estimation result can be consistent with the assumption of a smooth, convex adjustment cost function as long as γ_j is estimated to be positive and significant. However, if the parameter γ_j is not estimated to be positive and significant, then investment behavior exists that is at least partly inconsistent with a smooth, convex adjustment cost function (see Table 4.1 of Sect. 4.1 for the corresponding interpretations of the estimated γ_j for each data construction method).

If the parameters of the adjustment cost function are estimated to be significant, two hypotheses need to be verified. The first is whether the investment function based on the Multiple q model is more desirable than that based on the Single q model. We test the following two null hypotheses. Namely, among n kinds of capital goods, we state:

- **Hypothesis H_{A0}**: All γ_j are equal.
- **Hypothesis H_{B0}**: All γ_j are equal, and all a_j are equal.

If these null hypotheses are rejected, then investment functions based on the Multiple q model are more desirable. Note that the second null hypothesis, H_{B0}, is stronger than the first null hypothesis, H_{A0}, in theory in the sense that, if H_{A0} is rejected, H_{B0} must also be rejected. In other words, it is worth testing H_{B0} only when H_{A0} cannot be rejected. The test statistic can be the likelihood ratio computed from the sum of squared residuals of the estimated equation with and without homogeneity constraints on the parameters, which follows a χ^2 distribution with degrees of freedom equal to the number of constraints under a standard set of assumptions on the residual terms and for a large sample size.

Second, when the investment function based on the Multiple q model is more acceptable than that based on the Single q model, we must test whether the problems encountered in the empirical analysis of investment functions within the Single q model are fully attributable to the lack of consideration of the heterogeneity of capital goods. This point cannot be verified just by the significance of γ_j; we need to check the variables, such as the cash flow ratio and the interest-bearing debt ratio, that are inherently redundant within the framework of q theory. In other words, if these variables have no significant effect, we can conclude that the problems encountered during the empirical analysis of the investment function based on the Single q model are solved by considering the heterogeneity of capital goods (strictly speaking, we need to check other variables besides the cash flow and interest-bearing debt ratios, and, thus, the interpretation is not simple when the redundant variables have no significant effects).

4.2.2 Data Processing and Estimation Method

As described above, in what follows, we perform an empirical analysis after eliminating outliers from our sample. Specifically, we pool all data from FY 1998 to FY 2004 and process them to exclude the top and bottom 0.5% (= 1% in total for both sides) of Total q data from the sample (see Sect. 3.2.2). In addition, we exclude observations in the top 1% for the interest-bearing debt ratio and observations for which the total asset book value is over 1.5 or is less than 0.5 relative to the previous year's value. Because the denominator of the interest-bearing debt ratio is the capital stock, the upper outliers reflect a very small ratio of tangible fixed assets to total assets. In such cases, as with the upper outliers for Total q, we consider that Tobin's q, as defined in this analysis, does not inherently possess the functionality to signal investment incentives.

Lower outliers (large negative values) are frequently observed for the investment rate, but we do not eliminate them because such observations are an attribute of the beginning-of-period model. In our analysis in this section, which also examines the overcapacity elimination process, we consider that large-scale disinvestment is important information that is lost when such observations are uniformly treated as outliers. However, the fourth period (1998–04) also includes many cases of a large negative investment rate due to fundamental changes in the corporate management structure, such as forming a spin-off or a holding company. It is clearly misleading to treat such cases in the same manner as the elimination of overcapacity, as, in practical terms, the business itself continues unchanged. Thus, we consider observations for which the year-on-year change in the total asset size (including items other than tangible fixed assets) is less than 0.5 or greater than 1.5 to be unsuitable for analysis as going concerns, and, thus, we exclude them as outliers.

Regarding the empirical methodology, in addition to OLS estimations with fixed effect and random effect models, we also consider that the investment rate, cash flow ratio, and interest-bearing debt ratio may be simultaneously determined with Total q, and, thus, we also perform an estimation using instrumental variables, specifically system GMM, to avoid simultaneity biases. For the instrumental variables, we use data from three or more periods earlier for level variables and from two or more periods earlier for difference variables, as long as the overidentifying restrictions are satisfied, for each of the following: the dependent variable Total q and two explanatory variables "(investment rate) × (weighting): $\left(I_j/(1-\delta_j)K_j^{'}\right) \times s_j$" and "weighting: s_j."

The basic statistics for the data in each estimation period are shown in Table 4.2a, b, and c for the three data construction methods. However, because of the strong correlation between "(investment rate) × (weighting): $\left(I_j/(1-\delta_j)K_j^{'}\right) \times s_j$" and "weighting: s_j" for tools, furniture, and fixtures, we exclude "weighting: s_j" for tools, furniture, and fixtures from the explanatory variables. Thus, we cannot distinguish between γ_j and $\gamma_j a_j$ in the adjustment cost function for tools, furniture, and fixtures, and we must note that the coefficient on "(investment rate) × (weighting): $\left(I_j/(1-\delta_j)K_j^{'}\right) \times s_j$" has a different meaning in that case than it has for other capital goods.

4.2.3 Results of OLS Estimation

The estimation results for the fixed effect (FE) and random effect (RE) models are shown in Table 4.3. For the Hausman test for model identification between the fixed effect and random effect models, we obtain results indicating that the fixed effect model is better suited for all cases. Thus, in what follows, we mainly discuss the estimation results for the fixed effect model. We find no substantial differences in the results between the two models, and, thus, the results are robust.

Table 4.2 Basic statistics (a) Proportional method (b) Book-Value method (c) Zero method

	Variable name		Mean	S.D.	Min	Max	N of obs.
(a) Proportional method							
FY1982–86	(Tobin's $q-1$) × implicit deflator		1.824	4.431	−4.072	85.683	7,833
	Investment rate × share weighting	Buildings and structures	0.030	0.123	−5.515	0.741	7,833
		Machinery and equipment	0.040	0.387	−25.029	0.490	7,833
		Vessels and vehicles	0.003	0.058	−2.043	0.766	7,833
		Tools, furniture, and fixtures	0.006	0.963	−84.846	0.357	7,833
		Land	0.008	0.045	−1.174	0.483	7,833
	Share weighting	Buildings and structures	0.361	0.152	0	0.982	7,833
		Machinery and equipment	0.280	0.201	0	0.825	7,833
		Vessels and vehicles	0.036	0.121	0	0.999	7,833
		Tools, furniture, and fixtures	0.098	0.109	0	0.817	7,833
		Land	0.225	0.151	0	0.953	7,833
	Cash flow ratio		0.172	0.303	−10.933	11.092	7,833
	Interest-bearing debt ratio		1.693	3.365	0	45.420	7,833
FY1987–91	(Tobin's $q-1$) × implicit deflator		4.786	6.940	−1.921	86.630	8,762
	Investment rate × share weighting	Buildings and structures	0.019	2.642	−246.368	0.569	8,762
		Machinery and equipment	0.048	0.164	−9.675	0.469	8,762
		Vessels and vehicles	−0.048	4.423	−413.902	0.783	8,762
		Tools, furniture, and fixtures	0.001	1.137	−98.697	0.393	8,762
		Land	0.010	0.032	−0.693	0.541	8,762

(continued)

Table 4.2 (continued)

	Variable name		Mean	S.D.	Min	Max	N of obs.
	Share weighting	Buildings and structures	0.373	0.166	0	0.967	8,762
		Machinery and equipment	0.282	0.214	0	0.864	8,762
		Vessels and vehicles	0.029	0.106	0	0.991	8,762
		Tools, furniture, and fixtures	0.109	0.116	0	0.912	8,762
		Land	0.208	0.150	0	0.963	8,762
	Cash flow ratio		0.212	0.343	−4.466	10.628	8,762
	Interest-bearing debt ratio		1.717	3.364	0	44.900	8,762
FY1992–97	(Tobin's $q-1$) × implicit deflator		1.946	5.329	−4.222	89.441	12,497
	Investment rate × share weighting	Buildings and structures	0.030	0.269	−21.723	0.784	12,497
		Machinery and equipment	0.010	1.238	−116.723	0.531	12,497
		Vessels and vehicles	−0.001	0.165	−16.602	0.683	12,497
		Tools, furniture, and fixtures	0.008	0.287	−29.053	0.574	12,497
		Land	0.006	0.070	−6.291	0.541	12,497
	Share weighting	Buildings and structures	0.422	0.179	0	0.973	12,497
		Machinery and equipment	0.262	0.219	0	0.928	12,497
		Vessels and vehicles	0.021	0.087	0	0.981	12,497
		Tools, furniture, and fixtures	0.105	0.115	0	0.953	12,497
		Land	0.190	0.139	0	0.964	12,497
	Cash flow ratio		0.141	0.397	−12.258	14.458	12,497
	Interest-bearing debt ratio		1.551	3.126	0	44.870	12,497

(continued)

Table 4.2 (continued)

	Variable name		Mean	S.D.	Min	Max	N of obs.
FY1998–04	(Tobin's $q-1$) × implicit deflator		1.106	6.573	−4.253	89.510	15,733
	Investment rate × share weighting	Buildings and structures	−0.088	7.286	−780.989	0.777	15,733
		Machinery and equipment	−0.225	18.119	−2053.302	0.508	15,733
		Vessels and vehicles	−0.043	3.160	−379.012	0.511	15,733
		Tools, furniture, and fixtures	−0.008	0.679	−56.040	0.628	15,733
		Land	−0.132	12.207	−1518.407	0.558	15,733
	Share weighting	Buildings and structures	0.419	0.177	0	0.992	15,733
		Machinery and equipment	0.225	0.212	0	0.960	15,733
		Vessels and vehicles	0.014	0.071	0	0.962	15,733
		Tools, furniture, and fixtures	0.112	0.131	0	1.000	15,733
		Land	0.230	0.167	0	0.964	15,733
	Cash flow ratio		0.160	1.153	−13.614	88.228	15,733
	Interest-bearing debt ratio		1.194	2.649	0	44.431	15,733
(b) Book-Value method							
FY1982–86	(Tobin's $q-1$) × implicit deflator		1.629	3.812	−3.793	70.276	7,825
	Investment rate × share weighting	Buildings and structures	0.034	0.056	−0.661	0.732	7,825
		Machinery and equipment	0.049	0.219	−18.530	0.483	7,825
		Vessels and vehicles	0.005	0.057	−3.042	0.755	7,825
		Tools, furniture, and fixtures	0.022	0.032	−0.706	0.279	7,825
		Land	0.008	0.043	−1.079	0.439	7,825

(continued)

Table 4.2 (continued)

	Variable name		Mean	S.D.	Min	Max	N of obs.
	Share weighting	Buildings and structures	0.364	0.152	0	0.982	7,825
		Machinery and equipment	0.282	0.200	0	0.825	7,825
		Vessels and vehicles	0.038	0.122	0	0.999	7,825
		Tools, furniture, and fixtures	0.103	0.113	0	0.835	7,825
		Land	0.213	0.145	0	0.897	7,825
	Cash flow ratio		0.161	0.246	−8.603	4.418	7,825
	Interest-bearing debt ratio		1.539	2.805	0	36.657	7,825
FY1987–91	(Tobin's $q-1$) × implicit deflator		4.374	6.270	−1.921	71.623	8,763
	Investment rate × share weighting	Buildings and structures	0.050	0.067	−1.392	0.579	8,763
		Machinery and equipment	0.054	0.059	−0.925	0.466	8,763
		Vessels and vehicles	0.002	0.089	−5.401	0.782	8,763
		Tools, furniture, and fixtures	0.023	0.028	−0.364	0.366	8,763
		Land	0.010	0.030	−0.695	0.508	8,763
	Share weighting	Buildings and structures	0.372	0.166	0	0.967	8,763
		Machinery and equipment	0.284	0.213	0	0.864	8,763
		Vessels and vehicles	0.030	0.103	0	0.990	8,763
		Tools, furniture, and fixtures	0.118	0.123	0	0.918	8,763
		Land	0.195	0.141	0	0.906	8,763
	Cash flow ratio		0.198	0.295	−5.881	7.376	8,763
	Interest-bearing debt ratio		1.572	2.989	0	37.951	8,763

(continued)

Table 4.2 (continued)

	Variable name		Mean	S.D.	Min	Max	N of obs.
FY1992–97	(Tobin's $q-1$) × implicit deflator		1.726	4.700	−3.877	71.731	12,495
	Investment rate × share weighting	Buildings and structures	0.036	0.075	−4.034	0.778	12,495
		Machinery and equipment	0.032	0.201	−21.809	0.475	12,495
		Vessels and vehicles	0.000	0.232	−25.648	0.746	12,495
		Tools, furniture, and fixtures	0.016	0.026	−0.678	0.566	12,495
		Land	0.005	0.060	−5.277	0.393	12,495
	Share weighting	Buildings and structures	0.420	0.179	0	0.972	12,495
		Machinery and equipment	0.265	0.218	0	0.927	12,495
		Vessels and vehicles	0.022	0.084	0	0.976	12,495
		Tools, furniture, and fixtures	0.115	0.123	0	0.952	12,495
		Land	0.179	0.132	0	0.948	12,495
	Cash flow ratio		0.130	0.341	−8.907	11.685	12,495
	Interest-bearing debt ratio		1.425	2.746	0	37.025	12,495
FY1998–04	(Tobin's $q-1$) × implicit deflator		0.883	5.685	−3.937	75.061	15,736
	Investment rate × share weighting	Buildings and structures	0.016	0.305	−32.874	0.775	15,736
		Machinery and equipment	0.021	0.058	−3.402	0.607	15,736
		Vessels and vehicles	−10.523	1320.211	−165611.5	0.523	15,736
		Tools, furniture, and fixtures	0.013	0.219	−26.875	0.591	15,736
		Land	−0.127	11.994	−1493.245	0.545	15,736

(continued)

Table 4.2 (continued)

	Variable name		Mean	S.D.	Min	Max	N of obs.
	Share weighting	Buildings and structures	0.413	0.177	0	0.992	15,736
		Machinery and equipment	0.232	0.213	0	0.961	15,736
		Vessels and vehicles	0.016	0.069	0	0.960	15,736
		Tools, furniture, and fixtures	0.124	0.138	0	1.000	15,736
		Land	0.214	0.159	0	0.946	15,736
(c) Zero method							
FY1982–86	(Tobin's $q-1$) × implicit deflator		1.332	3.448	−2.541	56.597	7,828
	Investment rate × share weighting	Buildings and structures	0.038	0.047	0	0.704	7,828
		Machinery and equipment	0.053	0.053	0	0.551	7,828
		Vessels and vehicles	0.007	0.028	0	0.756	7,828
		Tools, furniture, and fixtures	0.022	0.029	0	0.277	7,828
		Land	0.013	0.030	0	0.445	7,828
	Share weighting	Buildings and structures	0.361	0.150	0	0.978	7,828
		Machinery and equipment	0.278	0.197	0	0.863	7,828
		Vessels and vehicles	0.039	0.123	0	0.997	7,828
		Tools, furniture, and fixtures	0.099	0.109	0	0.733	7,828
		Land	0.223	0.146	0	0.897	7,828
	Cash flow ratio		0.143	0.194	−4.959	3.863	7,828
	Interest-bearing debt ratio		1.250	1.912	0	21.574	7,828

(continued)

Table 4.2 (continued)

	Variable name		Mean	S.D.	Min	Max	N of obs.
FY1987–91	(Tobin's $q-1$) × implicit deflator		3.535	4.883	−1.921	60.655	8,749
	Investment rate × share weighting	Buildings and structures	0.051	0.060	0	0.582	8,749
		Machinery and equipment	0.054	0.055	0	0.459	8,749
		Vessels and vehicles	0.005	0.023	0	0.763	8,749
		Tools, furniture, and fixtures	0.023	0.028	0	0.408	8,749
		Land	0.010	0.026	0	0.457	8,749
	Share weighting	Buildings and structures	0.369	0.164	0.003	0.963	8,749
		Machinery and equipment	0.281	0.211	0	0.864	8,749
		Vessels and vehicles	0.032	0.108	0	0.989	8,749
		Tools, furniture, and fixtures	0.114	0.121	0	0.887	8,749
		Land	0.204	0.144	0	0.904	8,749
	Cash flow ratio		0.172	0.211	−2.244	5.812	8,749
	Interest-bearing debt ratio		1.251	1.991	0	21.696	8,749
FY1992–97	(Tobin's $q-1$) × implicit deflator		1.350	3.937	−3.469	60.007	12,505
	Investment rate × share weighting	Buildings and structures	0.039	0.058	0	0.778	12,505
		Machinery and equipment	0.034	0.043	0	0.643	12,505
		Vessels and vehicles	0.004	0.018	0	0.548	12,505
		Tools, furniture, and fixtures	0.017	0.025	0	0.558	12,505
		Land	0.008	0.023	0	0.459	12,505

(continued)

Table 4.2 (continued)

	Variable name		Mean	S.D.	Min	Max	N of obs.
	Share weighting	Buildings and structures	0.414	0.177	0.004	0.971	12,505
		Machinery and equipment	0.263	0.216	0	0.927	12,505
		Vessels and vehicles	0.024	0.092	0	0.969	12,505
		Tools, furniture, and fixtures	0.113	0.122	0	0.944	12,505
		Land	0.187	0.134	0	0.917	12,505
	Cash flow ratio		0.121	0.296	−6.079	13.307	12,505
	Interest-bearing debt ratio		1.170	1.913	0	21.686	12,505
FY1998–04	(Tobin's $q-1$) × implicit deflator		0.592	4.732	−3.499	59.527	15,745
	Investment rate × share weighting	Buildings and structures	0.029	0.050	0	0.708	15,745
		Machinery and equipment	0.025	0.038	0	0.680	15,745
		Vessels and vehicles	0.002	0.012	0	0.418	15,745
		Tools, furniture, and fixtures	0.016	0.030	0	0.600	15,745
		Land	0.009	0.027	0	0.396	15,745
	Share weighting	Buildings and structures	0.406	0.173	0	0.992	15,745
		Machinery and equipment	0.232	0.212	0	0.961	15,745
		Vessels and vehicles	0.017	0.075	0	0.958	15,745
		Tools, furniture, and fixtures	0.120	0.134	0	1.000	15,745
		Land	0.226	0.160	0	0.959	15,745
	Cash flow ratio		0.119	0.443	−5.119	23.350	15,745
	Interest-bearing debt ratio		0.831	1.478	0	21.169	15,745

Table 4.3 Estimation of Multiple q investment function (OLS) (a) Proportional method (b) Book-Value method (c) Zero method

		(a) Proportional method		(b) Book-Value method		(c) Zero method	
		FE model	RE model	FE model	RE model	FE model	RE model
FY1982–86							
γ	Buildings and structures	1.331 (4.98)***	1.736 (6.58)***	4.558 (7.95)***	5.491 (10.10)***	3.337 (4.77)***	4.620 (7.23)***
	Machinery and equipment	0.401 (4.20)***	0.416 (4.56)***	−0.212 (1.39)	−0.317 (2.34)**	1.882 (2.31)**	0.618 (0.82)
	Vessels and vehicles	0.491 (0.84)	0.689 (1.21)	0.699 (1.32)	0.677 (1.32)	1.748 (1.47)	2.005 (1.73)*
	Tools, furniture, and fixtures	0.012 (0.37)	0.025 (0.76)	12.051 (7.98)***	14.974 (10.37)***	24.074 (10.00)***	32.383 (14.65)***
	Land	3.906 (5.26)***	3.532 (4.86)***	2.358 (3.40)***	1.994 (3.00)***	5.042 (5.11)***	5.336 (5.70)***
$-\gamma{*}a$	Buildings and structures	−1.443 (0.93)	−6.097 (6.12)***	−0.461 (0.31)	−0.806 (0.94)	1.251 (0.83)	4.442 (5.37)***
	Machinery and equipment	−3.528 (2.06)**	−9.003 (8.94)***	−3.037 (1.81)*	−4.027 (4.72)***	1.660 (1.00)	1.899 (2.28)**
	Vessels and vehicles	2.260 (0.83)	−0.441 (0.25)	−0.222 (0.09)	2.045 (1.35)	3.010 (1.01)	6.020 (4.45)***
	Land	1.130 (0.70)	−6.476 (6.40)***	0.289 (0.18)	−2.339 (2.67)***	1.758 (1.13)	2.651 (3.19)***
Cash flow ratio		1.207 (8.22)***	1.895 (13.53)***	1.470 (9.21)***	2.267 (15.13)***	1.999 (9.71)***	3.119 (17.12)***
Interest-bearing debt ratio		0.334 (10.81)***	0.333 (15.13)***	0.368 (11.72)***	0.310 (13.97)***	0.480 (11.18)***	0.325 (11.57)***
Number of observations		7,833	7,833	7,825	7,825	7,828	7,828
Number of firms		1,672	1,672	1,670	1,670	1,668	1,668
R-squared: within		0.10	0.10	0.13	0.12	0.13	0.12
R-squared: between		0.13	0.27	0.17	0.29	0.22	0.39
R-squared: overall		0.07	0.18	0.12	0.21	0.16	0.27
H_{A0}: all $\gamma_j = \gamma$		18.05***	88.19***	42.35***	271.46***	18.76***	176.16***
H_{B0}: all $\gamma_j = \gamma$ & $a_j = a$		12.71***	122.88***	25.26***	298.80***	10.94***	217.93***
Hausman test		687.99***		577.48***		349.43***	

(continued)

Table 4.3 (continued)

		(a) Proportional method		(b) Book-Value method		(c) Zero method	
		FE model	RE model	FE model	RE model	FE model	RE model
FY1987–91							
γ	Buildings and structures	−0.020 (1.31)	−0.004 (0.26)	4.586 (6.49)***	6.059 (8.95)***	4.783 (7.25)***	7.023 (11.33)***
	Machinery and equipment	0.626 (2.51)**	0.786 (3.11)***	0.427 (0.44)	0.276 (0.29)	0.085 (0.09)	−0.140 (0.16)
	Vessels and vehicles	−0.019 (2.08)**	−0.035 (3.75)***	−1.890 (4.19)***	−2.466 (5.52)***	10.900 (6.36)***	10.184 (6.03)***
	Tools, furniture, and fixtures	0.614 (14.38)***	0.399 (9.64)***	30.363 (9.61)***	32.174 (10.67)***	22.958 (8.19)***	26.357 (10.16)***
	Land	21.604 (15.56)***	20.884 (15.05)***	17.247 (12.38)***	16.040 (11.66)***	13.788 (10.22)***	13.652 (10.45)***
$-\gamma * a$	Buildings and structures	−8.944 (4.55)***	−9.080 (7.67)***	−6.183 (3.00)***	0.106 (0.09)	−0.255 (0.15)	3.182 (3.37)***
	Machinery and equipment	−10.701 (4.72)***	−12.092 (9.60)***	−7.876 (3.31)***	−3.544 (2.93)***	−1.816 (0.96)	−0.893 (0.90)
	Vessels and vehicles	−13.338 (4.02)***	−3.677 (1.64)	−38.882 (13.19)***	−17.604 (9.14)***	11.149 (3.28)***	6.606 (3.54)***
	Land	4.429 (2.00)**	−2.835 (2.21)**	2.722 (1.18)	4.679 (3.74)***	4.827 (2.58)***	2.790 (2.75)***
Cash flow ratio		1.939 (9.03)***	3.657 (18.67)***	2.746 (12.48)***	4.432 (22.23)***	3.975 (14.95)***	5.628 (24.37)***
Interest-bearing debt ratio		0.15 (3.84)***	0.29 (10.38)***	0.35 (9.20)***	0.33 (11.54)***	0.23 (4.94)***	0.24 (6.96)***
Number of observations		8,762	8,762	8,763	8,763	8,749	8,749
Number of firms		1,913	1,913	1,908	1,908	1,905	1,905
R-squared: within		0.17	0.15	0.20	0.18	0.17	0.16
R-squared: between		0.10	0.30	0.06	0.33	0.17	0.37
R-squared: overall		0.12	0.25	0.06	0.26	0.15	0.30
H_{A0}: all $\gamma_j = \gamma$		117.02***	349.56***	85.06***	409.00***	28.65***	140.54***
H_{B0}: all $\gamma_j = \gamma$ & $a_j = a$		83.92***	447.52***	98.61***	638.11***	20.33***	223.68***
Hausman test		1257.89***		668.58***		199.67***	

(continued)

Table 4.3 (continued)

		(a) Proportional method		(b) Book-Value method		(c) Zero method	
		FE model	RE model	FE model	RE model	FE model	RE model
FY1992–97							
γ	Buildings and structures	0.392 (3.52)***	0.459 (4.15)***	1.243 (3.06)***	1.574 (4.05)***	3.322 (6.82)***	3.565 (7.90)***
	Machinery and equipment	−0.020 (0.79)	−0.026 (1.05)	0.045 (0.34)	−0.012 (0.09)	0.233 (0.31)	−0.285 (0.40)
	Vessels and vehicles	0.173 (0.98)	0.137 (0.78)	−0.045 (0.41)	−0.047 (0.43)	5.386 (3.82)***	4.940 (3.53)***
	Tools, furniture, and fixtures	0.144 (1.39)	0.140 (1.37)	17.840 (9.67)***	23.925 (13.65)***	25.794 (13.39)***	34.791 (19.55)***
	Land	0.772 (1.82)*	1.052 (2.49)**	0.725 (1.67)*	0.902 (2.09)**	5.978 (5.38)***	6.314 (5.97)***
$-\gamma *a$	Buildings and structures	−11.006 (8.60)***	−9.791 (11.92)***	−6.964 (5.66)***	−3.506 (4.58)***	3.192 (2.82)***	2.650 (4.02)***
	Machinery and equipment	−14.866 (9.52)***	−12.943 (14.41)***	−8.271 (5.50)***	−5.975 (7.25)***	0.872 (0.65)	0.231 (0.33)
	Vessels and vehicles	28.116 (9.01)***	8.063 (4.11)***	−15.025 (6.98)***	−8.575 (5.77)***	23.132 (9.77)***	11.218 (7.80)***
	Land	−11.510 (8.45)***	−10.220 (11.63)***	−7.083 (5.39)***	−3.760 (4.52)***	1.750 (1.46)	1.014 (1.43)
Cash flow ratio		1.778 (15.44)***	2.169 (20.78)***	2.291 (17.48)***	2.551 (22.03)***	2.993 (21.06)***	3.212 (27.78)***
Interest-bearing debt ratio		0.199 (6.65)***	0.228 (10.05)***	0.266 (8.16)***	0.275 (11.60)***	0.200 (5.05)***	0.162 (5.82)***
Number of observations		12,497	12,497	12,495	12,495	12,505	12,505
Number of firms		2,278	2,278	2,278	2,278	2,279	2,279
R-squared: within		0.10	0.09	0.10	0.10	0.14	0.13
R-squared: between		0.06	0.21	0.14	0.25	0.11	0.33
R-squared: overall		0.04	0.17	0.11	0.20	0.09	0.28
H_{A0}: *all* $\gamma_j = \gamma$		4.82***	27.44***	28.69***	222.77***	36.97***	317.53***
H_{B0}: *all* $\gamma_j = \gamma$ & $a_j = a$		33.90***	162.04***	19.64***	256.57***	37.84***	414.94***
Hausman test		351.35***		246.03***		255.50***	

(continued)

Table 4.3 (continued)

		(a) Proportional method		(b) Book-Value method		(c) Zero method	
		FE model	RE model	FE model	RE model	FE model	RE model
FY1998–04							
γ	Buildings and structures	0.038 (5.23)***	0.065 (9.36)***	0.216 (2.19)**	0.251 (2.56)**	6.629 (9.65)***	7.133 (11.04)***
	Machinery and equipment	0.004 (2.04)**	0.004 (2.20)**	0.455 (0.78)	0.745 (1.30)	−3.680 (3.64)***	−2.969 (3.10)***
	Vessels and vehicles	0.001 (0.05)	−0.001 (0.13)	0.000 (2.19)**	0.000 (4.01)***	−0.437 (0.16)	−0.137 (0.05)
	Tools, furniture, and fixtures	0.470 (7.53)***	0.491 (7.96)***	0.215 (1.59)	0.281 (2.08)**	28.971 (18.73)***	35.514 (25.06)***
	Land	0.001 (0.30)	0.002 (0.86)	0.002 (0.75)	0.004 (1.58)	1.694 (1.65)*	1.918 (1.96)*
$-\gamma{*}a$	Buildings and structures	−15.876 (13.53)***	−15.140 (19.74)***	−11.894 (9.80)***	−11.194 (15.80)***	−2.049 (1.73)*	−1.975 (3.15)***
	Machinery and equipment	−20.739 (14.54)***	−17.998 (21.25)***	−15.544 (10.24)***	−13.403 (17.26)***	−6.346 (4.56)***	−3.576 (5.40)***
	Vessels and vehicles	12.148 (3.07)***	−6.343 (2.80)***	−7.470 (1.87)*	−11.371 (5.49)***	−5.811 (1.61)	−4.312 (2.52)**
	Land	−17.375 (15.88)***	−16.171 (22.44)***	−12.217 (10.99)***	−11.458 (17.43)***	−3.857 (3.51)***	−3.062 (5.17)***
Cash flow ratio		0.634 (12.65)***	0.941 (20.36)***	1.014 (10.53)***	1.653 (21.07)***	1.157 (10.14)***	2.144 (26.10)***
Interest-bearing debt ratio		0.000 (0.00)	0.102 (4.03)***	0.140 (3.72)***	0.176 (5.52)***	0.171 (3.75)***	0.221 (6.67)***
Number of observations		15,733	15,733	15,736	15,736	15,745	15,745
Number of firms		2,529	2,529	2,528	2,528	2,527	2,527
R-squared: within		0.06	0.05	0.04	0.04	0.08	0.07
R-squared: between		0.18	0.38	0.27	0.39	0.43	0.54
R-squared: overall		0.09	0.22	0.14	0.23	0.23	0.33
H_{A0}: *all* $\gamma_j = \gamma$		29.34***	214.27***	2.27***	15.21***	78.20***	516.84***
H_{B0}: *all* $\gamma_j = \gamma$ & $a_j = a$		29.22***	257.53***	3.40***	30.17***	46.59***	544.07***
Hausman test		1788.38***		266.57***		262.54***	

Note Absolute *t*-values are shown in parenthesis. *, **, and *** denote significance at the 10%, 5%, and 1% level, respectively

First, under the Proportional method described in panel (a), we find no capital goods whose estimated parameter γ_j of the adjustment cost function is significantly positive across all four periods. However, positive and significant estimations are obtained for buildings and structures, machinery and equipment, and land in the majority of periods, with the following exceptions: the second period (1987–91) for buildings and structures, the third period (1992–97) for machinery and equipment, and the fourth period (1998–04) for land. The following relationship holds for the magnitude of the estimated value of the parameter γ_j:

$$\text{machinery and equipment} < \text{buildings and structures} < \text{land}.$$

The estimated value turns out to be extremely large with respect to land during the second period (1987–91), which overlaps with the bubble period. In the fourth period (1998–04), the parameter values for buildings and structures and machinery and equipment are considerably smaller than those in other periods. In addition, the estimation results for $-\gamma_j a_j$ (excluding those for tools, furniture, and fixtures) in cases in which γ_j is positive and significant are negative and significant except in the following cases: the first period (1982–86) for buildings and structures and land and the second period (1987–91) for land. This result suggests that a_j is generally positive.

Regarding hypothesis testing, the null hypothesis stating that the parameters of the adjustment cost function are equal for each capital good is significantly rejected in all sample periods. Thus, the investment functions based on the Multiple q model are preferable to those based on the Single q model. However, the coefficients on the cash flow and interest-bearing debt ratios are significantly estimated in almost all subsample periods. Thus, even if we consider the heterogeneity of capital goods, factors remain that cannot be fully explained within the framework of Tobin's q theory.

Next, for the Book-Value method described in panel (b), γ_j is positive and significantly estimated for buildings and structures across all four periods. We estimate that γ_j is also positive and significant for tools, furniture, and fixtures and land in all periods except the fourth period (1998–04). However, the estimations for machinery and equipment and vessels and vehicles are either insignificant or negative in all subsample periods. As is the case with the Proportional method, the estimated value of γ_j is considerably larger for land in the second period (1987–91), which overlaps with the bubble period. The adjustment cost parameter γ_j is large for tools, furniture, and fixtures, but, as discussed, because s_j is excluded from the explanatory variables only for tools, furniture, and fixtures, we cannot simply compare these values with the γ_j values for other capital goods. However, the high correlation between "(investment rate) × (weighting): $\left(I_j/(1-\delta_j)K_j^{'}\right) \times s_j$" and "weighting: s_j" signifies that the fluctuation in the investment rate is relatively small, and we can infer that, if they are distinguishable, γ_j is highly likely to take a large value.

The estimation results for $-\gamma_j a_j$ (excluding that of tools, furniture, and fixtures) in cases for which the parameter γ_j is positive and significant are negative and significant, suggesting that a_j is positive, as in the Proportional method, except in the following cases: the first period (1982–86) for buildings and structures and land and the second period (1987–91) for land. The coefficients on the cash flow and interest-bearing debt ratios are significant in nearly all subsample periods, and the results of the hypothesis test are the same as those in the Proportional method.

From the above, we can summarize conclusions from the somewhat robust results obtained by the Proportional and Book-Value methods, which assess the behaviors around new acquisitions and sales and retirements in a symmetric, mutually additive manner. The first is that buildings and structures in all periods and land in periods other than the fourth period (1998–2004), which follows the financial crisis, can be explained within the framework of a smooth, convex adjustment cost function. The second is that the investment function based on the Multiple q model is preferable to that based on the Single q model, but factors remain that cannot be explained within the framework of Tobin's q theory.

Under the Zero method described by panel (c), which only assesses the behavior for new acquisitions, the number of cases in which γ_j is significantly positive is greater than under the Proportional and Book-Value methods. This relationship holds for all four sampled periods for buildings and structures; tools, furniture, and fixtures; and land. However, γ_j is positive and significant for machinery and equipment only in the first period (1982–86) and for vessels and vehicles only in the second (1987–91) and third periods (1992–97); its estimated values in the other periods are insignificant or negative.

For land, the largest value of γ_j appears in the second period (1987–91) and the smallest appears in the fourth period (1998–04). In contrast, for buildings and structures, the largest value appears in the fourth period (1998–04). The estimation results for $-\gamma_j a_j$ (excluding tools, furniture, and fixtures) in cases of positive and significant γ_j differ from the Proportional and Book-Value methods in that the estimates are significantly positive for vessels and vehicles and for land in the second period (1987–91) and for buildings and structures and for vessels and vehicles in the third period (1992–97). This result implies that, in these cases, a_j is negative. The hypothesis test results and the coefficients on the cash flow and interest-bearing debt ratios are similar to those obtained by the Proportional and Book-Value methods.

4.2.4 Results of System-GMM Estimation

In addition to the investment rate, the cash flow and interest-bearing debt ratios are determined simultaneously with Tobin's q. As a result, estimation bias may occur in the OLS estimation results in the previous subsection. Thus, we next report the estimation results using system GMM (Table 4.4). In the estimations for the first period (1982–86), the pre-bubble period, we suspect that second-order serial correlation exists based on Arellano and Bond's (1991) serial correlation test. We believe this correlation may arise because the instrumental variables adopted for this estimation are weak instruments, as this period is still impacted by the benchmark. However, we do not observe any particular estimation problems from the second period (1987–91) onwards.

First, we note that under the Proportional method described by panel (a), the adjustment cost function parameter γ_j is only positive and significant for land in the first (1982–86) and second periods (1987–91). Under the Book-Value method described by panel (b), we observe more positive and significant coefficients to a certain degree. However, from the third period onwards, only tools, furniture, and fixtures in the third period (1992–97) has a positive and significant coefficient, and the levels of the estimated values are fairly unstable. When we consider this result together with the results for the Proportional method in panel (a), as far as the behaviors of new acquisitions and sales and retirements are lumped together, we cannot robustly conclude in any case that the data are consistent with the framework of a smooth, convex adjustment cost function.

However, under the Zero method, as shown in panel (c), γ_j is estimated to be positive and significant for buildings and structures and for tools, furniture, and fixtures across all four periods. The trend in the magnitude of the estimated value of γ_j for buildings and structures is similar to that in the investment rate, with the largest value in the second period (1987–91) and the smallest value in the fourth period (1998–04). Moreover, $-\gamma_j a_j$ is positive and significantly estimated for buildings and structures with the exception of the third period (1992–97), suggesting that a_j is negative.

Finally, we can significantly reject the null hypothesis—that the parameters of the adjustment cost function are equal for each capital good—in all periods, indicating that the investment function based on the Multiple q model is preferable to that based on the Single q model. However, at least one of the coefficients on the cash flow and interest-bearing debt ratios is significantly estimated in all four periods. Thus, factors remain that cannot be explained within the framework of a simple Multiple q theory that merely considers the heterogeneity of capital goods.

Table 4.4 Estimation of the Multiple q investment function (system GMM)

		(a) Proportional method	(b) Book-Value method	(c) Zero method	(a) Proportional method	(b) Book-Value method	(c) Zero method
		FY1982–86			FY1987–91		
γ	Buildings and structures	8.369 (1.42)	10.450 (1.70)*	30.068 (3.55)***	2.513 (0.63)	99.927 (2.31)**	49.432 (2.47)**
	Machinery and equipment	−0.517 (0.12)	14.549 (3.70)***	3.882 (0.63)	−1.356 (0.32)	−27.210 (0.58)	−20.199 (2.11)**
	Vessels and vehicles	−1.693 (0.26)	−0.079 (0.09)	0.641 (0.32)	−0.380 (1.53)	11.594 (1.91)*	30.894 (1.69)*
	Tools, furniture, and fixtures	−0.552 (0.13)	7.288 (1.65)*	36.281 (2.53)**	−0.166 (0.35)	175.702 (1.74)*	111.922 (2.81)***
	Land	33.436 (2.15)**	1.567 (0.24)	2.966 (0.28)	63.988 (2.02)**	29.168 (0.64)	23.578 (0.52)
$-\gamma{*}a$	Buildings and structures	−5.588 (1.75)*	4.250 (1.45)	7.696 (2.45)**	−9.846 (2.13)**	13.251 (0.53)	17.053 (2.53)**
	Machinery and equipment	−5.861 (1.74)*	−9.887 (2.96)***	5.904 (1.66)*	−8.797 (1.68)*	28.155 (1.39)	23.381 (3.28)***
	Vessels and vehicles	−5.746 (1.74)*	−3.898 (1.58)	7.369 (2.50)**	5.224 (0.68)	36.353 (2.18)**	19.963 (1.82)*
	Land	−0.423 (0.11)	−11.876 (2.72)***	4.050 (1.25)	−14.106 (1.63)	15.450 (0.70)	13.834 (1.40)
Cash flow ratio		11.973 (2.28)**	7.296 (3.39)***	10.924 (5.16)***	14.859 (4.20)***	−7.278 (0.61)	4.481 (1.52)
Interest-bearing debt ratio		0.370 (1.59)	0.306 (1.72)*	0.656 (2.61)***	1.455 (3.52)***	1.532 (1.99)**	1.211 (2.25)**
Number of observations		7,833	7,825	7,828	8,762	8,763	8,749
Number of firms		1,672	1,670	1,668	1,913	1,908	1,905
Allerano Bond AR(2) test		−1.91*	−2.03**	−2.55**	0.33	1.53	1.44
p-values of Sargan test		0.374	0.013	0.411	0.079	0.112	0.111
H_{A0}: all $\gamma_j = \gamma$		6.25	30.13***	31.63***	6.09	17.13**	25.49***
H_{B0}: all $\gamma_j = \gamma$ & $a_j = a$		13.25*	49.61***	38.58***	12.00	25.89*	31.53***

(continued)

Table 4.4 (continued)

		(a) Proportional method	(b) Book-Value method	(c) Zero method	(a) Proportional method	(b) Book-Value method	(c) Zero method
			FY1982–86			FY1987–91	
γ	Buildings and structures	−3.581 (0.43)	14.887 (0.88)	24.574 (2.35)**	0.910 (0.69)	0.596 (0.30)	19.838 (3.44)***
	Machinery and equipment	−0.295 (0.25)	0.463 (0.06)	54.517 (2.56)**	−0.123 (0.91)	0.295 (0.07)	−6.481 (0.93)
	Vessels and vehicles	−4.281 (0.21)	0.651 (0.19)	−18.649 (0.73)	−0.179 (0.68)	0.001 (0.29)	−4.421 (0.87)
	Tools, furniture, and fixtures	−0.258 (0.02)	93.196 (2.15)**	55.886 (2.18)**	2.022 (1.09)	0.762 (0.26)	61.981 (3.38)***
	Land	21.046 (0.66)	21.409 (0.65)	59.186 (2.04)**	0.169 (0.22)	0.011 (0.12)	2.744 (0.44)
$-\gamma*a$	Buildings and structures	−26.175 (2.99)***	10.615 (1.31)	4.978 (1.52)	−17.212 (2.49)**	−5.858 (2.41)**	5.362 (1.75)*
	Machinery and equipment	−27.715 (3.15)***	13.931 (1.84)*	−1.655 (0.37)	−17.172 (2.55)**	−7.473 (2.77)***	6.406 (1.99)**
	Vessels and vehicles	−25.083 (2.91)***	11.118 (1.48)	7.732 (2.02)**	−0.972 (0.12)	−6.896 (2.94)***	6.038 (2.08)**
	Land	−17.145 (1.80)*	3.443 (0.34)	−1.084 (0.24)	−17.926 (2.67)***	−8.190 (3.01)***	5.300 (1.85)*
Cash flow ratio		−1.070 (0.37)	27.084 (4.86)***	3.791 (1.56)	1.743 (3.28)***	2.258 (1.61)	2.020 (2.92)***
Interest-bearing debt ratio		−0.006 (0.04)	1.339 (2.07)**	0.612 (2.00)**	0.557 (2.29)**	0.199 (0.95)	0.212 (1.01)
Number of observations		12,497	12,495	12,505	15,733	15,736	15,745
Number of firms		2,278	2,278	2,279	2,529	2,528	2,527
Allerano Bond AR(2) test		0.29	−0.89	0.70	0.83	0.94	−0.91
p-values of Sargan test		0.469	0.99	0.484	0.251	0.201	0.941
H_{A0}: all $\gamma_j = \gamma$		0.84	7.50	7.83*	2.77	0.32	26.67***
H_{B0}: all $\gamma_j = \gamma$ & $a_j = a$		7.29	8.65	19.04***	4.42	3.99	31.40***

Note Absolute z-values are shown in parenthesis. *, **, and *** denote significance at the 10%, 5%, and 1% level, respectively

4.2.5 Overcapacity Elimination Process After the Mid-1990s

We now reinterpret the system GMM estimation results from the perspective of clarifying the overcapacity elimination process after the mid-1990s, and we note several implications. The goodness of fit of the parameter γ_j of the adjustment cost function using the Zero method is highest in the third period (1992–97), or the post-bubble collapse period, and it is positive and significant for all capital goods except vessels and vehicles. In other words, the data in this period are the most consistent with the framework of a smooth, convex adjustment cost function for new acquisitions of capital goods as assessed by the Zero method. In the third period (1992–97), although there was an adjustment to the overcapacity that had built up during the bubble period, the financial crisis was not yet apparent. Thus, the estimation results can be seen as revealing the prudency in increasing new investments, and its suppression was also gradual. At the same time, however, this period still includes few cases in which sales and retirements of capital goods served to eliminate overcapacity. Nevertheless, in terms of clarifying the overcapacity elimination process, a limitation of the framework of a smooth, convex adjustment cost function is also clear, as the explanations do not perform well if we treat sales and retirements as symmetric to and mutually additive with new acquisitions, as in the Proportional or Book-Value methods.

In the fourth period (1998–04), after the financial crisis became apparent, new investments were drastically suppressed, and sales and retirements clearly surged. The number of listed companies, such as ICT-related businesses, also saw an unprecedented increase. Thus, it would not be surprising for the explanatory power to decline in the framework of the continuous convex adjustment cost function. Conversely, despite these circumstances, buildings and structures and tools, furniture, and fixtures maintained robust results under the Zero method.

4.2.6 Summary Discussion

This section estimated investment functions based on the Multiple q model using financial data from listed companies in Japan since the 1980s. We attempted to verify whether investment behavior (by capital good), and, in particular, the overcapacity elimination process after the mid-1990s followed a smooth, convex adjustment cost function. We simultaneously used three methods, taken from prior research, to prepare the capital investment and capital stock data for each capital good to estimate the investment functions based on the Multiple q model. These methods differ in their calculations of the market value for sold or retired capital goods in the absence of observable data. These methods are the Proportional method, which multiplies the book value by the ratio of market-to-book value; the Book-Value method, which uses the book value as is; and the Zero method, which uniformly sets these values equal to zero. By incorporating these differences into the analysis, we clarified the differences between new acquisition behavior and sale and retirement behavior.

The following points became clear from the estimation results of the investment function based on the Multiple q model. First, as long as we assume a smooth, convex adjustment cost function, an investment function based on the Multiple q framework is preferable to one based on the Single q framework. However, an investment function based on the Multiple q model does not necessarily provide a good fit, and, particularly for estimations in which the new acquisition and sale and retirement behaviors of capital goods are combined, the explanatory power of investment functions based on the Multiple q model is not necessarily high.

Second, even for estimations with relatively high explanatory power targeting only new acquisitions of capital goods, theoretically redundant variables, such as the cash flow and interest-bearing debt ratios, have significant effects within the framework of Tobin's original q theory. This result confirms that factors still remain that cannot be explained within the framework of a simple Multiple q theory that only considers the heterogeneity of capital goods. The constraints of MM theory (Modigliani & Miller, 1958), which is an implicit precondition for Tobin's q theory, need to be lifted, and the relevance of issues facing companies, such as liquidity constraints and the agency cost problem caused by asymmetrical information, need to be reaffirmed, as Asako, Kuninori, Inoue, and Murase (1991) and Miyagawa (2005) address. Relatedly, it is also important to conduct empirical analyses that incorporate the impacts of various uncertainties, as stressed by Abel and Eberly (1994) and Tanaka (2016).

Third, if we consider the differences in investment behavior by capital good, the new acquisition behavior observed for buildings and structures and for tools, furniture, and fixtures is consistent with a smooth, convex adjustment cost function regardless of the sample period. However, we did not consistently obtain significant results regarding new acquisition behavior for other capital goods, such as machinery and equipment, or for sale and retirement behavior in general. When we considered the results by period, we observed the largest number of capital goods types with significant adjustment cost function parameters pertaining to new acquisition behavior in the mid-1990s (1992–97), following the collapse of the bubble economy.

Finally, we describe the challenges to address in the future. First, it is understood that new acquisitions of buildings and structures and tools, furniture, and fixtures can be explained within the framework of a smooth, convex adjustment cost function, even during the overcapacity elimination process after the mid-1990s. However, new acquisitions of machinery and equipment, which, along with buildings and structures, have a large composition ratio with respect to capital stock and capital investment, are not explained well by the analysis in this section. More detailed analyses are needed to clarify the reasoning for this result or to understand the difference of investment behaviors for machinery and equipment from those for buildings and structures.

Second, when we consider investment behavior including sale and retirement behavior, we do not obtain stably significant estimation results across all capital goods. Thus, cases that investment behavior has certain sections that cannot be explained within the framework of a smooth, convex adjustment cost function must be examined. Examples of such cases include the presence of a fixed portion in the adjustment cost (e.g., when a lump-sum investment is implemented after the marginal profit of the investment exceeds a certain threshold, which is the so-called lumpy investment model) and the case in which asymmetrical adjustment costs are incurred for positive and negative investments. Prior studies along these lines include those by Bertola and Caballero (1990), Shima (2005), and Miyagawa (2005). These studies do not incorporate the heterogeneity of capital and should be extended to the Multiple q framework.

Further, in this section, we addressed the concept of capital stock as a quasi-fixed production factor with unique adjustment costs, and we analyzed this notion by limiting capital stock to that around traditional tangible fixed assets. However, as shown above, in recent years, the number of outliers that must be excluded from the analysis is increasing. One typical example is ICT-related businesses whose sources of corporate value are mostly intangible assets, some of which do not even appear on financial statements. If we extend our target of analysis to the 2010s and later, we will need to closely examine the concept of capital stock and conduct analyses by industry to deal with these new situations. Studies along these lines include that of Miyagawa and Kim (2008), among others.[1]

4.3 Test of the Homogeneity of Capital

4.3.1 Partial Homogeneity

In the previous section, we tested two null hypotheses, H_{A0} and H_{B0}, which state that the parameters related to the adjustment costs of the five categories of capital goods, including land, are all equal. In almost every case that the parameters are estimated to significantly positive, these hypotheses are rejected in all four sample periods, which we can observe from the significant test statistics in the respective cells of

---

[1] We will touch on these issues more in detail in Chap. 7, the concluding chapter of this book.

Tables 4.3 and 4.4. These statistics are derived from the sum of squared residuals of the estimated equation with and without parameter constraints for homogeneity. This heterogeneity, first tested by Tonogi et al. (2010), is observed regardless of the method used to evaluate sales and retirements of capital goods and the selected estimation method (i.e., OLS with either a fixed effects model or system GMM).[2] These hypothesis tests, however, do not identify the source of this rejection of homogeneity. Thus, as briefly mentioned in Chap. 2, Asako and Tonogi (2010) consider the possibility of partial homogeneity and test the homogeneity between "certain capital goods" and the "other four capital goods that are regarded tentatively as homogeneous." They also conduct a pairwise test in which any two of the capital goods are homogeneous.

First, for a given capital good j ($j = 1, \ldots, n$), we tentatively assume that the remaining capital goods are homogeneous and can be included among the capital goods indexed ($n-j$) through direct aggregation. Then, similar to the two null hypotheses H_{AO} and H_{BO}, we raise two null hypotheses H_{CO} and H_{DO} regarding the parameters of the investment function given by Eq. (4.1) as follows:

- **Hypothesis H_{CO}**: The corresponding γ_j and $\gamma_{(n-j)}$ are equal.
- **Hypothesis H_{DO}**: The corresponding γ_j and $\gamma_{(n-j)}$ are equal, and a_j and $a_{(n-j)}$ are equal.

By testing these two null hypotheses, we can identify the capital goods that are most responsible for generating the heterogeneity of capital goods in Japan.

Second, for any pair of two capital goods i and $j(i, j = 1, \ldots, n)$, we test the following two null hypotheses H_{EO} and H_{FO}:

- **Hypothesis H_{EO}**: The corresponding γ_i and γ_j are equal.
- **Hypothesis H_{FO}**: The corresponding γ_i and γ_j are equal, and a_i and a_j are equal.

Through this test, any pairwise partial homogeneity between two categories of capital goods can be detected and, thus, the source of the heterogeneity of capital goods is identified.

The test results are summarized in Table 4.5 for H_{CO} and H_{DO} and in Table 4.6 for H_{EO} and H_{FO}. Following the discussions of the estimation results in Sect. 4.2, we only discuss the results from the OLS model with fixed effects (FE model) but the results are robust throughout the estimations using the random effects model (RE model).

A glance at these tables indicates that, as in Table 4.3, which provides results for the null hypotheses H_{AO} and H_{BO}, the majority of cells contain significant test statistics, implying a rejection of the respective null hypotheses. Although partial homogeneity is not rejected in certain cases, these cases are not uniform across the sample period and the data construction method regarding gross investment and capital stock. Thus, overall, we can conclude that the Multiple q model should be used based on the assumption that these five capital goods are fundamentally heterogeneous.

---

[2]We find exceptions in some subsample periods for estimations using system GMM and with the Proportional and Book-Value methods in panels (a) and (b), respectively, of Table 4.4. With the Zero method, shown in panel (c), we find no exceptions, at least at the 10% significance level.

Table 4.5 Test results for H_{C0} and H_{D0} (a) Proportional method (b) Book-Value method (c) Zero method

		Buildings and structures		Machinery and equipment		Vessels and vehicles		Tools, furniture, and fixtures		Land	
		FE model	RE model	FE model	RE model	FE model	RE model	FE model	RE model	FE model	RE model
(a) Proportional method											
FY1982–1986											
γ	Capital good concerned	0.572 (1.85)*	0.809 (2.62)***	0.235 (2.36)**	0.246 (2.48)**	0.413 (0.64)	0.612 (0.95)	0.002 (0.08)	−0.004 (0.11)	2.827 (3.14)***	2.840 (3.17)***
	Other four capital goods	3.217 (9.42)***	3.860 (11.40)***	3.595 (11.68)***	4.523 (14.82)***	2.947 (11.96)***	3.557 (14.59)***	3.105 (11.83)***	3.710 (14.43)***	2.812 (8.73)***	3.472 (10.87)***
$-\gamma{*}a$	Capital good concerned	−3.522 (3.44)***	−3.423 (3.52)***	−5.835 (4.70)***	−7.582 (6.58)***	1.525 (0.51)	5.087 (1.82)*			0.771 (0.62)	−1.096 (0.94)
	Other four capital goods	−3.819 (3.48)***	−4.029 (3.92)***	−3.610 (2.79)***	−4.482 (3.84)***	−0.456 (0.15)	−0.905 (0.31)	−2.058 (1.33)	−8.353 (9.15)***	−0.693 (0.54)	−0.077 (0.06)
Cash flow ratio		1.151 (8.35)***	1.863 (14.08)***	1.306 (8.98)***	2.051 (14.74)***	1.172 (8.55)***	1.891 (14.34)***	1.054 (7.73)***	1.762 (13.52)***	1.132 (8.25)***	1.847 (14.02)***
Interest-bearing debt ratio		0.342 (11.16)***	0.353 (15.96)***	0.354 (11.55)***	0.356 (16.33)***	0.351 (11.42)***	0.356 (16.25)***	0.345 (11.24)***	0.347 (15.80)***	0.344 (11.24)***	0.357 (16.13)***
Number of observations		7,833	7,833	7,833	7,833	7,833	7,833	7,833	7,833	7,833	7,833
Number of firms		1,672	1,672	1,672	1,672	1,672	1,672	1,672	1,672	1,672	1,672
R-squared: within		0.10	0.10	0.11	0.11	0.11	0.10	0.11	0.10	0.11	0.10
R-squared: between		0.17	0.24	0.19	0.27	0.18	0.26	0.19	0.27	0.16	0.25
R-squared: overall		0.10	0.16	0.11	0.19	0.10	0.17	0.11	0.18	0.10	0.17
H_{C0}: $\gamma_j = \gamma_{(n-j)}$		24.57***	32.81***	97.14***	159.45***	12.50***	16.91***	135.96***	203.40***	0.00	0.35
H_{D0}: $\gamma_j = \gamma_{(n-j)}$ & $a_j = a_{(n-j)}$		12.30***	32.84***	50.28***	188.43***	6.48**	29.21***			0.99	2.78
Hausman test		702.83***		997.25***		430.85***		370.98***		417.00***	
FY1987–1991											

(continued)

Table 4.5 (continued)

		Buildings and structures		Machinery and equipment		Vessels and vehicles		Tools, furniture, and fixtures		Land	
		FE model	RE model	FE model	RE model	FE model	RE model	FE model	RE model	FE model	RE model
γ	Capital good concerned	0.013 (0.830)	0.017 (1.090)	0.815 (2.90)***	0.904 (3.21)***	0.038 (3.04)***	0.010 (0.81)	0.584 (13.43)***	0.367 (8.69)***	24.436 (16.45)***	25.206 (17.05)***
	Other four capital goods	0.695 (5.25)***	0.394 (2.96)***	0.079 (3.04)***	0.069 (2.66)***	0.066 (2.56)**	0.060 (2.28)**	0.074 (2.83)***	0.076 (2.85)***	−0.028 (1.08)	−0.027 (1.04)
$-\gamma * a$	Capital good concerned	−7.229 (6.91)***	−5.814 (5.98)***	−4.732 (3.02)***	−5.495 (3.88)***	13.700 (3.74)***	22.409 (6.28)***			17.190 (12.80)***	13.162 (10.61)***
	Other four capital goods	−2.311 (2.28)**	−4.620 (4.83)***	−0.011 (0.010)	1.070 (0.75)	29.139 (7.22)***	23.044 (6.08)***	−0.346 (0.17)	−5.154 (4.48)***	6.786 (4.78)***	9.529 (7.29)***
Cash flow ratio		1.744 (7.88)***	3.665 (18.41)***	2.004 (9.32)***	3.694 (19.11)***	2.215 (10.00)***	3.922 (19.80)***	1.673 (7.81)***	3.444 (17.61)***	2.198 (10.46)***	3.801 (19.94)***
Interest-bearing debt ratio		0.173 (4.27)***	0.319 (11.08)***	0.161 (3.97)***	0.299 (10.43)***	0.148 (3.67)***	0.307 (10.77)***	0.159 (3.97)***	0.322 (11.34)***	0.199 (4.92)***	0.328 (11.34)***
Number of observations		8,762	8,762	8,762	8,762	8,762	8,762	8,762	8,762	8,762	8,762
Number of firms		1,913	1,913	1,913	1,913	1,913	1,913	1,913	1,913	1,913	1,913
R-squared: within		0.10	0.09	0.10	0.09	0.10	0.09	0.12	0.11	0.14	0.13
R-squared: between		0.10	0.31	0.25	0.33	0.06	0.32	0.10	0.29	0.13	0.30
R-squared: overall		0.09	0.24	0.19	0.26	0.06	0.25	0.12	0.23	0.14	0.25
$H_{C0}: \gamma_j = \gamma_{(n-j)}$		25.98***	7.83***	6.79***	8.67***	0.95	2.93*	97.25*	32.63***	269.63***	289.59***
$H_{D0}: \gamma_j = \gamma_{(n-j)}$ & $a_j = a_{(n-j)}$		23.68***	10.31***	7.70**	67.95***	13.08***	3.15			175.28***	322.81***
Hausman test		263.03***		261.44***		377.74***		987.73***		203.88***	
FY1992–1997											
γ	Capital good concerned	0.319 (2.73)***	0.340 (2.92)***	−0.047 (1.84)*	−0.057 (2.28)**	0.475 (2.65)***	0.536 (2.99)***	−0.030 (0.30)	−0.053 (0.52)	0.111 (0.25)	0.234 (0.53)

(continued)

Table 4.5 (continued)

		Buildings and structures		Machinery and equipment		Vessels and vehicles		Tools, furniture, and fixtures		Land	
		FE model	RE model	FE model	RE model	FE model	RE model	FE model	RE model	FE model	RE model
	Other four capital goods	1.673 (7.40)***	1.860 (8.33)***	1.591 (10.07)***	1.765 (11.28)***	1.212 (8.76)***	1.344 (9.80)***	1.788 (11.31)***	1.945 (12.46)***	1.600 (10.46)***	1.715 (11.31)***
$-\gamma*a$	Capital good concerned	−3.002 (3.87)***	−2.383 (3.27)***	−7.132 (5.88)***	−7.462 (6.79)***	52.223 (16.30)***	42.697 (15.01)***			−5.649 (6.12)***	−5.994 (6.99)***
	Other four capital goods	−0.981 (1.15)	−1.467 (1.91)*	−3.761 (3.08)***	−3.502 (3.17)***	21.754 (7.50)***	29.668 (10.83)***	−3.430 (2.53)**	−7.506 (9.44)***	−4.571 (4.79)***	−5.370 (6.10)***
Cash flow ratio		1.797 (15.45)***	2.239 (21.32)***	1.780 (15.30)***	2.226 (21.24)***	1.759 (15.34)***	2.182 (20.98)***	1.780 (15.29)***	2.176 (20.77)***	1.785 (15.38)***	2.227 (21.25)***
Interest-bearing debt ratio		0.267 (8.81)***	0.271 (11.78)***	0.264 (8.75)***	0.259 (11.34)***	0.258 (8.66)***	0.272 (11.95)***	0.259 (8.45)***	0.256 (11.23)***	0.258 (8.54)***	0.267 (11.64)***
Number of observations		12,497	12,497	12,497	12,497	12,497	12,497	12,497	12,497	12,497	12,497
Number of firms		2,278	2,278	2,278	2,278	2,278	2,278	2,278	2,278	2,278	2,278
R-squared: within		0.07	0.07	0.08	0.08	0.10	0.09	0.08	0.08	0.08	0.08
R-squared: between		0.11	0.19	0.16	0.21	0.03	0.19	0.17	0.23	0.14	0.20
R-squared: overall		0.09	0.16	0.13	0.17	0.03	0.16	0.13	0.17	0.11	0.16
$H_{C0}: \gamma_j = \gamma_{(n-j)}$		25.02***	32.17***	102.08***	128.68***	10.49***	12.68***	89.99***	111.17***	9.37***	9.35***
$H_{D0}: \gamma_j = \gamma_{(n-j)}$ & $a_j = a_{(n-j)}$		16.37***	36.47***	55.26***	176.34***	54.13***	59.82***			5.53*	10.74***
Hausman test		136.32***		179.74***		227.19***		132.84***		247.47***	
FY1998–2004											
γ	Capital good concerned	0.035 (3.54)***	0.050 (5.06)***	0.005 (2.73)***	0.005 (2.59)***	0.002 (0.17)	0.000 (0.01)	0.298 (4.60)***	0.279 (4.38)***	0.001 (0.36)	0.003 (1.01)
	Other four capital goods	0.022 (4.26)***	0.033 (6.50)***	0.031 (10.13)***	0.046 (15.78)***	0.022 (9.92)***	0.032 (15.50)***	0.019 (7.37)***	0.030 (12.06)***	0.030 (10.02)***	0.044 (15.54)***

(continued)

Table 4.5 (continued)

		Buildings and structures		Machinery and equipment		Vessels and vehicles		Tools, furniture, and fixtures		Land	
		FE model	RE model	FE model	RE model	FE model	RE model	FE model	RE model	FE model	RE model
$-\gamma*a$	Capital good concerned	0.500 (0.62)	−0.032 (0.04)	−2.674 (2.30)**	−3.065 (2.81)***	34.112 (7.44)***	11.991 (3.12)***			−3.629 (5.48)***	−3.515 (5.48)***
	Other four capital goods	1.485 (1.83)*	1.991 (2.60)***	0.476 (0.410)	0.590 (0.54)	0.476 (0.13)	1.327 (0.38)	−9.127 (8.75)***	−12.319 (18.25)***	−0.309 (0.46)	−0.155 (0.24)
Cash flow ratio		0.761 (14.29)***	1.126 (23.09)***	0.733 (13.92)***	1.096 (22.67)***	0.715 (13.62)***	1.078 (22.30)***	0.700 (13.32)***	1.014 (21.09)***	0.722 (13.67)***	1.077 (22.19)***
Interest-bearing debt ratio		0.008 (0.25)	0.100 (3.88)***	0.004 (0.12)	0.092 (3.59)***	0.005 (0.14)	0.098 (3.75)***	(0.033) (0.98)	0.070 (2.78)***	(0.012) (0.36)	0.100 (3.90)***
Number of observations		15,733	15,733	15,733	15,733	15,733	15,733	15,733	15,733	15,733	15,733
Number of firms		2,529	2,529	2,529	2,529	2,529	2,529	2,529	2,529	2,529	2,529
R-squared: within		0.03	0.03	0.03	0.03	0.04	0.03	0.04	0.04	0.03	0.03
R-squared: between		0.22	0.32	0.21	0.32	0.02	0.31	0.29	0.38	0.17	0.32
R-squared: overall		0.09	0.18	0.10	0.18	0.01	0.17	0.14	0.22	0.07	0.18
$H_{C0}: \gamma_j = \gamma_{(n-j)}$		0.90	1.50	49.08*	134.29***	3.00***	8.11*	17.97***	14.84***	50.44***	108.02***
$H_{D0}: \gamma_j = \gamma_{(n-j)}$ & $a_j = a_{(n-j)}$		1.24	14.96***	29.04***	169.86***	39.10***	30.57***			42.90***	167.16***
Hausman test		1641.69***		7385.21***		200.48***		544.29***		※	

Notes

Absolute *t*-values are shown in parenthesis. *, **, and *** denote significance at the 10%, 5%, and 1% level, respectively

※ the statistic takes a negative sign suggesting the possibility that the assumption of the Hausman test is not satisfied

(b) Book-Value method

FY1982–1986

γ	Capital good concerned	3.702 (4.53)***	4.910 (6.08)***	−0.187 (1.260)	−0.254 (1.75)*	0.503 (0.81)	0.357 (0.58)	12.812 (8.19)***	14.972 (9.72)***	1.097 (1.27)	1.160 (1.35)

(continued)

Table 4.5 (continued)

		Buildings and structures		Machinery and equipment		Vessels and vehicles		Tools, furniture, and fixtures		Land	
		FE model	RE model	FE model	RE model	FE model	RE model	FE model	RE model	FE model	RE model
	Other four capital goods	3.053 (6.70)***	3.031 (6.75)***	3.903 (12.74)***	4.489 (14.87)***	3.675 (13.37)***	4.123 (15.24)***	2.505 (9.41)***	2.841 (10.98)***	3.834 (10.78)***	4.222 (12.05)***
$-\gamma * a$	Capital good concerned	−1.173 (0.99)	0.324 (0.29)	−5.436 (4.50)***	−6.256 (5.62)***	−0.829 (0.26)	1.404 (0.47)			−1.614 (1.33)	−3.281 (2.91)***
	Other four capital goods	−1.207 (0.94)	−0.675 (0.55)	−4.289 (3.44)***	−3.557 (3.16)***	−1.828 (0.57)	−3.026 (0.99)	4.326 (2.69)***	−1.617 (1.90)*	−3.751 (3.01)***	−3.263 (2.75)***
Cash flow ratio		1.440 (9.05)***	2.240 (14.96)***	1.390 (8.72)***	2.184 (14.58)***	1.462 (9.19)***	2.248 (15.02)***	1.446 (9.13)***	2.196 (14.74)***	1.388 (8.73)***	2.160 (14.43)***
Interest-bearing debt ratio		0.378 (12.09)***	0.324 (14.33)***	0.375 (11.97)***	0.315 (14.01)***	0.376 (12.03)***	0.321 (14.23)***	0.377 (12.06)***	0.316 (14.08)***	0.373 (11.92)***	0.318 (14.02)***
Number of observations		7,825	8,763	7,825	7,825	7,825	7,825	7,825	7,825	7,825	7,825
Number of firms		1,670	1,670	1,670	1,670	1,670	1,670	1,670	1,670	1,670	1,670
R-squared: within		0.12	0.12	0.12	0.12	0.12	0.12	0.13	0.12	0.12	0.12
R-squared: between		0.14	0.24	0.15	0.26	0.15	0.25	0.12	0.27	0.12	0.24
R-squared: overall		0.10	0.18	0.11	0.20	0.11	0.19	0.09	0.20	0.09	0.18
H_{C0}: $\gamma_j = \gamma_{(n-j)}$		0.32	2.72*	138.75*	192.41***	19.91***	28.85***	39.25***	56.27***	6.45***	8.23**
H_{D0}: $\gamma_j = \gamma_{(n-j)}$ & $a_j = a_{(n-j)}$		0.16	6.98**	69.45***	222.03***	9.99***	36.88***			5.26*	8.37**
Hausman test		365.72***		426.96***		※		322.42***		339.07***	
FY1987–1991											
γ	Capital good concerned	9.350 (9.46)***	10.388 (10.69)***	0.590 (0.500)	0.838 (0.71)	0.118 (0.22)	−1.129 (2.14)**	36.470 (10.30)***	41.265 (12.39)***	17.547 (10.66)***	17.712 (10.82)***
	Other four capital goods	2.272 (4.31)***	1.934 (3.72)***	5.360 (13.11)***	5.539 (13.82)***	6.417 (17.20)***	6.825 (18.31)***	3.341 (9.39)***	3.253 (9.45)***	2.681 (5.90)***	3.104 (6.93)***

(continued)

Table 4.5 (continued)

		Buildings and structures		Machinery and equipment		Vessels and vehicles		Tools, furniture, and fixtures		Land	
		FE model	RE model	FE model	RE model	FE model	RE model	FE model	RE model	FE model	RE model
$-\gamma{*}a$	Capital good concerned	1.634 (1.15)	3.447 (2.60)***	−7.273 (3.89)***	−8.602 (5.06)***	−16.209 (4.45)***	−4.274 (1.18)			12.228 (7.21)***	6.687 (4.20)***
	Other four capital goods	3.975 (2.67)***	2.696 (1.88)*	−5.332 (2.74)***	−3.364 (1.83)*	28.720 (7.28)***	18.421 (4.76)***	2.551 (1.07)	3.836 (3.10)***	−3.956 (2.14)**	−0.730 (0.42)
Cash flow ratio		2.283 (10.00)***	4.319 (21.21)***	2.241 (9.88)***	4.200 (20.76)***	2.928 (13.23)***	4.545 (22.66)***	2.215 (9.77)***	4.078 (20.13)***	2.412 (10.79)***	4.295 (21.30)***
Interest-bearing debt ratio		0.448 (11.35)***	0.381 (13.33)***	0.464 (11.76)***	0.371 (13.01)***	0.357 (9.32)***	0.342 (12.09)***	0.472 (12.03)***	0.398 (14.00)***	0.390 (9.91)***	0.347 (12.03)***
Number of observations		8,763	8,763	8,763	8,763	8,763	8,763	8,763	8,763	8,763	8,763
Number of firms		1,908	1,908	1,908	1,908	1,908	1,908	1,908	1,908	1,908	1,908
R-squared: within		0.13	0.12	0.13	0.12	0.18	0.16	0.14	0.13	0.15	0.14
R-squared: between		0.17	0.33	0.21	0.35	0.01	0.30	0.20	0.34	0.12	0.31
R-squared: overall		0.16	0.26	0.19	0.27	0.02	0.24	0.18	0.26	0.12	0.25
H_{C0}: $\gamma_j = \gamma_{(n-j)}$		29.15***	42.84***	11.93***	11.78***	84.66***	136.47***	81.41***	121.14***	62.03***	60.74***
H_{D0}: $\gamma_j = \gamma_{(n-j)}$ & $a_j = a_{(n-j)}$		15.83***	49.54***	7.35**	82.40***	266.09***	363.69***			117.81***	165.70***
Hausman test		386.55***		381.37***		639.27***		360.66***		623.61***	
FY1992–1997											
γ	Capital good concerned	−0.380 (0.760)	−0.104 (0.210)	−0.279 (2.05)**	−0.373 (2.74)***	−0.470 (3.56)***	−0.437 (3.52)***	14.910 (7.64)***	21.408 (11.55)***	−0.049 (0.11)	−0.128 (0.28)
	Other four capital goods	5.406 (12.94)***	5.985 (14.50)***	4.533 (16.12)***	5.209 (18.81)***	3.284 (13.49)***	3.753 (15.67)***	2.840 (11.61)***	2.977 (12.48)***	3.970 (13.65)***	4.522 (15.78)***
$-\gamma{*}a$	Capital good concerned	−3.813 (4.41)***	−3.260 (3.95)***	−7.457 (5.93)***	−9.366 (8.09)***	−12.278 (6.70)***	−13.214 (7.64)***			−3.892 (4.26)***	−4.384 (5.15)***

(continued)

Table 4.5 (continued)

		Buildings and structures		Machinery and equipment		Vessels and vehicles		Tools, furniture, and fixtures		Land	
		FE model	RE model	FE model	RE model	FE model	RE model	FE model	RE model	FE model	RE model
	Other four capital goods	−3.705 (3.79)***	−3.927 (4.34)***	−7.529 (5.82)***	−6.830 (5.80)***	−14.129 (5.98)***	−13.557 (6.84)***	−3.224 (2.31)**	−3.268 (4.17)***	−2.673 (2.81)***	−4.160 (4.72)***
Cash flow ratio		2.444 (18.48)***	2.698 (23.10)***	2.356 (18.38)***	2.630 (23.17)***	2.342 (18.22)***	2.623 (22.91)***	2.302 (17.89)***	2.531 (22.28)***	2.374 (18.49)***	2.647 (23.18)***
Interest-bearing debt ratio		0.317 (9.75)***	0.310 (12.95)***	0.342 (10.53)***	0.315 (13.30)***	0.312 (9.61)***	0.307 (12.86)***	0.312 (9.58)***	0.305 (12.93)***	0.315 (9.71)***	0.310 (12.97)***
Number of observations		12,495	12,495	12,495	12,495	12,495	12,495	12,495	12,495	12,495	12,495
Number of firms		2,278	2,278	2,278	2,278	2,278	2,278	2,278	2,278	2,278	2,278
R-squared: within		0.10	0.10	0.10	0.10	0.10	0.10	0.10	0.10	0.10	0.10
R-squared: between		0.14	0.20	0.17	0.23	0.15	0.21	0.19	0.25	0.14	0.21
R-squared: overall		0.13	0.18	0.14	0.19	0.13	0.18	0.16	0.20	0.13	0.18
$H_{C0}: \gamma_j = \gamma_{(n-j)}$		54.79***	62.24***	209.26***	288.39***	174.20***	229.14***	35.34***	91.47***	45.78***	61.94***
$H_{D0}: \gamma_j = \gamma_{(n-j)}$ & $a_j = a_{(n-j)}$		28.01***	62.26***	104.63***	322.19***	89.92***	234.68***			24.20***	62.72***
Hausman test		199.07***		441.35***		198.92***		207.97***		228.79***	
FY1998–2004											
γ	Capital good concerned	0.027 (0.240)	0.036 (0.320)	0.040 (0.060)	0.030 (0.05)	0.000 (2.40)**	0.000 (3.87)***	0.209 (1.54)	0.266 (1.97)**	0.001 (0.54)	0.004 (1.49)
	Other four capital goods	0.972 (4.98)***	1.093 (5.75)***	0.878 (6.66)***	0.981 (7.61)***	0.722 (6.05)***	0.783 (6.69)***	0.734 (6.09)***	0.857 (7.38)***	1.871 (9.05)***	2.315 (11.53)***
$-\gamma * a$	Capital good concerned	−1.815 (2.19)**	−2.570 (3.26)***	−3.536 (2.73)***	−4.177 (3.39)***	9.085 (1.81)*	3.339 (0.74)			−2.099 (3.46)***	−2.232 (3.80)***
	Other four capital goods	−1.579 (1.85)*	−1.389 (1.72)*	−1.161 (0.860)	−0.980 (0.77)	3.750 (0.81)	3.987 (0.91)	−6.024 (5.48)***	−9.777 (15.58)***	−0.866 (1.38)	−0.310 (0.52)

(continued)

Table 4.5 (continued)

		Buildings and structures		Machinery and equipment		Vessels and vehicles		Tools, furniture, and fixtures		Land	
		FE model	RE model	FE model	RE model	FE model	RE model	FE model	RE model	FE model	RE model
Cash flow ratio		1.001 (10.61)***	1.725 (22.22)***	0.990 (10.51)***	1.712 (22.11)***	1.028 (10.66)***	1.768 (22.41)***	0.948 (10.00)***	1.572 (20.25)***	1.043 (11.08)***	1.743 (22.50)***
Interest-bearing debt ratio		0.168 (4.53)***	0.188 (6.84)***	0.181 (4.92)***	0.192 (7.05)***	0.183 (4.83)***	0.206 (7.41)***	0.144 (3.92)***	0.168 (6.28)***	0.190 (5.15)***	0.214 (7.89)***
Number of observations		15,736	15,736	15,736	15,736	15,736	15,736	15,736	15,736	15,736	15,736
Number of firms		2,528	2,528	2,528	2,528	2,528	2,528	2,528	2,528	2,528	2,528
R-squared: within		0.03	0.03	0.03	0.03	0.03	0.03	0.03	0.03	0.04	0.03
R-squared: between		0.22	0.34	0.22	0.35	0.18	0.34	0.31	0.39	0.25	0.36
R-squared: overall		0.11	0.20	0.11	0.20	0.09	0.20	0.16	0.23	0.13	0.21
$H_{C0}: \gamma_j = \gamma_{(n-j)}$		12.99***	16.85***	1.61	2.11	36.60*	44.76***	8.25***	10.86***	81.78***	132.33***
$H_{D0}: \gamma_j = \gamma_{(n-j)}$ & $a_j = a_{(n-j)}$		6.63**	23.67***	3.69	37.09***	19.19***	44.88***			44.45***	155.20***
Hausman test		312.66***		300.52***		311.38***		415.94***		341.43***	

Notes
Absolute *t*-values are shown in parenthesis. *, **, and *** denote significance at the 10%, 5%, and 1% level, respectively
※, the statistic test takes a negative sign suggesting the possibility that the assumption of the Hausman test is not satisfied

(c) Zero method											
FY1982–1986											
γ	Capital good concerned	3.728 (3.68)***	4.307 (4.35)***	1.785 (1.68)*	1.054 (1.01)	2.423 (1.79)*	3.035 (2.25)**	26.938 (10.38)***	35.530 (14.44)***	4.487 (3.57)***	4.586 (3.72)***
	Other four capital goods	3.875 (6.82)***	4.683 (8.42)***	4.377 (10.79)***	5.588 (14.10)***	3.765 (13.02)***	4.342 (15.36)***	2.283 (7.47)***	2.379 (8.05)***	3.853 (9.42)***	4.590 (11.40)***
$-\gamma*a$	Capital good concerned	−1.843 (1.46)	−0.604 (0.51)	−2.303 (1.60)	−4.238 (3.11)***	2.346 (0.61)	4.666 (1.32)			−1.770 (1.45)	−3.284 (2.90)***

(continued)

Table 4.5 (continued)

		Buildings and structures		Machinery and equipment		Vessels and vehicles		Tools, furniture, and fixtures		Land	
		FE model	RE model	FE model	RE model	FE model	RE model	FE model	RE model	FE model	RE model
	Other four capital goods	−1.017 (0.73)	−2.226 (1.68)*	−3.271 (1.95)*	−2.161 (1.41)	1.339 (0.35)	2.389 (0.65)	4.867 (2.89)***	4.002 (4.66)***	−2.178 (1.62)	−3.079 (2.47)**
Cash flow ratio		2.047 (9.90)***	3.246 (17.63)***	2.052 (9.93)***	3.294 (17.96)***	2.058 (9.95)***	3.246 (17.62)***	2.017 (9.82)***	3.136 (17.19)***	2.038 (9.86)***	3.232 (17.54)***
Interest-bearing debt ratio		0.478 (11.09)***	0.332 (11.54)***	0.481 (11.16)***	0.316 (11.14)***	0.479 (11.10)***	0.326 (11.35)***	0.480 (11.21)***	0.325 (11.55)***	0.478 (11.07)***	0.329 (11.38)***
Number of observations		7,828	7,828	7,828	7,828	7,828	7,828	7,828	7,828	7,828	7,828
Number of firms		1,668	1,668	1,668	1,668	1,668	1,668	1,668	1,668	1,668	1,668
R-squared: within		0.12	0.11	0.12	0.11	0.12	0.11	0.13	0.12	0.12	0.11
R-squared: between		0.15	0.33	0.16	0.35	0.16	0.33	0.21	0.37	0.15	0.32
R-squared: overall		0.12	0.23	0.13	0.25	0.13	0.23	0.16	0.26	0.12	0.22
H_{C0}: $\gamma_j = \gamma_{(n-j)}$		0.01	0.07	3.86*	12.33**	0.89	0.85	81.59*	163.91***	0.18	0.00
H_{D0}: $\gamma_j = \gamma_{(n-j)}$ & $a_j = a_{(n-j)}$		0.41	10.20***	2.00	56.04***	0.50	3.94			0.20	0.16
Hausman test		341.97***		463.43***		321.24***		324.96***		413.65***	
FY1987–1991											
γ	Capital good concerned	4.699 (4.60)***	6.371 (6.38)***	−3.747 (3.17)***	−4.304 (3.70)***	12.169 (6.80)***	11.883 (6.72)***	24.297 (7.73)***	29.495 (10.08)***	12.564 (7.68)***	12.615 (7.86)***
	Other four capital goods	6.624 (9.75)***	6.906 (10.37)***	8.451 (18.83)***	9.537 (21.82)***	5.025 (15.09)***	5.767 (17.73)***	4.608 (12.96)***	4.947 (14.41)***	4.992 (10.28)***	6.051 (12.81)***
$-\gamma*a$	Capital good concerned	−4.173 (3.22)***	−0.402 (0.33)	−10.789 (6.66)***	−13.292 (9.02)***	17.503 (4.32)***	15.693 (4.13)***			1.378 (0.88)	−2.419 (1.67)*
	Other four capital goods	−1.437 (1.00)	−2.919 (2.11)**	−10.528 (6.08)***	−10.607 (6.49)***	13.551 (3.05)***	14.179 (3.47)***	1.819 (0.97)	3.030 (2.93)***	−3.760 (2.20)**	−4.077 (2.55)**

(continued)

Table 4.5 (continued)

		Buildings and structures		Machinery and equipment		Vessels and vehicles		Tools, furniture, and fixtures		Land	
		FE model	RE model	FE model	RE model	FE model	RE model	FE model	RE model	FE model	RE model
Cash flow ratio		4.030 (15.05)***	5.788 (24.91)***	4.176 (15.75)***	5.796 (25.27)***	4.106 (15.43)***	5.738 (24.76)***	4.070 (15.27)***	5.615 (24.18)***	4.105 (15.44)***	5.759 (24.85)***
Interest-bearing debt ratio		0.243 (5.12)***	0.261 (7.68)***	0.267 (5.67)***	0.233 (6.92)***	0.241 (5.08)***	0.242 (7.09)***	0.279 (5.89)***	0.266 (7.85)***	0.241 (5.07)***	0.237 (6.88)***
Number of observations		8,749	8,749	8,749	8,749	8,749	8,749	8,749	8,749	8,749	8,749
Number of firms		1,905	1,905	1,905	1,905	1,905	1,905	1,905	1,905	1,905	1,905
R-squared: within		0.15	0.15	0.16	0.16	0.16	0.15	0.16	0.15	0.16	0.15
R-squared: between		0.18	0.36	0.32	0.38	0.24	0.34	0.29	0.35	0.23	0.34
R-squared: overall		0.15	0.28	0.26	0.31	0.20	0.27	0.23	0.28	0.20	0.28
H_{C0}: $\gamma_j = \gamma_{(n-j)}$		1.57	0.13	70.36*	94.14***	14.80***	11.16***	35.67***	63.88***	15.54***	12.17***
H_{D0}: $\gamma_j = \gamma_{(n-j)}$ & $a_j = a_{(n-j)}$		6.48**	18.03***	36.85***	178.43***	8.79**	13.57***			19.80***	22.99***
Hausman test		236.00***		151.94***		139.08***		63.20***		179.80***	
FY1992–1997											
γ	Capital good concerned	3.053 (4.68)***	3.517 (5.51)***	−1.605 (1.84)*	−2.112 (2.45)**	7.872 (5.45)***	8.145 (5.66)***	27.301 (12.82)***	35.257 (18.20)***	2.508 (1.86)*	1.803 (1.37)
	Other four capital goods	5.128 (9.67)***	6.068 (11.70)***	5.515 (18.13)***	6.326 (21.33)***	3.407 (14.09)***	4.002 (16.91)***	2.628 (10.10)***	2.718 (10.85)***	4.831 (14.60)***	5.624 (17.38)***
$-\gamma^*a$	Capital good concerned	−1.482 (1.68)*	−0.842 (1.01)	−7.319 (5.92)***	−8.535 (7.39)***	32.903 (12.32)***	27.328 (11.19)***			−6.287 (6.67)***	−7.286 (8.31)***
	Other four capital goods	−1.868 (1.85)*	−1.914 (2.04)**	−6.481 (4.74)***	−6.824 (5.47)***	19.346 (7.69)***	21.442 (8.86)***	4.092 (3.10)***	1.904 (2.75)***	−5.169 (5.05)***	−6.721 (7.03)***
Cash flow ratio		3.115 (21.72)***	3.403 (29.03)***	3.165 (22.17)***	3.436 (29.53)***	3.131 (22.03)***	3.406 (29.16)***	3.067 (21.47)***	3.280 (28.33)***	3.121 (21.82)***	3.402 (29.04)***

(continued)

Table 4.5 (continued)

		Buildings and structures		Machinery and equipment		Vessels and vehicles		Tools, furniture, and fixtures		Land	
		FE model	RE model	FE model	RE model	FE model	RE model	FE model	RE model	FE model	RE model
Interest-bearing debt ratio		0.221 (5.54)***	0.173 (6.09)***	0.239 (6.03)***	0.167 (5.92)***	0.215 (5.43)***	0.172 (6.05)***	0.219 (5.52)***	0.168 (6.03)***	0.216 (5.42)***	0.170 (5.95)***
Number of observations		12,505	12,505	12,505	12,505	12,505	12,505	12,505	12,505	12,505	12,505
Number of firms		2,279	2,279	2,279	2,279	2,279	2,279	2,279	2,279	2,279	2,279
R-squared: within		0.12	0.11	0.12	0.12	0.13	0.13	0.13	0.13	0.12	0.12
R-squared: between		0.19	0.26	0.22	0.28	0.10	0.25	0.24	0.32	0.18	0.26
R-squared: overall		0.19	0.24	0.21	0.26	0.09	0.24	0.22	0.28	0.18	0.24
H_{C0}: $\gamma_j = \gamma_{(n-j)}$		3.85**	6.07**	47.55**	69.11***	9.08***	7.87***	121.21***	254.99***	2.29	6.50*
H_{D0}: $\gamma_j = \gamma_{(n-j)}$ & $a_j = a_{(n-j)}$		1.96	9.53***	25.61***	113.59***	26.31***	31.64***			2.39	9.23***
Hausman test		171.92***		198.17***		213.66***		178.31***		172.55***	
FY1998–2004											
γ	Capital good concerned	9.348 (10.73)***	9.045 (10.73)***	−3.641 (3.16)***	−4.605 (4.10)***	0.388 (0.13)	−1.561 (0.52)	32.172 (20.13)***	38.573 (25.94)***	−6.985 (5.31)***	−8.500 (6.55)***
	Other four capital goods	2.220 (3.53)***	4.610 (7.56)***	6.710 (18.37)***	8.548 (24.16)***	4.811 (16.52)***	6.163 (21.66)***	2.274 (7.21)***	2.889 (9.43)***	7.369 (17.73)***	9.387 (23.30)***
$-\gamma * a$	Capital good concerned	3.530 (3.11)***	0.886 (0.82)	−8.320 (6.46)***	−10.183 (8.32)***	−1.549 (0.30)	−7.825 (1.66)*			−9.235 (10.93)***	−11.380 (13.93)***
	Other four capital goods	4.115 (3.31)***	1.764 (1.49)	−5.422 (3.87)***	−8.660 (6.57)***	0.893 (0.18)	−6.539 (1.36)	5.970 (5.04)***	−0.292 (0.49)	−11.055 (12.02)***	−11.463 (13.02)***
Cash flow ratio		1.191 (10.34)***	2.390 (28.54)***	1.202 (10.45)***	2.383 (28.67)***	1.191 (10.32)***	2.394 (28.58)***	1.184 (10.37)***	2.187 (26.52)***	1.191 (10.36)***	2.365 (28.28)***
Interest-bearing debt ratio		0.191 (4.14)***	0.243 (7.09)***	0.213 (4.62)***	0.242 (7.12)***	0.196 (4.24)***	0.247 (7.20)***	0.197 (4.30)***	0.225 (6.77)***	0.194 (4.21)***	0.238 (6.99)***

(continued)

Table 4.5 (continued)

	Buildings and structures		Machinery and equipment		Vessels and vehicles		Tools, furniture, and fixtures		Land	
	FE model	RE model	FE model	RE model	FE model	RE model	FE model	RE model	FE model	RE model
Number of observations	15,745	15,745	15,745	15,745	15,745	15,745	15,745	15,745	15,745	15,745
Number of firms	2,527	2,527	2,527	2,527	2,527	2,527	2,527	2,527	2,527	2,527
R-squared: within	0.06	0.05	0.06	0.05	0.05	0.05	0.07	0.07	0.06	0.05
R-squared: between	0.38	0.46	0.33	0.48	0.40	0.47	0.43	0.54	0.40	0.48
R-squared: overall	0.20	0.28	0.17	0.30	0.20	0.28	0.22	0.34	0.20	0.29
$H_{C0}: \gamma_j = \gamma_{(n-j)}$	26.88***	11.16***	60.52***	103.34***	2.05	6.44*	302.53**	493.91***	85.56***	137.71***
$H_{D0}: \gamma_j = \gamma_{(n-j)}$ & $a_j = a_{(n-j)}$	13.45***	12.22***	38.84***	153.46***	1.33	8.24**			45.51***	141.18***
Hausman test	602.35***		563.96***		569.42***		375.00***		540.66***	

Note Absolute *t*-values are shown in parenthesis. *, **, and *** denote significance at the 10%, 5%, and 1% level, respectively

Table 4.6 Pairwise homogeneity test results (H_{E0} and H_{F0}) (a) Proportional method (b) Book-Value method (c) Zero method

(a) Proportional method

FY1982-86 (upper right) / FY1987-91 (lower left)

	H_0	Buildings and structures	Machinery and equipment	Vessels and vehicles	Tools, furniture, and fixtures	Land
Buildings and structures	H_{E0}		10.49***	1.70	23.87***	9.94***
	H_{F0}		6.04**	2.69		6.58**
Machinery and equipment	H_{E0}	6.66***		0.02	14.67***	21.87***
	H_{F0}	4.80*		2.57		15.44***
Vessels and vehicles	H_{E0}	0.00	6.66***		0.67	12.92***
	H_{F0}	1.33	3.56			7.25**
Tools, furniture, and fixtures	H_{E0}	193.71***	0.00	211.82***		
	H_{F0}					
Land	H_{E0}	241.91***	220.13***	242.49***	228.07***	
	H_{F0}	169.65***	140.59***	134.15***		

FY1992-97 (upper right) / FY1998-04 (lower left)

	H_0	Buildings and structures	Machinery and equipment	Vessels and vehicles	Tools, furniture, and fixtures	Land
Buildings and structures	H_{E0}		12.77***	1.10	2.62	0.72
	H_{F0}		12.37***	99.91***		0.61
Machinery and equipment	H_{E0}	20.49***		1.17	2.36	3.45*
	H_{F0}	20.47***		107.74***		5.57*
Vessels and vehicles	H_{E0}	8.11***	0.10		0.02	1.70
	H_{F0}	32.86***	37.06***			99.36***
Tools, furniture, and fixtures	H_{E0}	43.84***	55.66***	54.90***		2.08
	H_{F0}					
Land	H_{E0}	23.16***	0.83	0.00	56.44***	
	H_{F0}	14.12***	7.67**	31.47***		

(b) Book-Value method

FY1982-86 (upper right) / FY1987-91 (lower left)

	H_0	Buildings and structures	Machinery and equipment	Vessels and vehicles	Tools, furniture, and fixtures	Land
Buildings and structures	H_{E0}		63.23***	24.39***	19.75***	4.86**
	H_{F0}		31.71***	13.06***		3.92
Machinery and equipment	H_{E0}	10.23***		2.72*	65.23***	13.17***
	H_{F0}	5.27*		1.63		8.55**
Vessels and vehicles	H_{E0}	59.13***	4.68**		50.29***	3.56*
	H_{F0}	130.87***	77.60***			1.80
Tools, furniture, and fixtures	H_{E0}	58.95***	77.13***	102.25***		33.21***
	H_{F0}					
Land	H_{E0}	56.47***	97.15***	170.57***	14.06***	
	H_{F0}	43.03***	58.99***	249.19***		

(continued)

Table 4.6 (continued)

FY1992-97 (upper right) / FY1998-04 (lower left)

Buildings and	H_{E0}		7.69***	9.37***	73.51***	0.65
structures	H_{F0}		4.12	14.33***		0.32
Machinery and	H_{E0}	0.15		0.27	92.31***	2.22
equipment	H_{F0}	5.83*		6.00**		1.46
Vessels and	H_{E0}	4.78**	0.60		93.72***	2.96*
vehicles	H_{F0}	3.08	2.47			11.45***
Tools, furniture,	H_{E0}	0.00	0.16	2.52		81.39***
and fixtures	H_{F0}					
Land	H_{E0}	4.70**	0.60	0.53	2.48	
	H_{F0}	2.44	6.90**	1.05		

(c) Zero method

FY1982-86 (upper right) / FY1987-91 (lower left)

	H_0	Buildings and structures	Machinery and equipment	Vessels and vehicles	Tools, furniture, and fixtures	Land
Buildings and	H_{E0}		1.40	1.31	63.34***	1.61
structures	H_{F0}		0.94	1.07		0.81
Machinery and	H_{E0}	13.51***		0.01	69.19***	6.03**
equipment	H_{F0}	7.05**		0.13		3.12
Vessels and	H_{E0}	10.91***	30.41***		67.17***	4.45**
vehicles	H_{F0}	12.46***	22.84***			2.64
Tools, furniture,	H_{E0}	36.66***	56.57***	13.37***		51.66***
and fixtures	H_{F0}					
Land	H_{E0}	32.33***	67.21***	1.73	8.31***	
	H_{F0}	22.43***	38.66***	3.10		

FY1992-97 (upper right) / FY1998-04 (lower left)

Buildings and	H_{E0}		10.08***	1.91	117.93***	4.01**
structures	H_{F0}		6.83**	49.59***		5.74*
Machinery and	H_{E0}	58.38***		10.45***	143.25***	18.12***
equipment	H_{F0}	34.83***		57.49***		9.06**
Vessels and	H_{E0}	6.53**	1.29		71.64***	0.11
vehicles	H_{F0}	3.62	0.65			52.92***
Tools, furniture,	H_{E0}	149.02***	287.77***	90.57***		76.98***
and fixtures	H_{F0}					
Land	H_{E0}	12.59***	13.89***	0.55	216.58***	
	H_{F0}	7.91**	9.83***	0.40		

4.3.2 Breaking Away from Homogeneity

As we touched on earlier in the discussion of H_{A0} and H_{B0}, the null hypothesis H_{D0}, which requires the equality of a_j in addition to that of γ_j is, in principle, stronger than H_{C0}, which only requires the equality of γ_j. However, the realized value of the χ^2 statistic of the likelihood ratio and the number of asterisks or symbols "*" corresponding to the significance level at which the null hypothesis is rejected indicate the opposite result in some cells. This outcome can occur in practice because of differences in the degrees of freedom of the χ^2 distribution and differences in the correlations with and between the additional explanatory variables included depending on the sample period and the construction method for sales and retirements. Because of this finding, we conclude in the below analysis that capital goods are not homogeneous whenever either H_{CO} or H_{DO} is rejected at the 1% significance level.

Several notable features are evident from Table 4 5. First, the null hypotheses are not always rejected, although the number of cases in which homogeneity is rejected surpasses that of cases of acceptance (i.e., not rejection). Second, the estimates of equations indicate that although the coefficient γ_j is insignificant in some cases, the coefficient $\gamma_{(n-j)}$, which corresponds to the remaining homogeneous capital, is always significant regardless of the sample period or data construction method for sales and retirements of capital. Third, when we consider the heterogeneity of land, on which Asako, Kuninori, Inoue, and Murase (1989, 1997) focus, we find that some results in Table 4.5 suggest that homogeneity with other productive capital is not rejected. Specifically, these results include those for the pre-bubble period (1982–86) with the Proportional method and those for the pre-bubble (1982–86) and post-bubble collapse periods (1992–97) with the Zero method. We identify no such cases for the Book-Value method, implying that land is consistently heterogeneous to the other types of productive capital as a whole.

Fourth, the capital types that are judged to be homogeneous with the aggregate remaining other capital types include tools, furniture, and fixtures in the second period (1987–91) and buildings and structures in the fourth period (1998–04) under the Proportional method; buildings and structures in the first period (1982–86) and machinery and equipment in the fourth period (1998–04) under the Book-Value method; and buildings and structures; machinery and equipment; vessels and vehicles; and tools, furniture, and fixtures in the first period (1982–86) and vessels and vehicles and tools, furniture, and fixtures in the fourth period (1998–04) under the Zero method. Buildings and structures in the second (1987–91) and third periods (1992–97) are also homogeneous at the less stringent 5% significance level.

In sum, we can interpret the above results as follows: capital goods are basically heterogeneous; but for some sample periods and combinations of capital goods, the marginal adjustment costs of investing in respective capital goods can fall in a comparable range; in that case, different capital goods are aggregable as if they are homogeneous. As obviously seen in Figs. 3.1 and 3 2 in Chap. 3, each capital good category has its own dynamics with both long-term trends and short-term cycles over time in terms of its composition ratio and investment rate. However, depending on the timing of phase-change, there occur possibilities that different capital goods can be aggregated directly. Note that the different results stemming from the three data construction methods imply that not only new investments but also disinvestments in the form of sales and retirements are responsible for the observed homogeneity or heterogeneity of capital goods.

4.3.3 Pairwise Homogeneity Test

The test results for the null hypotheses H_{E0} and H_{F0} summarized in Table 4.6 share many similarities with those for H_{C0} and H_{D0} in Table 4.5. In Table 4.6, panels (a), (b), and (c) summarize the test results for H_{E0} and H_{F0} for four sample periods and for every pair of capital goods, amounting to 10 ($= {}_5C_2$) combinations. For each data construction method, the test results in each panel are divided into two matrices according to the sample periods. Within each matrix, the cells in the upper diagonal part of the matrix display results for the earlier of the two sample periods, whereas those in the lower diagonal part of the matrix display results for the later of the two sample periods. Each cell reports the test results for H_{E0} and H_{F0}, and we conclude that capital goods i and j are not homogeneous if, in cell (i, j), where i represents the i-th row and j represents the j-th column of the matrix, either H_{E0} or H_{F0} is rejected at the 1% significance level. Computing the likelihood ratio obtained from the sum of squared residuals of the estimated equation with and without parameter homogeneity constraints yields a χ^2 statistic with degrees of freedom equal to the number of constraints, as the sample size is large enough.

We point out several notable features of Table 4.6. First, the test results regarding the rejection or acceptance of the null hypotheses vary depending on the data construction method, the sample period, and the selected combination of two capital goods, as they do for H_{C0} and H_{D0}. Second, if we focus on land, we obtain mixed results. Specifically, under the Proportional method, described in panel (a), pairwise homogeneity is not rejected when land is paired with buildings and structures and with tools, furniture, and fixtures in the third period (1992–97), and the same is true for land's paring with machinery and equipment at a less stringent significance level. Under the Book-Value method, described in panel (b), pairwise homogeneity is not rejected when land is paired with buildings and structures and machinery and equipment in the third period (1992–97), nor is it rejected when land is paired with any of the four other capital goods in the fourth period (1998–04). Under the Zero method, described in panel (c), although pairwise homogeneity is rejected when land is paired with the other capital goods in the third period (1992–97), land's pairwise homogeneity with buildings and structures is not rejected in the first period (1982–86) and the same result holds in the same period for land and machinery and equipment at a less stringent significance level. Additionally, pairwise homogeneity between land and vessels and vehicles is not rejected for the entire sample period. In summary, the heterogeneity between land and the other types of capital goods is confirmed rather robustly for the bubble period (1987–91), but this property is weaker in the other periods.

Third, we consider capital goods other than land, with a particular focus on the pair of two categories, buildings and structures and machinery and equipment, which share two of the highest weights in any period and for any data construction method for sales and retirements, as is seen in Fig. 3.1 in Chap. 3. The null hypotheses of pairwise homogeneity are not rejected for this pair of capital goods in only two cases: in the fourth period for the Book-Value method and the first period for the

Zero method. Interestingly, we therefore find that two of the most commonly and undoubtedly aggregated capital goods are basically heterogeneous.

4.4 Non-convex Adjustment Costs and Lumpy Investment

The analyses of the previous section conclude that it is preferable to use an investment function from the Multiple q framework that considers the heterogeneity of capital goods rather than an investment function from the Single q framework given the assumption of a smooth, convex adjustment cost function. However, applying an investment function from the Multiple q framework is not suitable in every case, and the explanatory power of such a function tends to be low in cases that take the net value of new acquisitions and sales and retirements.

Even in estimates targeting only new acquisitions, for which the q theory framework's explanatory power is relatively high, variables that should not have explanatory power in the q theory framework (as q becomes a sufficient statistic)—namely, the cash flow and interest-bearing debt ratios—are estimated as having significant effects. We therefore confirm that only considering the heterogeneity of capital goods and maintaining the convex adjustment cost framework unchanged leads to remaining factors that cannot be explained.[3]

4.4.1 Augmentations to the Non-linear Model

Based on the above observation and inspired by Tonogi et al. (2010), Asako and Tonogi (2010) allow the adjustment cost function to have a non-convex part that results in lumpy and intermittent or infrequent investment, and they estimate the augmented Multiple q-type investment function. Specifically, they aim to combine fixed costs and convex adjustment costs, as was discussed in Chap. 1 within a Single q framework, and they consider two models. The first is an "inner-fixed outer-convex" model that severs the correlation between the investment rate and q in the area where the absolute value of the investment rate is normally assumed to be small, leading to an N-shaped investment function with a jump, as in Fig. 4.1.[4] The second is an "inner-

[3]Moreover, when we look at differences in investment behavior according to capital good types, we find that new acquisitions of buildings and structures and tools, furniture, and fixtures consistently follow a smooth, convex adjustment cost function regardless of the time period. However, we obtain no such consistent and significant results for newly acquisitions of other capital goods, such as machinery and equipment, or for overall sale and retirement behavior.

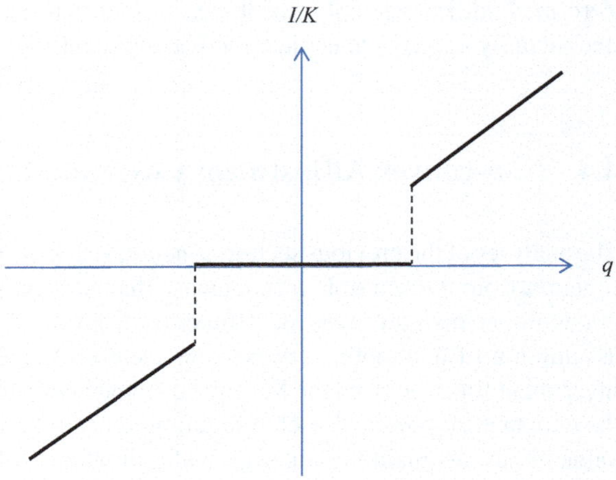

Fig. 4.1 Inner-fixed outer-convex investment function (N-shaped with jumps) *Note* The standard origin corresponds to $q = 1$, $I/K = 0$

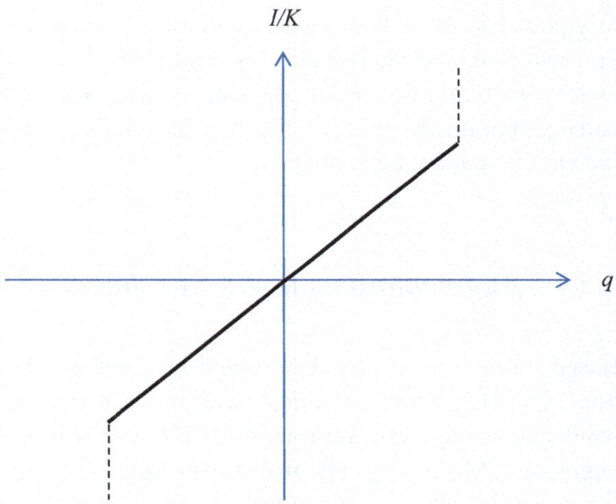

Fig. 4.2 Inner-convex outer-fixed investment function *Note* The stabdard origin corresponds to $q = 1$, $I/K = 0$

convex outer-fixed" model, as is shown in Fig. 4.2, that severs the correlation between the investment rate and q in the area where the absolute value of the investment rate is large.[5]

[4]In Fig. 4.1, when the absolute value of the investment rate is small, it is drawn as a horizontal line, representing inaction or zero investment. However, in the inner-fixed outer-convex formulation itself, the only condition that is imposed is that of no correlation between investment rates within the investment rate threshold and q. Thus, the possibility that the function takes another shape cannot be excluded.

[5]In Fig. 4.2, when the absolute value of the investment rate is large, it is drawn as a line that jumps up and down, representing a lumpy investment and disinvestment. However, in the inner-convex outer-fixed formulation, the only condition imposed is that of no correlation between investment rates outside of the investment rate threshold and q. Thus, the possibility that the function takes

The two large and small threshold values for the investment rate, which becomes non-continuous in relation to q, are estimated as percentile values of the distribution of the data set for the investment rate. As these threshold values cannot be estimated directly within standard statistical estimation models, the selection must rely on a goodness-of-fit measure, such as the highest coefficient of determination (R^2) when using the grid search method. However, Asako and Tonogi (2010) only provide an overview of this process using a fairly rough grid, as main purpose of their analysis is testing hypotheses regarding the heterogeneity of capital goods. In this section, following the analytical method of Asako and Tonogi (2010), we use a more detailed grid to clarify the non-continuity of the investment function of each capital good.

4.4.2 From the Linear Model to the Non-linear Model

We introduce non-linear relationships and shift our focus to the non-linear Multiple q model while retaining the background assumptions of perfect competition and constant returns to scale of the investment adjustment cost function that are part of standard q theory. We also provide an additional assumption regarding the non-convexity of the adjustment cost function that results in the non-continuity of the investment function.

We begin with the same framework that yielded the investment function of the Multiple q model given by Eq. (2.9) under the adjustment cost function in Eq. (2.3) in Chap. 2, and we only replace Eq. (2.3) by

$$C\left(K_1',\ldots,K_n',K_1,\ldots,K_n\right)=\begin{cases}\sum_{j=1}^{n}\frac{\gamma_j}{2}\left(Z_j-a_j\right)^2\left(1-\delta_j\right)K_j' & \text{if } \left|Z_j\right|\geq m_j\\ \sum_{j=1}^{n}\frac{\gamma_j}{2}\left(m_j-a_j\right)^2\left(1-\delta_j\right)K_j' & \text{otherwise}\end{cases} \tag{4.2}$$

to create the non-linear investment function. In other words, this phase-dividing formulation assumes only the fixed amount applies to the investment adjustment cost until the absolute value of the investment rate reaches m_j, and when m_j is exceeded, quadratic convex adjustment costs are imposed additionally for the investment rate in excess of the threshold. This function is the "inner-fixed outer-convex" model described by Asako and Tonogi (2010).[6]

Alternatively, we can also consider the non-convex type, for which the usual quadratic convex adjustment costs apply in the area in which the absolute value of

another shape cannot be excluded, and this condition does not contradict an S-shaped investment function, as in Fig. 1.4 in Chap. 1.

[6]As the fixed cost part in Eq. (4.2) is also proportional to capital stock K_j', the linear homogeneity of adjustment costs with regards to K_j' $(j=1,\ldots,n)$ provided by the overall Eq. (4.2) is maintained, and this model does not go beyond the framework of q theory.

the investment rate is small. In this case, conversely, even when the threshold is exceeded, additional adjustment costs are not generated. Thus, the adjustment cost function can be expressed by replacing the inequality $|Z_j| \geq m_j$ in Eq. (4.2) with the opposite inequality $|Z_j| \leq m_j$. This model reflects the "inner-convex outer-fixed" type described in Asako and Tonogi (2010).[7]

We can intuitively express the differences between the inner-fixed outer-convex and inner-convex outer-fixed types as follows. The unresponsive area with regards to q (in other words, the area that cannot be explained by q) in the former is assumed to represent small-scale investments, as is shown in Fig. 4.1, whereas the unresponsive area in the latter is assumed to represent large-scale investments, as is shown in Fig. 4.2.

4.5 Estimation Results and Implications of the Non-linear Multiple q Model

We take the following steps to estimate the threshold forming the boundary between the fixed and convex portions. First, in the case of the inner-fixed outer-convex type (inner-convex outer-fixed type), we compare the best fit of the estimation equation in terms of coefficient of determination, using the combination of the five capital goods, for any of the ten symmetrical investment rate distribution pairs. These pairs are separated by percentiles in 5% intervals such that the interior (exterior) term represents the fixed cost, that is, (0, 100%) (5, 95%)... (40, 60%) (45, 55%). The symmetry assumption is introduced to lessen the burden of grid-search computation before Sect. 4.5.3.

This process determines the optimal interval from among 10^5 combinations (see Fig. 4.3).[8] Using this interval as a base case, we test other variations, including cases in which the inner-fixed outer-convex and the inner-convex outer-fixed types are mixed across capital good types. We use OLS for the estimation method, and we report only the results for the fixed effects model in all cases as before, based on the results of the Hausman test.[9]

---

[7]Unlike the inner-fixed outer-convex type, the formulation of the inner-convex outer-fixed type may not satisfy convexity globally, and the formulation itself departs from the q theory framework. Nonetheless, even if the sufficient condition of global convexity is not satisfied, the possibility remains that the formulation does not contradict the local maximization of enterprise value.

[8]Asako and Tonogi (2010) only conduct estimations for three symmetric intervals separated by percentiles in 10% increments: (0, 100%), (10, 90%), and (20, 80%). In the following, from the estimated percentiles, it is possible to specifically calculate m_j, the investment rate threshold in Eq. (4.2), but we leave this calculation for future discussion as Asako and Tonogi (2010) did, as it would require the verification and specification of the probability distribution function conforming to the investment rate.

[9]The basic settings, such as, for example, the inclusion of the cash flow and interest-bearing debt ratios as additional explanatory variables, are the same as those of Tonog et al. (2010) and Asako and Tonogi (2010). We include the cash flow and interest-bearing debt ratios not to verify the financial

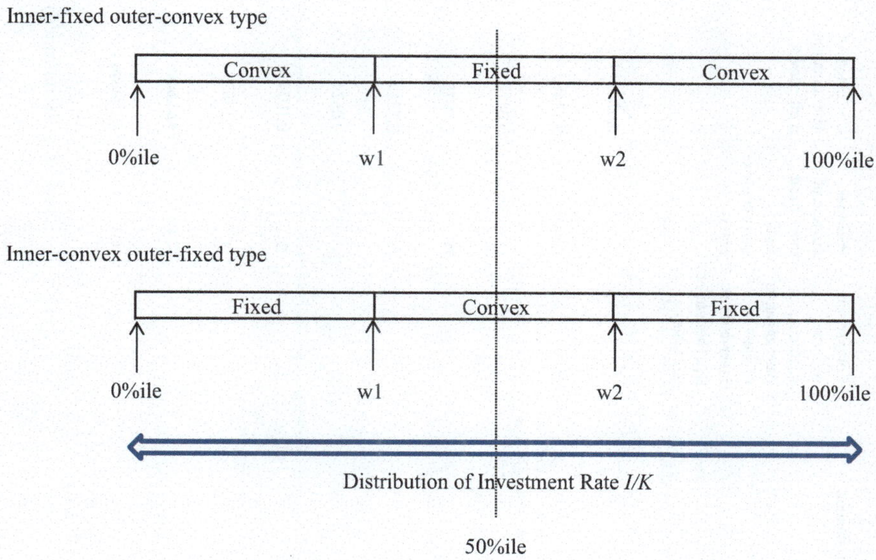

Fig. 4.3 Estimating the boundary percentiles (base case)

4.5.1 Estimation Results of the Base Case

Table 4.7 shows the estimation results for the inner-fixed outer-convex and inner-convex outer-fixed types (i.e., the percentile combinations that maximize the coefficients of determination).[10] Owing to repeated references in the text, we refer to the inner-fixed outer-convex type as the "inner-fixed type" and to the inner-convex outer-fixed type as the "inner-convex type" in the following discussion. In the table, the estimated fixed-cost range is identified. For the inner-fixed type, (w_1–w_2), where $w_2 = 100 - w_1$, indicates that the investment rate Z obeys standard q theory for the area $Z < w_1$ and $w_2 < Z$ in terms of percentiles, but it remains constant for $w_1 < Z < w_2$. For the inner convex type, (–w_1_w_2–) indicates that the investment rate Z remains constant for the area $Z < w_1$ and $w_2 < Z$ but obeys standard q theory for $w_1 < Z < w_2$.

In general, the introduction of non-linearity improves fit. In other words, except in the case of the inner-fixed type, the Zero method, and the first period (1982–86), the coefficient of determination increases relative to the usual Multiple q model,

constraints hypothesis but to control unresolved problems in the estimation, such as measurement error, as outlined in Chap. 1.

[10]The coefficient of determination is calculated to the 11th decimal place and allows for simultaneous listings if this still causes multiple percentile combinations to line up.

Table 4.7 Estimation results in the base case: selected percentiles

		Buildings and structures	Machinery and equipment	Vessels and vehicles	Tools, furniture, and fixtures	Land	Coefficient of determination	Comparison with the coefficient of determination of the inner-convex type(bottom of this table)	Potential mixture of inner-fixed and inner-convex types	Coefficient of determination if all-convex
Inner-fixed outer-convex type, 5% intervals										
(a) Proportional method	1st period (1982–86)	10–90	10–90	5–95	35–65	10–90	0.0947			0.0743
	2nd period (1987–91)	20–80	45–55	20–80	All fixed	15–85	0.2095	○	○	0.1245
	3rd period (1992–97)	5–95	45–55	20–80	35–65	35–65	0.1188		○	0.0422
	4th period (1998–2004)	5–95	45–55	5–95	45–55	30–70	0.1023		○	0.0875
(b) Book-Value method	1st period (1982–86)	10–90	5–95	All fixed	45–55	40–60	0.1296		○	0.1214
	2nd period (1987–91)	20–80	All fixed	5–95	20–80	15–85	0.2152	○		0.0624
	3rd period (1992–97)	5–95	45–55	5–95	45–55	25–75	0.1673		○	0.1074
	4th period (1998–2004)	5–95	45–55	40–60	25–75	35–65	0.1411		○	0.1362
	(tie)	As above	As above	As above	As above	40–60	As above		(○)	As above
	(tie)	As above	As above	As above	As above	45–55	As above		(○)	As above

(continued)

Table 4.7 (continued)

		Buildings and structures	Machinery and equipment	Vessels and vehicles	Tools, furniture, and fixtures	Land	Coefficient of determination	Comparison with the coefficient of determination of the inner-convex type (bottomo f this table)	Potential mixture of inner-fixed and inner-convex types	Coefficient of determination if all-convex
(c) Zero method	1st period (1982–86)	30–70	All fixed	5–95	45–55	10–90	0.1604		○	0.1644
	2nd period (1987–91)	45–55	All fixed	10–90	15–85	45–55	0.2528	○	○	0.1539
	3rd period (1992–97)	45–55	5–95	25–75	15–85	All fixed	0.2298		○	0.0930
	4th period (1998–2004)	45–55	5–95	30–70	45–55	40–60	0.2922	○	○	0.2338
		Buildings and structures	Machinery and equipment	Vessels and vehicles	Tools, furniture, and fixtures	Land	Coefficient of determination	Comparison with the coefficient of determination of the inner-fixed type (top of this table)	Potential mixture of inner-fixed and inner-convex types	Coefficient of determination if all-convex
Inner convex outer-fixed type, 5% interval										
(a) Proportional method	1st period (1982–86)	All convex	-5_95-	-15_85-	-5_95-	-5_95-	0.0979	○		0.0743
	2nd period (1987–91)	-5_95-	All convex	-20_80-	-30_70-	-15_85-	0.2066			0.1245
	3rd period (1992–97)	-10_90-	-5_95-	-45_55-	-5_95-	-25_75-	0.1310	○	○	0.0422
	4th period (1998–2004)	All convex	-5_95-	-45_55-	-5_95-	-10_90-	0.1544	○	○	0.0875

(continued)

Table 4.7 (continued)

		Buildings and structures	Machinery and equipment	Vessels and vehicles	Tools, furniture, and fixtures	Land	Coefficient of determination	Comparison with the coefficient of determination of the inner-fixed type (top of this table)	Potential mixture of inner-fixed and inner-convex types	Coefficient of determination if all-convex
(b) Book-Value method	1st period (1982–86)	All convex	-5_95-	-5_95-	All convex	-5_95-	0.1404	○		0.1214
	2nd period (1987–91)	All convex	All convex	-10_90-	-45_55-	-15_85-	0.2054		○	0.0624
	3rd period (1992–97)	-10_90-	All convex	-25_75-	All convex	-25_75-	0.1786	○		0.1074
	4th period (1998–2004)	-15_85-	-5_95-	-45_55-	-5_95-	-5_95-	0.1691	○	○	0.1362
(c) Zero method	1st period (1982–86)	All convex	-25_75-	-40_60-	All convex	-10_90-	0.1795	○		0.1644
	2nd period (1987–91)	-5_95-	All convex	-5_95-	-15_85-	-15_85-	0.2311			0.1539
	3rd period (1992–97)	All convex	-5_95-	-25_75-	All convex	-40_60-	0.2442	○		0.0930
	4th period (1998–2004)	All convex	-45_55-	-20_80-	All convex	All convex	0.2884		○	0.2338

Notes
1. In the inner-fixed type, the inside of the displayed percentile, and in the inner-convex type, the outside of the displayed percentile, correspond to the range of fixed-cost type
2. The ○ marks in the fields comparing the coefficients of determination indicate that the coefficient of determination is higher than the target of comparison
3. The shaded fields indicate that the (45%ile, 55%ile) combination has been selected. The selection of this percentile for any of the 5 capital goods suggests the intermingling of inner-fixed and inner-convex types (see text)

which assumes convex adjustment costs across the entire investment rate.[11] In addition, when we compare this increase across sample periods, we find a large overall improvement in fit in the second and third periods (1987–91, 1992–97) from introducing non-linearity. In particular, the fit noticeably improves in the second period (1987–91) for the Proportional and Book-Value methods, which integrate sales and retirements of capital goods; and in the third period (1992–97) for the Zero method, which captures only new acquisitions of capital goods.

As a whole, similar to the estimations of the all-convex model, the Zero method provides a better fit than the Proportional and Book-Value methods do. However, when considering non-linearity, the advantages of the Zero method become quite small regarding the second period (1987–91). This result may be related to the fact that the second period (1987–91) is centered on the economic bubble, when relatively few sales and retirements occurred.

Neither the inner-fixed type nor the inner-convex type absolutely dominates with regards to fit. However, because the coefficient of determination of the inner-fixed type exceeds that of the inner-convex type in only four out of twelve cases, we conclude that the inner-convex type is relatively dominant. Interestingly, in the first and third periods (1982–86, 1992–97), the inner-convex type is superior for all three methods, whereas in the second period (1987–91), the inner-fixed type is superior for all three methods. In other words, when controlling non-linearity, the timing of the investment rather than the method for handling sales and retirements is crucial for the goodness of fit. The second period (1987–91) is considered a period of many large-scale investments, but these investments can be explained by the usual convex adjustment cost rather than by the lumpy investment model. However, we must be wary that stock prices at the time may have included elements of an economic bubble.

Next, we examine the intervals corresponding to the fixed costs selected by each of the inner-fixed type and inner-convex type models. The selected percentiles for the Proportional and Book-Value methods, which integrate sales and retirements of capital goods, largely deviate from those for the Zero method, which captures only new acquisitions. This result is natural considering that the scope of the investment rate is completely different among the three definitions. This trend is particularly strong for the inner-fixed type, for which inconsistent results can be observed even between the Proportional and Book-Value methods.

Within the inner-fixed type, the new acquisition behavior of machinery and equipment is relatively stable under the Zero method. Specifically, the optimal case in the first and second periods (1982–86, 1987–91) is fixed costs for the entire area, and even in the third and fourth periods (1992–97, 1998–04), fixed costs are optimal for the pair (5, 95%), or almost the entire area. As long as we assume the inner-fixed type, this result suggests a very weak relationship between new acquisitions of machinery and equipment and q. However, for new acquisitions of buildings and structures, although the optimal case in the first period (1982–86) is (30, 70%), it is (45, 55%) in the second period onwards, implying that the fixed costs portion is narrow and

[11] However, for the inner-convex type, it is self-evident that the coefficient of determination increases because the entirely-convex type is included as a special case.

the portion explained by convex adjustment costs is broad. The selection results for buildings and structures are nearly the same for the Proportional and Book-Value methods. Among the five categories of capital goods, the above estimation results of buildings and structures are particularly stable, as also evidenced by the increase in the fixed cost portion when integrating sale and retirement behavior.[12]

For the inner-convex type, we obtain fairly consistent results for the Proportional and Book-Value methods in each category of goods excluding vessels and vehicles. We do not see as large a deviation from the Zero method as we observe for the inner-fixed type. For buildings and structures, a very narrow percentile range is chosen for the fixed-cost part across the three methods and four periods, and in some cases an entirely convex function is chosen. Tools, furniture, and fixtures shows a similar trend, although some exceptions arise. These results are consistent with those of Tonogi et al. (2010), who postulate all-convex adjustment costs and who most significantly estimate new acquisition behavior for these two categories of goods. However, with regards to machinery and equipment, we observe large variations across periods for the Zero method, although the all-convex or (5, 95%) cases are almost always chosen for the Proportional and Book-Value methods. Tonogi et al. (2010) find that the performance of estimations for machinery and equipment are not generally favorable, suggesting the possibility that the fit improved here through the consideration of the fixed portion. As is the case for machinery and equipment, nearly the same results are obtained by the Proportional and Book-Value methods for land, even though the intervals of the fixed portions are slightly wider than for machinery and equipment.

Thus far, we have observed the characteristics of the estimation results in the base case. We note that (45, 55%) is selected in a significant proportion of cases. In particular, this trend arises strongly for the inner-fixed type. For all twelve combinations of three methods and four periods, with the exception of the Proportional method in the first period (1982–86) and the Book-Value method in the second period (1987–91), this percentile is selected for one or more categories of capital goods. In addition, for the inner-convex type, this percentile is selected for one or more categories of capital goods in five out of twelve cases. The percentile (45, 55%) is only one step short of (50, 50%), that is, it is very close to convexity across all areas for the inner-fixed type and to all areas being fixed for the inner-convex type.[13] In the base case, to compare the merits and demerits of the inner-fixed and inner-convex types, we set the search range from (0, 100%) to (45, 55%) under the constraint that all categories of goods must belong to the same type. Thus, (45, 55%) represents a type of boundary solution, and the fact that it has been selected many times suggests that the goods in the

[12]The portion of buildings and structures explained by convex adjustment costs is larger than that of machinery and equipment, and the estimation results for buildings and structures are more stable. This result is not consistent with the empirical studies using data from the United States and Italy, as discussed in Chap. 1. However, we cannot make a simple comparison, as, in our data set, differently from the previous studies, machinery and equipment and tools, furniture, and fixtures are treated as different capital goods.

[13]In actuality, in many of the inner-fixed type cases for which (45, 55%) is selected as the fixed portion, select all-convex or a similar percentile is selected in the inner-convex types.

inner-fixed and inner-convex types may be intermingled. Therefore, we next try an inner-fixed and inner-convex hybrid type.

4.5.2 *Inner-Fixed and Inner-Convex Hybrid Type*

The inner-fixed and inner-convex hybrid type requires immense amounts of calculation, and, thus, we expand the grid increments to 10% rather than 5%. Table 4.8 summarizes the estimation results.

Excluding the Book-Value and Zero methods in the first-period (1982–86), in which a percentile of the inner-convex type is selected for all categories of capital goods, inner-fixed and inner-convex types are intermingled across capital goods in 10 out of 12 cases. In general, this result backs the prediction of the preceding subsection. However, the coefficient-of-determination levels only improve slightly, if at all, when compared to the maximum estimation value in the base case (with no intermingling). Even discounting the impact from expanding grid increments, it is difficult to argue that this improvement is a significant change. Comparing the inner-fixed and inner-convex types, of the 5 capital goods $\times$ 12 cases $=$ 60 sets of percentiles, the inner-convex type was selected 39 times (except when simultaneous listings select different types). Thus, as in the base case, the inner-convex type is relatively superior.

Next, we consider the results by category of capital goods. The percentiles of the inner-convex type are selected in following cases: 11 cases for machinery and equipment, excluding the fourth period of the Zero method; 10 cases for tools, furniture, and fixtures, excluding the second period of the Book-Value and Zero methods. Thus, essentially, the investment behavior for these two categories of capital goods can be explained consistently by the inner-convex type. In other words, q theory fits within a certain range of investment rate in terms of absolute values, but it cannot explain large new acquisitions or sales and retirements. In contrast, the inner-fixed type is dominant for the Proportional and Book-Value methods in the case of vessels and vehicles. The investment rate is independent of q for a certain range in terms of absolute values, but for large new acquisitions or sales and retirements, q theory fits. Finally, it is difficult to identify distinct characteristics, such as those described above, for buildings and structures and land.

Moreover, if we view the characteristics by sample period, the inner-convex type is particularly dominant in the first period (1982–86), and the majority of the selected percentiles have narrow external fixed portions. In addition, the dominance of the inner-convex type is also significant in the third period (1992–97), except for vessels and vehicles. The majority of selected percentiles, excluding those for land, have narrow external fixed portions. In contrast, in the second and fourth periods (1987–91, 1998–04) the inner-fixed type is also selected to some extent. The second and fourth periods represent periods when stock prices reached extreme optimism and pessimism, respectively (although the fourth period includes a period of optimism

Table 4.8 Estimation results for the inner-fixed and inner-convex hybrid type

		Buildings and structures	Machinery and equipment	Vessels and vehicles	Tools, furniture, and fixtures	Land	Coefficient of determination	Coefficient of determination of the base case (5%ile intervals)	
								Inner-fixed type	Inner-convex type
(a) Proportional method	1st Period (1982–86)	10–90	-10_90-	-10_90-	-10_90-	10–90	0.0998	0.0947	0.0979
	2nd Period (1987–91)	20–80	-20_80-	20–80	-10_90-	40–60	0.2105	0.2095	0.2066
	3rd Period (1992–97)	10–90	-10_90-	20–80	-10_90-	-30_70-	0.1257	0.1188	0.1310
	4th Period (1998–2004)	All convex	All convex	All fixed	-10_90-	-10_90-	0.1243	0.1023	0.1544
(b) Book-Value method	1st Period (1982–86)	All convex	-10_90-	-10_90-	All convex	-10_90-	0.1391	0.1296	0.1404
	2nd Period (1987–91)	-20_80-	All convex	10–90	20–80	10–90	0.2279	0.2152	0.2054
	3rd Period (1992–97)	-10_90-	All convex	10–90	All convex	-30_70-	0.1790	0.1673	0.1786

(continued)

Table 4.8 (continued)

		Buildings and structures	Machinery and equipment	Vessels and vehicles	Tools, furniture, and fixtures	Land	Coefficient of determination	Coefficient of determination of the base case (5%ile intervals)	
								Inner-fixed type	Inner-convex type
	4th Period (1998–2004)	10–90	-10_90-	40–60	-10_90-	All convex	0.1490	0.1411	0.1691
	(tie)	As above	As above	As above	As above	40–60	As above		
(c) Zero method	1st Period (1982–86)	All convex	-20_80-	-40_60-	All convex	-10_90-	0.1794	0.1604	0.1795
	2nd Period (1987–91)	20–80	All convex	-20_80-	20–80	-10_90-	0.2585	0.2528	0.2311
	3rd Period (1992–97)	All convex	-10_90-	30–70	All convex	-40_60-	0.2468	0.2298	0.2442
	4th Period (1998–2004)	30–70	10–90	-20_80-	All convex	20–80	0.2936	0.2922	0.2884

Note In the inner-fixed type (unshaded), the inside of the displayed percentile, and in the inner-convex type (shaded), the outside of the displayed percentile, correspond to the range of the fixed-cost type

during the ICT bubble), and this result may also be interpreted as the investment rate within a certain range arising steadily and independently of these fad moves.

4.5.3 Estimation Results for Other Derivative Cases

The estimations thus far have assumed in both the base case and the hybrid type that the three intervals bounded by the two thresholds appear symmetrically at the center of the investment rate distribution. However, we can also set up a model in which the assumption of symmetry on both sides is removed such that the width of the middle of the three intervals is set to, say, 50 percentage points and the thresholds are shifted by five percentiles to the left and right (the fixed-width of 50 percentage points model).

By estimating this fixed-width model for the inner-fixed and inner-convex types and comparing the coefficients of determination for all possible cases of both types, Asako, Nakamura, and Tonogi (2016) obtain interesting results. Namely, first, similar to the base case, the inner-convex type is relatively dominant for the Proportional method, whereas the inner-fixed type is superior for the Book-Value and Zero methods. Second, however, in comparison to the base case model, the fixed-width model is only superior in only one out of the 24 total cases of the inner-fixed and inner-convex types: the inner-fixed type with the Book-Value method in the second period (1987–91). The reason that the inner-fixed type is superior for the fixed-width model is just only that its coefficient of determination decreased from the base case model by less than that of the inner-convex type did. Thus, the previous assumption of bilateral symmetry with the 50th percentile serving as the position of the middle of the three intervals is not incorrect, and the selection of the width is more important.

Furthermore, Asako et al. (2016) show that the fixed-width model largely results in boundary cases in which one of the thresholds is 5% or 95%. Thus, we remove the assumption of a fixed width and instead estimate two cases, a degeneration into binary patterns (upper and lower) with a single threshold. In other words, we estimate a "lower-fixed type," for which the lower side of the distribution is a fixed portion and the upper side is a convex portion, and an "upper-fixed type," for which the lower side of the distribution is a convex portion and the upper side is a fixed portion. The results are summarized in Table 4.9.

Taking the greater of the upper-fixed and lower-fixed types, this model's coefficients of determination exceed those of inner-fixed, inner-convex hybrid type model with bilateral symmetry, which has the highest coefficients of determination so far, in 11 out of 12 cases, excluding the Zero method in the third period. For the Proportional and Book-Value methods, the assumption of bilateral symmetry means that, typically, the same model is applied for both large-scale new acquisitions and sales and retirements. However, higher coefficient of determination for the upper-fixed and lower-fixed types suggests instead that it is better to fit different models for large-scale new acquisitions and sales and retirements.

Table 4.9 Estimation results for the lower-fixed and upper-fixed types

		Buildings and structures	Machinery and equipment	Vessels and vehicles	Tools, furniture, and fixtures	Land	Coefficient of determination	Comparison with the coefficient of determination of the lower-fixed type (bottom of this table)	Comparison with the coefficient of determination of the inner-fixed/inner-convex hybrid type (Table 4.8)
Upper-fixed type, 10% intervals									
(a) Proportional method	1st period (1982–86)	90–100	90–100	80–100	90–100	90–100	0.1163	○	○
	2nd period (1987–91)	90–100	All convex	70–100	All fixed	90–100	0.2103		
	3rd period (1992–97)	80–100	90–100	20–100	60–100	20–100	0.1282	○	○
	4th period (1998–2004)	90–100	All convex	30–100	All convex	90–100	0.1280		○
	(tie)	As above	As above	40–100	As above	As above	As above		(○)
(b) Book-Value method	1st period (1982–86)	All convex	90–100	80–100	All convex	90–100	0.1438		○
	2nd period (1987–91)	All convex	All convex	10–100	70–100	90–100	0.2055		

(continued)

Table 4.9 (continued)

		Buildings and structures	Machinery and equipment	Vessels and vehicles	Tools, furniture, and fixtures	Land	Coefficient of determination	Comparison with the coefficient of determination of the lower-fixed type (bottom of this table)	Comparison with the coefficient of determination of the inner-fixed/inner-convex hybrid type (Table 4.8)
	3rd period (1992–97)	80–100	All convex	All fixed	All convex	20–100	0.1826		○
	4th period (1998–2004)	90–100	All convex	40–100	All convex	90–100	0.1508		○
(c) Zero method	1st period (1982–86)	All convex	10–100	30–100	All convex	40–100	0.1898	○	○
	2nd period (1987–91)	90–100	All convex	90–100	80–100	90–100	0.2410		
	3rd period (1992–97)	All convex	90–100	10–100	All convex	All fixed	0.2422		
	(tie)	As above	As above	20–100	As above	As above	As above		
	4th period (1998–2004)	All convex	10–100	80–100	All convex	All convex	0.2885		
	(tie)	As above	20–100	As above	As above	As above	As above		

(continued)

Table 4.9 (continued)

		Buildings and structures	Machinery and equipment	Vessels and vehicles	Tools, furniture, and fixtures	Land	Coefficient of determination	Comparison with the coefficient of determination of the upper-fixed type (top of this table)	Comparison with the coefficient of determination of the inner-fixed/inner-convex hybrid type (Table 4.8)
Lower-fixed type, 10% intervals									
(a) Proportional method	1st period (1982–86)	0–60	0–70	0–70	0–30	0–90	0.1110		○
	2nd period (1987–91)	0–80	0–90	0–90	All fixed	0–90	0.2135	○	○
	3rd period (1992–97)	0–90	0–90	0–90	0–60	0–20	0.1259		○
	4th period (1998–2004)	0–90	0–20	0–90	0–30	0–80	0.2468	○	○
	(tie)	As above	0–30	As above	As above	As above	As above	(○)	(○)
(b) Book-Value method	1st period (1982–86)	0–40	All fixed	0–80	0–10	0–90	0.1456	○	○
	2nd period (1987–91)	0–90	All convex	0–90	0–80	0–90	0.2304	○	○
	3rd period (1992–97)	0–90	All convex	0–80	0–10	0–30	0.1877	○	○

(continued)

Table 4.9 (continued)

		Buildings and structures	Machinery and equipment	Vessels and vehicles	Tools, furniture, and fixtures	Land	Coefficient of determination	Comparison with the coefficient of determination of the upper-fixed type (top of this table)	Comparison with the coefficient of determination of the inner-fixed/inner-convex hybrid type (Table 4.8)
	(tie)	As above	As above	As above	As above	0–40	As above	(○)	(○)
	(tie)	As above	As above	As above	As above	0–50	As above	(○)	(○)
	4th period (1998–2004)	0–90	0–20	0–90	All convex	All convex	0.1526	○	○
(c) Zero method	1st period (1982–86)	All convex	All fixed	0–90	All convex	All fixed	0.1785		
	2nd period (1987–91)	0–80	0–10	0–90	0–80	0–90	0.2618	○	○
	3rd period (1992–97)	All convex	All fixed	0–80	All convex	All fixed	0.2443	○	
	4th period (1998–2004)	0–10	0–90	0–90	All convex	0–80	0.2950	○	○

Notes
1. The displayed percentiles all correspond within the range of fixed-cost types
2. The ○ marks in the fields comparing the coefficients of determination indicate that the coefficient of determination is higher than the target of comparison

Comparing the coefficients of determination between the upper-fixed and lower-fixed types, the latter are higher in nine of the twelve cases. However, with regards to this model, the following points are more important than the comparison of the two types. Specifically, the intervals of the fixed portion suggested by the upper-fixed and lower-fixed types include cases for which completely consistent results are obtained, as in the first and third periods (1982–86, 1992–96) for buildings and structures with the Zero method or in the first, third, and fourth periods (1982–86, 1992–04) for tools, furniture, and fixtures with the Zero method, whereas other cases have completely inconsistent results.

"Completely inconsistent" refers to the condition that the threshold values are the same but the convex and fixed portions are completely interchanged, as in the first and second periods (1982–91) for land with the Proportional method, for which the upper-fixed type model obtains results of 0–90% in the convex portion and 90–100% in the fixed portion, whereas the lower-fixed type model finds 0–90% in the fixed portion and 90–100% in the convex portion.[14] In addition, in even more cases, the threshold values slightly deviate but these types of interchanges occur. Overall, the upper-fixed type tends to estimate a broader convex portion, and the lower-fixed type tends to estimate a broader fixed portion.

At first glance, this situation seems difficult to interpret. However, even in completely inconsistent cases, if we focus on the fact that the estimated threshold itself is consistent, then the results are by no means inexplicable. In other words, we obtain consistent estimation results with respect to the boundary for changes in investment behavior, but the selection of the convex side differs across models. In this way, we can see that the threshold of changes in investment behavior for inconsistent cases is roughly in the 70–100th percentiles, namely, the upper portion of the distribution of the investment rate, or the range of large-scale investments. If the true structure of the adjustment cost in these cases is such that both of the two portions fit the convex type but with different parameters, the upper-fixed and lower-fixed types would estimate one of them as the fixed portion.

As described above, the estimation results for the Multiple q model investment function that allows for the non-convexity of adjustment costs reveals clear differences in the appropriate functional type depending on capital goods, periods, and whether new acquisitions and sales and retirements are handled in a symmetric, mutually additive manner. This result is fully consistent with the conclusion of Cooper and Haltiwanger (2006), discussed in Chap. 1 of this book, that "the differing types of capital have differing and corresponding processes of adjustment," which they find after estimating comprehensive investment functions with single capital goods data encompassing the main models of capital investment research subsequent to q theory as special cases.

---

[14]In cases of such phenomena, there is a strong tendency for the fixed portion indicated by the inner-fixed type to be inconsistent with the fixed portion indicated by the inner-convex type, even for estimation results in the base case (Table 4.7). For example, in the first period (1982–86) for land with the Proportional method, as shown in Table 4.7, the fixed portion indicated by the inner-fixed type is the 10–90 percentile interval, whereas the fixed portion indicated by the inner-convex type is the 0–5 percentile and 95–100 percentile intervals.

4.6 Concluding Remarks

In this chapter, we conducted empirical analyses within the framework of the Multiple q model (an extension of q theory to the case of multiple capital goods). We considered important background themes with regards to the coexistence of new and old theories, such as the heterogeneity of capital goods and the heterogeneity in investment behaviors for new acquisitions and sales and retirements.

The estimation results of the Multiple q model, which was extended to include the possibility that the adjustment cost function contains a non-convex portion, further highlight the variety of investment functions forms, depending on the capital goods category, the estimation period, and whether new acquisition behavior is considered alone or is integrated with the sale and retirement behavior. That is, although we observed that a proportion of cases fit purely convex adjustment cost functions, we confirmed that the majority of cases fit functions with non-convex portions. Moreover, the non-convex areas of the investment rate distribution varied considerably depending on the categories of capital goods and the estimation period. However, we have still only tested a small portion of possible adjustment processes created by various forms of heterogeneity.

In particular, the estimations of the best-fitting models in the analysis thus far—the upper-fixed and lower-fixed types—imply that the next step to be attempted is estimating models that apply two convex adjustment costs with differing parameters to each of the two intervals. The performance of these models can test the necessity of applying fixed-cost types. For example, if a case consisting of two types of convex adjustment costs is more desirable than a combination of convex and fixed types, then we may need to apply differing convex adjustment costs to the outer two of the three intervals based on the inner-fixed type model. By continuing these sorts of searches, we believe that we can identify models with greater explanatory power with regards to the adjustment processes of different capital goods.

We also consider an agenda for further research for the empirical analysis of capital investment using the Multiple q model. In addition to due inquiries into capital market imperfections, this agenda includes performing an estimation that more explicitly incorporates non-linearity; analyzing the adjustment process of sale and retirement behavior on its own; extending the scope of capital stock as a quasi-fixed factor of production to such components as inventory and intangible assets; and relabeling the notion of heterogeneity to include not only differences in physical attributes but also qualitative characteristics of capital, such as classifications by enterprise size and by forms of capital acquisition. The last item will be taken up as an extension of the basic Multiple q framework in the following two chapters of this book.

References

Abel, A. B., & Eberly, J. C. (1994). A Unified model of investment under uncertainty. *American Economic Review, 84,* 1369–1384.

Arellano, M., & Bond, S. (1991). Some tests of specification for panel data: Monte carlo evidence and an application to employment equations. *Review of Economic Studies, 58,* 277–297.

Asako, K., Kuninori, M., Inoue, T., & Murase, H. (1989), Land evaluation and measurement of Tobin's *q* theory/Estimation of Multiple *q*. *Economics Today, 10*(3). (In Japanese).

Asako, K., Kuninori, M., Inoue, T., & Murase, H. (1991). Capital investment and financing: Estimation by the simultaneous equations model. *Economics Today, 11*(4). (In Japanese).

Asako, K., M. Kuninori, T. Inoue, and H. Murase (1997), Capital investment and land investment: 1977–1994, In K. Asako and M. Otaki eds., *Dynamics of modern macroeconomics*, University of Tokyo Press, pp. 323–349. (In Japanese).

Asako, K., Nakamura, J., & Tonogi, K. (2016). The Development of Investment Research and Multiple *q* in Japan. *International Journal of Finance and Accounting, 5*(5A), 1–29.

Asako, K., & Tonogi, K. (2010). Heterogeneity of capital stock and Multiple *q*. *The Economic Review, 61,* 325–341. (In Japanese).

Bertola, G., & Caballero, R. J. (1990). Kinked adjustment costs and aggregate dynamics. In O. Blanchard, & S. Fischer (Eds.), *NBER Macroeconomics Annual 1990* (pp. 237–295). MIT press.

Cooper, R., & Haltiwanger, J. C. (2006). On the nature of capital adjustment costs. *Review of Economic Studies, 73,* 611–633.

Hori, K., Saito, M., & Ando, K. (2006). What caused fixed investment to stagnate during the 1990s in Japan? Evidence from panel data of listed companies. *Japanese Economic Review, 57,* 283–306.

Miyagawa, T. (2005). *The economics of long-term stagnation–Globalization and the transformation of industrial structure*. University of Tokyo Press. (In Japanese).

Miyagawa, T., & Kim, Y. (2008). Measuring organizational capital in Japan: An empirical assessment using firm-level data. *Seoul Journal of Economics, 21,* 171–193.

Modigliani, F., & Miller, M. (1958). The cost of capital, corporation finance and the theory of investment. *American Economic Review, 48,* 261–297.

Shima, K. (2005). Lumps in equipment investment of Japanese firms: A hazard analysis. *The Electric Economic Review, 54,* 1–17. (In Japanese).

Tanaka, K. (2016). Industrial characteristics and the investment-uncertainty relationship: A panel study of data on Japanese firms. *International Journal of Finance and Accounting, 5*(5A), 36–48.

Tonogi, K., Nakamura, J., & Asako, K. (2010). Estimation of Multiple *q* models of investment: Investment behavior over heterogeneous capital goods during the period of excess capacity reduction. *Economics Today, 31*(2). (In Japanese).

Wildasin, D. E. (1984). The *q* theory of investment with many capital goods. *American Economic Review, 74,* 203–210.

Chapter 5
Extensions of the Multiple q Model: (I) Heterogeneity by Enterprise Size

Abstract This chapter extends the Multiple q model to individual firm data that include small and medium-sized enterprises as well as large ones. To do so in a feasible way, we divide capital goods into land and other tangible fixed assets. Our estimation results for the sample period 2004–2013 show that land should be treated as an independent capital good that incurs unique adjustment costs regardless of enterprise size. However, we also find that some variables that are considered redundant under the standard Tobin's q theory, such as debt ratio and tangibility, have significant explanatory power and that lumpy investment behaviors exist that cannot be handled by a smooth investment adjustment cost function. The lumpiness of investment behaviors is higher for smaller firms, suggesting that capital market imperfections constrain some lumpy investments.

Keywords Heterogeneity of capital · Multiple q model · SMEs · Survey slip data · Capital market imperfection · Lumpy investment

5.1 Investment Behaviors by Capital Good and Enterprise Size

In this chapter, we explore whether the explanatory power of the q theory framework can be improved by expanding the dataset to include unlisted, smaller firms in our sample. We can analyze such firms by using individual survey slip data from the Financial Statements Statistics of Corporations by Industry (FSSCI) released by Ministry of Finance, Japan. The analysis period is set as ten years, from fiscal year 2004 to fiscal year 2013, to continue sequentially from the period covered in the previous chapters. Analyzing this period enables us to see whether the effects of the heterogeneity of capital goods have changed since fiscal year 2004 for the major enterprises.

This chapter is a shortened and reorganized version of Nakamura, Tonogi, and Asako (2017). The content of and opinions in this chapter are solely attributable to the authors and are unrelated to any organizations with which the authors are affiliated.

K. Asako et al., *Multiple q and Investment in Japan*,
https://doi.org/10.1007/978-981-15-2981-8_5

Much of the research thus far on investment behavior across sample periods has incorporated the possibility that capital markets are imperfect, including studies on small and medium-sized enterprises (SMEs), but all of these studies assume a single capital good. After controlling for the heterogeneity of capital goods, we expect to obtain new findings on the effect of the imperfect nature of capital markets on investment behavior by considering differences by enterprise size in the relationships with and significance of financial variables, such as leverage, which should be inherently redundant for perfect capital markets.

The FSSCI has fewer survey items than those disclosed on a firm's financial statements and is also affected by replacements of sample firms. Thus, we cannot simply apply conventional analysis methods based on panel data. Thus, the techniques developed to construct a dataset of acceptable quality under these constraints is another important contribution of this study.

5.1.1 Analysis by Corporate Size Using Individual Survey Slip Data

The individual survey slip data from the FSSCI include only two categories of information on tangible fixed assets, "land" and "capital goods other than land," and it is difficult to form panel data over a long period of time because the data for smaller enterprises are collected through random sampling. Our dataset also has various restrictions, such as the absence of market evaluations of firm value and the impossibility of using the perpetual inventory method to construct the capital stock data. However, it targets enterprises of a wide range of sizes, from large listed firms to micro enterprises with equity capital of less than ten million yen. Thus, our dataset has several advantages for estimating the Multiple q model.

First, one reasons that the Multiple q investment function is not always a good fit in studies of listed firms is that most listed firms have several business units belonging to different industries, and it may be impossible to capture their investment behavior with a single function. Moreover, q theory is premised on perfect competition, which may not be even close to reality for listed firms. These problems are less serious for smaller firms. If an investment function that is a poor fit for major enterprises is found to have significant explanatory power for SMEs, then the conjecture described above is likely supported. Conversely, an analysis of the investment behavior of manufacturing business establishments in the United States by Doms and Dunne (1998) finds that the smaller an establishment is, the more pronounced its characteristics of so-called lumpy investment behavior are. As we scrutinized to a certain extent in Chap. 4 of this book, lumpy investments cannot be analyzed within the framework of the smooth, convex adjustment cost function that is assumed by the standard Multiple q model. Thus, if this effect is strong, the standard Multiple q model would have a rather poorer fit for SMEs than major enterprises.

Second, by comparing the Single q model and the Multiple q model based on the assumption that the convex adjustment cost function framework has a certain degree of real world validity, we can test for each firm size whether land is a capital good with an adjustment cost, and, if so, whether any intrinsic heterogeneity exists between land and capital stock other than land. For instance, if the land-acquisition behaviors of small enterprises are fundamentally synonymous with the acquisition of new buildings and the expansion of business establishments, land may be homogeneous with capital stock other than land. Otherwise, the adjustment cost may remain within a negligible range, as small enterprises tend to acquire small parcels of land.

Third, the fact that the cash flow and interest-bearing debt ratios are estimated to be significant in the investment function was formerly considered evidence that imperfect aspects of the capital market, such as liquidity constraints, influence investment behavior. However, these variables still have robustly significant effects even among listed enterprises, which should easily be able to access the capital market, and even after controlling for the simultaneity problems that can cause spurious correlation, thus casting doubt on this interpretation. Alternative explanations include, for example, non-negligible measurement error in the q ratio or information on future investment opportunities contained in cash flows, although this issue has not yet been settled. Comparing major enterprises and SMEs, which differ in accessibility to the capital market, would help to address this point, as would analyzing the period of the global financial crisis in which even major enterprises faced liquidity constraints. Although such research has already been carried out to some extent, this study seems to be the first analysis within a framework that includes land investment with features specific to Japanese enterprises and that takes the heterogeneity of capital goods into consideration.

5.1.2 Basic Framework of the Empirical Analysis

In the basic framework for the analysis described below, we straightforwardly estimate an equation that includes several control variables, such as the cash flow and interest-bearing debt ratios, as well as year, industry, and other dummy variables on the right-hand side of Eq. (2.9) in Chap. 2 or Eq. (4.1) in Chap. 4 using individual survey slip data from the FSSCI (for all industries except the financial and insurance industries). Note that Eq. (2.9), which we renumber in this chapter as Eq. (5.1),

$$(q-1)P = \sum_{j=1}^{n} \gamma_j Z_j s_j - \sum_{j=1}^{n} \gamma_j a_j s_j \tag{5.1}$$

is derived from the optimization behavior of a firm that maximizes its market value. In Eq. (5.1), q, P, Z_j and s_j stand, respectively, for Total q, the implicit deflator of the aggregated capital stock, the investment rate, and the ratio of the jth capital goods in the aggregated capital stock. Additionally, $\gamma_j > 0$ represents the degree and size of the adjustment cost for each capital good, and a_j denotes the parameter corresponding to the investment rate in which the adjustment cost takes its minimum value.

Individual survey slip data from the FSSCI have various restrictions that differ from those for listed firms. Because it is not possible to simply apply conventional analytical methods that assume panel data based on financial statements, we develop appropriate techniques to deal with the data constraints in the empirical analysis. Analyzing the FSSCI data faces three major constraints compared to analyses using data on listed firms: (i) it is not possible to calculate the average q using equity prices, (ii) it is not possible to construct capital stock data using the perpetual inventory method due to the difficulty in forming a panel, and (iii) the data include only two categories of capital goods: land and capital goods other than land.

Regarding the first two constraints, we need to identify an appropriate proxy variable for the marginal q that substitutes for the average q as the dependent variable, and we also need to construct the capital stock using various techniques, such as taking the market-to-book-value ratio and the deflator for each capital good by industry from listed firms' data. The rest of this section explains the basic ideas behind the proxy of the marginal q. Also, Sect. 5.2 describes the basic ideas behind the construction of the parameters that are necessary for calculating q and the capital stock and investment-related data.

In conventional q theory, which was developed with the assumption of a single capital good, the marginal q is defined as the sum of the discounted present value of the expected marginal earnings that will be newly created in the future by adding one unit of capital stock in the current period (i.e., the shadow price of capital) divided by the replacement cost of one unit of capital goods. When it is problematic to use the average q based on market equity prices to estimate the investment function if, for example, an equity-price bubble exists, some proxy for marginal q is used instead. For example, if linear homogeneity is assumed with regards to the value function, marginal earnings are equivalent to average earnings; thus, many previous studies estimate the marginal q with a vector autoregression (VAR) model using data on the current average return on capital (or the profit rate) obtained from the accounting values under the assumption that the stochastic process for the past profit and discount rates estimated from the VAR model will be stable over time.[1] However, this method cannot be applied in this study, as panel data cannot be used. Thus, in the following, the marginal q is estimated assuming a steady state in which the static expectations formation becomes a rational expectations formation.

In general, when assuming a steady state, two estimation methods can be considered depending on whether the capital depreciation rate is included in expected marginal earnings (*EME*), which is the numerator of marginal q. Thus, with ρ as the current period's profit rate, δ as the depreciation rate, r as the discount rate, and g as the expected growth rate, *EME* is expressed by the net method as

$$EME = \frac{\rho}{r-g}K, \tag{5.2}$$

[1]See, for example, Abel and Blanchard (1986) and Otaki and Suzuki (1986).

and by the gross method, which considers capital depreciation, as

$$EME = \frac{\rho + \delta}{r + \delta - g} K. \tag{5.3}$$

Although it is not clear which expression is the main focus of investors and of enterprises, when we use actual data, the estimates of marginal q, which are implicitly computable from Eqs. (5.2) and (5.3) as the ratio EME/K, do not exist if any of the denominators or numerators are negative. Such cases are left out of our sample. Thus, following Suzuki (2001), we use the gross method to reduce the probability that this non-existence problem occurs. For the expected growth rate, g, no candidate proxies are available in our dataset based on the FSSCI except for the growth rate of the book value of total assets (*BTA*). However, this variable is a rather noisy proxy, and the possibility that the denominator of Eq. (5.3) is negative may increase. Taking these shortcomings into account, we uniformly set g equal to zero for all samples without estimation.

5.1.3 Control Variables and the Estimation Equation

The above calculation is the backbone of the investment function based on Tobin's q theory. In addition, following Tonogi, Nakamura, and Asako (2010) and the analyses of the previous chapters of this book, we introduce some control variables that should be redundant in the framework of q theory and check their significance to investigate the validity of q theory and its assumption of a perfect capital market. To do so, we first include the following additional variables, which are often employed in estimations of the investment function, among the explanatory variables:

$$\textit{Interest-bearing debt ratio}\ (D/BTA) = \frac{\text{interest-bearing debt } (D)}{\text{book value of total assets} (BTA)},$$

$$\begin{aligned} &\textit{Tangibility}\ (BK/BTA) \\ &\quad = \frac{\text{total book value of land and other tangible fixed assets} (BK)}{\text{book value of total assets } (BTA)}, \end{aligned}$$

$$\begin{aligned} &\textit{Enterprise size} \\ &\quad = \text{book value of total assets' logarithmic value } \ln(BTA). \end{aligned}$$

Needless to say, the lower limit of the *interest-bearing debt ratio* (*D/BTA*) is zero; however, the number of zero-leverage firms that have reached this limit, has recently increased regardless of enterprise size. Therefore, we also add a *zero-leverage dummy* (*ZLD*) to our list of explanatory variables to capture this effect. Incidentally, the cash flow, which is frequently used in estimations of the investment function, almost always overlaps in terms of its numerical value with the numerator of marginal q

in this study's dataset. To avoid improving the model's explanatory power only in appearance (i.e., purely for technical reasons related to data construction), we decided not to include cash flow among our explanatory variables.

In the Multiple q model investment function given by Eqs. (2.9) and (5.1), if these control variables are estimated to have significant effects along with the theoretically derived q because, for instance, the capital market is imperfect, we establish the following interpretations of their signs.

First, concerning the coefficient on the *zero-leverage dummy* and the *interest-bearing debt ratio*, if, for example, (i) the supply-side factors in the capital market (i.e., the higher the profit rate, the greater a bank's willingness to lend), (ii) the disciplinary effects of debt (i.e., the higher the debt rate, the higher the profit rate from the effects of discipline), and (iii) the tax-saving effects of debt (i.e., the income deduction from interest expenses) are predominant, the coefficient on the *zero-leverage dummy* should be significantly negative, and the coefficient on the *interest-bearing debt ratio* should be significantly positive. Conversely, if, for example, (iv) demand-side factors in the capital market (i.e., high debt ratios owing to past low profitability with serial correlations in profit rates) and (v) the risk of bankruptcy (i.e., the higher the debt ratio, the higher the discount rate) are predominant, the coefficient on the *zero-leverage dummy* should be significantly positive, and the coefficient on the *interest-bearing debt ratio* should be significantly negative.[2]

Second, *tangibility* (*BK/BTA*) is used as a proxy variable for pledgeability, which is considered to promote the use of external debt, in research on the determinants of the capital structure. In the Multiple q model investment function, if pledgeability has the effect of easing borrowing constraints, it is expected that the possibility of realizing earnings opportunities increases, implying that *tangibility* is positive and significant with regards to q. Conversely, *tangibility* may have another role in controlling the effects of intangible assets, which are not considered in our framework. In this case, it is expected that the coefficient on *tangibility* should be negative and significant for the reasons described below.

To clarify the underlying mechanism for this negative effect, we consider a firm consisting only of tangible fixed assets including land (K), and intangible fixed assets (R). For simplicity, real, nominal, and book values are assumed to be always consistent. As assumed in our framework, if intangible fixed assets' Partial q_R is always equal to one, tangible fixed assets' Partial q_K is calculated as follows:

$$q_K = \frac{V - R}{K}, \tag{5.4}$$

where V denotes firm value. However, if intangible fixed assets should also be considered as capital stock with an adjustment cost (a quasi-fixed production factor) in practice and, thus, q_R deviates from one, the firm value should be expressed as follows:

[2]In the estimations of the Multiple q model by Tonogi et al. (2010), the coefficient on the *interest-bearing debt ratio* is robustly positive and significant. However, making a straightforward comparison with this study is difficult because the *zero-leverage dummy* is not included in the list of control variables and they target listed firms and use the average q for the dependent variable.

$$V = q_K K + q_R R. \tag{5.5}$$

Then, Eq. (5.4) is replaced by

$$q_K = \frac{V - R}{K} - \frac{(q_R - 1)R}{K}, \tag{5.6}$$

which indicates that q_K in Eq. (5.4) deviates from the true Partial q_K by the margin of the second term in the right-hand side of Eq. (5.6), which is negative including the negative sign insofar as $q_R > 1$.

Meanwhile, because *tangibility* $= K/(K + R)$ is negatively correlated with the intangible-to-tangible capital assets ratio, R/K, by definition, the second term on the right-hand side of Eq. (5.6), including the negative sign, correlates positively with *tangibility*. Thus, in summary, the variable *tangibility* absorbs the introduced upward bias in q_K from its true value, implying that the estimated coefficient on *tangibility* should be negative. Thus, if this negative effect is greater than the pledgeability effect of tangible fixed assets, the coefficient on *tangibility* is likely to be negative and significant.

Third, *enterprise asset size*, ln(*BTA*), usually results in the easing of borrowing constraints owing to effects such as the diversification of the business portfolio. It is therefore expected to be positive. Conversely, if *enterprise asset size* is positively correlated with the company's degree of maturity (i.e., if it is negatively correlated with growth potential), it may be negative.

Finally, *year dummies*, *industry dummies*, and *capital size dummies* are used as dummy variables in the constant term of the estimation equation. The *industry dummies* are based on the FSSCI industry classification table, and the *capital size dummies* are based on equity capital and are grouped into four categories: 1 billion yen or more (major enterprises), 100 million yen to 1 billion yen (medium-sized enterprises), 10 million yen to 100 million yen (small enterprises), and less than 10 million yen (micro enterprises).

The final investment function given by Eq. (2.9) or Eq. (5.1) is therefore estimated with additional control variables as follows:

$$\begin{aligned}(q-1)P = &\gamma_K Z_K s_K + \gamma_L Z_L s_L - \gamma_K a_K s_K - \gamma_L a_L s_L \\ &+ C_0 ZLD + C_1 \frac{D}{BTA} + C_2 \frac{BK}{BTA} + C_3 \ln(BTA) \\ &+ C_4\, \textit{year dummies} + C_5\, \textit{industry dummies} \\ &+ C_6\, \textit{capital size dummies},\end{aligned} \tag{5.7}$$

where the subscripts K and L correspond to capital goods other than land and land, respectively.

5.2 Data Overview

5.2.1 Data Construction and Elimination of Outliers

The investment-related data for each category of capital goods and the parameters necessary for calculating the q ratio are constructed according to the process described below.

(i) **Nominal investment**

As in the studies subsequent to Asako, Kuninori, Inoue, and Murase (1997), we adopt in this analysis the concept of "gross investment" for the investment rate, which is calculated by

$I_K =$ the difference in the book value of non-land tangible fixed assets between the beginning and end of the fiscal period + depreciation expenses.
$I_L =$ the difference in the book value land between the beginning and end of the fiscal period.

In the survey slip of the FSSCI, special depreciation expenses are also surveyed; however, they are often not directly deducted from the book value in the accounting treatment, and we determined that noise would increase if they were included, so we exclude these expenses. In the survey slip, depreciation expenses include those of intangible fixed assets, which should be excluded from depreciation expenses in our model. However, as the breakdown across asset types is unknown, these expenses are difficult to estimate. Therefore, abnormal value processing is used to exclude observations with the ratio of intangible fixed assets to tangible fixed assets above a certain threshold.

(ii) **Nominal capital stock**

As mentioned, it is difficult to construct sufficient panel data to apply the perpetual inventory method using the survey slip data of the FSSCI. Therefore, based on listed firms' financial data, we construct a nominal capital stock series by industry and by capital good type from 1977 onwards using the perpetual inventory method, and we make calculations by multiplying the book value of the survey slip data by the industry's market-value-to-book-value ratio, which is the industry's nominal capital stock value divided by the corresponding book value.

(iii) **Deflator**

For the capital stock deflator, we create a real capital stock series by industry and by capital good type from 1977 onwards based on the listed firms' financial data using the perpetual inventory method, and we make calculations by dividing this value by the nominal capital stock constructed in (ii). We attempted to create a deflator for investment flows using data on listed firms' real and nominal capital investment, but we did not obtain a stable series. Thus, we also use the capital stock deflator in place of the deflator for investment flow.

(iv) **Capital depreciation rate δ**

The capital depreciation rate δ is obtained by multiplying the depreciation rate of non-land capital stock by the weight of capital stock other than land in real capital stock (as it is natural to consider the depreciation rate of land to be zero). The weighted averages of the depreciation rates by capital goods type derived from Hulten and Wykoff (1977, 1981)[3] are used for the depreciation rate of non-land capital stock. We create the weights of real capital stock by industry and by capital good type from 1977 onwards using the perpetual inventory method based on listed firms' financial data. When calculating the Single q that does not include land, the depreciation rate of non-land capital stock (not multiplied by the weight) is used for δ.

(v) **Profit rate ρ**

For each firm and for each year, the ratio of the after-tax gross current profit to capital, that is,

$$\frac{\text{(current profit before depreciation and interest payment)} - \text{(taxes paid)}}{\text{nominal capital stock at the beginning of the fiscal period}}$$

is used. Taxes paid are calculated by subtracting the after-tax profit from the pre-tax profit. When calculating the Single q that does not include land, land is excluded from the nominal capital stock in the denominator.

(vi) **Discount rate r**

In the same way, for each firm and for each year, the values obtained from

$$\frac{\text{interest and discount paid}}{\text{(interest-bearing debt)} + \text{(the notes receivable discount balance)}}$$

are used. However, the discount rate of zero-leverage firms is replaced with the minimum value (>0) among the relevant firms in each year, and we apply Winsorizing processing for values exceeding 20%, with an upper ceiling of 20%.

We consider that some observations include errors caused by respondents' misunderstanding of the question items or mistaken entries; moreover, transcription or input errors may have occurred when the collected questionnaires were processed, and such values are also considered outliers.

Specifically, the variables for which outliers must be eliminated based on theoretical or empirical grounds are as follows. First, if $Q = (q-1)P \geq 10$, the contribution of intangible assets to enterprise value is too large, which is difficult to explain within the framework of this study; second, observations with $Q = (q-1)P \leq -10$ sample are meaningless, as the expression includes a proxy variable for q that should theoretically be positive; third, observations with

[3]The corresponding values for buildings, structures, machinery and equipment, vessels and vehicles, and tools, furniture, and fixtures are 0.047, 0.0564, 0.09489, 0.1470, and 0.08838, respectively.

(depreciation expenses/assets subject to depreciation) ≥1 likely include mistaken entries, such as entries of the accumulated depreciation amount in current depreciation expenses; fourth, regarding the book value of total assets, observations with large discontinuities such that (end of fiscal period/beginning of fiscal period) ≥1.5 are likely due to mergers and acquisitions rather than ordinary economic activities. Thus, observations meeting any of these criteria are excluded from the estimations.

5.2.2 Summary Statistics

As is described in Table 5.1, a total of 105,470 observations are obtained after outlier processing for the ten-year period from fiscal year 2004 to fiscal year 2013. Medium-sized enterprises (with capital of 100 million yen to 1 billion yen) account for the greatest portion, with major enterprises (with capital of over 1 billion yen) and small enterprises (with capital of 10 million yen to 100 million yen) a close second and third. The sample includes 3,800 micro enterprises (with capital of less than 10 million yen), which is less than 4% of the total. Around 40% of firms are from the manufacturing industry, and around 60% are from the non-manufacturing industry. The manufacturing percentage increases as the size of the firm's equity capital grows, and it slightly exceeds 50% for major enterprises.

Table 5.2 shows the basic summary statistics of variables for the regression equation of the Multiple q model in Eq. (5.7). Specifically, this table includes $(q-1)P$ as the dependent variable; $Z_K s_K$ and $Z_L s_L$ as the products of the investment rate and the ratio of capital stock with regards to non-land tangible fixed assets and land, respectively; s_K and s_L as the ratios of capital; and major control variables.

The average value of dependent variable, $(q-1)P$, is 0.95, and its median value is 0.55 for the whole sample, which seem plausible. These values grow as capital size increases. At the industry level, the manufacturing industry average is 0.62, whereas the non-manufacturing industry average is 1.19, nearly twice as high. The average value of $Z_K s_K$, the product of the investment rate in non-land tangible fixed assets and the ratio of its capital stock, is 0.055, whereas the average value of $Z_L s_L$, the product of the investment rate in land and the ratio of its capital stock, is slightly negative

Table 5.1 Number of samples by capital size and industry (FY 2004–13)

	Major enterprises	Medium-sized enterprises	Small enterprises	Micro enterprises	Total
Manufacturing	16,499	15,122	11,046	1,157	43,824
Non-manufacturing	16,196	24,685	18,122	2,643	61,646
All industries	32,695	39,807	29,168	3,800	105,470

Note Major enterprises have capital of 1 billion yen and above, medium-sized enterprises have capital of 100 million yen to 1 billion yen, small enterprises have capital of 10 million yen to 100 million yen, and micro enterprises have capital of less than 10 million yen

Table 5.2 Summary statistics by capital size and industry (FY 2004–13)

		$(q-1)P$	$Z_K s_K$	$Z_L s_L$	s_K	s_L	*D/BTA*	*ZLD*	*BK/BTA*
All enterprises	Mean	0.951	0.055	−0.003	0.508	0.492	0.371	0.114	0.405
	Median	0.547	0.030	0.000	0.494	0.506	0.325	0.000	0.361
	S.D.	1.990	0.118	0.074	0.250	0.250	0.456	0.318	0.240
Major enterprises	Mean	1.105	0.066	−0.004	0.561	0.439	0.239	0.137	0.350
	Median	0.673	0.046	0.000	0.563	0.437	0.199	0.000	0.297
	S.D.	1.975	0.120	0.071	0.235	0.235	0.223	0.344	0.222
Medium-sized enterprises	Mean	1.010	0.055	−0.004	0.511	0.489	0.350	0.125	0.409
	Median	0.575	0.029	0.000	0.491	0.509	0.319	0.000	0.363
	S.D.	1.988	0.121	0.078	0.247	0.247	0.315	0.330	0.244
Small enterprises	Mean	0.764	0.045	0.000	0.450	0.550	0.506	0.081	0.441
	Median	0.403	0.017	0.000	0.421	0.579	0.504	0.000	0.413
	S.D.	1.951	0.110	0.073	0.252	0.252	0.670	0.273	0.235
Micro enterprises	Mean	0.445	0.040	0.004	0.475	0.525	0.689	0.045	0.571
	Median	0.219	0.005	0.000	0.452	0.548	0.672	0.000	0.580
	S.D.	2.245	0.106	0.052	0.279	0.279	0.682	0.207	0.252
Manufacturing	Mean	0.616	0.058	−0.002	0.567	0.433	0.346	0.102	0.350
	Median	0.420	0.041	0.000	0.578	0.422	0.291	0.000	0.322
	S.D.	1.400	0.088	0.048	0.227	0.227	0.564	0.302	0.181
Non-manufacturing	Mean	1.189	0.052	−0.003	0.467	0.533	0.389	0.122	0.445
	Median	0.693	0.021	0.000	0.426	0.574	0.354	0.000	0.409
	S.D.	2.291	0.135	0.088	0.257	0.257	0.358	0.328	0.267

overall. Because the composition ratio value is always positive, we understand that the investment rate in non-land tangible fixed assets is correspondingly positive on average, whereas the investment rate in land is negative on average, reflecting, understandably, the falling trend in land prices over the sample period.

The overall average values of s_K and s_L indicate that the ratios of capital stock of non-land tangible fixed assets and land are basically half and half. For major and medium-sized enterprises and manufacturing firms, s_K is greater than 0.5, whereas for small and micro enterprises and non-manufacturing firms, s_L is greater than 0.5. The *interest-bearing debt ratio* (*D/BTA*) grows as capital size decreases; it is 0.24 for major enterprises and reaches 0.69 for micro enterprises. It is slightly higher for the non-manufacturing industry. The ratio of zero-leverage enterprises ($ZLD = 1$) is 11.4%, which decreases as capital size decreases. However, even for micro enterprises, 4.5% are zero-leveraged. This ratio is slightly higher for the non-manufacturing industry. *Tangibility* (*BK/BTA*) grows as capital size decreases, and it is higher for the non-manufacturing industry.

5.3 Main Estimation Results and Interpretation

5.3.1 Baseline Model for All Sample Enterprises

In estimating Eq. (5.7), or the Multiple q investment function, we run for all sample enterprises three types of regressions as baseline model depending on the included control variables. Specifically, we include none of the control variables, which we call the "no control variable" case; we include all of the control variables but the *zero-leverage dummy*, which we call the "not including *zero-leverage dummy*" case; and we include all of the control variables, which we call the "including *zero-leverage dummy*" case. Table 5.3 shows the results of the standard OLS (ordinary least squares) estimations for these baseline models.

First, for the estimates of γ_K, γ_L, $-\gamma_K a_K$, $-\gamma_L a_L$ in the three types of regressions, the γ parameter is significantly positive for non-land tangible fixed assets in all cases, whereas the γ parameter of land is significantly negative in all cases. The fact that γ_K is positive indicates that the investment behavior for non-land tangible fixed assets does not necessarily contradict the smooth, convex adjustment cost framework. However, the fact that the control variables also have significant effects in estimates including these variables is not consistent with q theory. All of the estimated values of $-\gamma_K a_K$, $-\gamma_L a_L$ are positive and significant, suggesting that the investment rate a that minimizes the adjustment cost is negative for non-land tangible fixed assets and positive for land.

The fact that parameter γ_L is negative is in line with the result obtained by Asako, Kuninori, Inoue, and Murase (1989, 1997), but it is inconsistent with the result obtained by Tonogi et al. (2010). Tonogi et al. (2010) use a more detailed classification for capital goods other than land, but it is unlikely that this distinction affects the

Table 5.3 Baseline model results (FY 2004–13)

	No control variable	Not including *zero-leverage dummy*	Including *zero-leverage dummy*
γ_K	3.05**	2.25**	2.35**
γ_L	−1.75**	−1.80**	−1.87**
$-\gamma_K a_K$	1.60**	1.22**	1.95**
$-\gamma_L a_L$	1.70**	1.37**	2.05**
C_0			−1.39**
C_1		0.20**	−0.05
C_2		−2.55**	−2.90**
C_3		0.13**	0.10**
R-squared	0.280	0.337	0.373
No of obs.	105,470	105,470	105,470

Notes
1. Standard errors are heteroscedasticity robust (Huber–White estimator), with * and ** denoting significance at the 10% and 5% levels, respectively
2. The results of the year dummies, industry dummies, and capital size dummies are omitted from the table

estimates for land. The difference is more likely partly attributable to their use of panel analysis with controlling for firm fixed effects.

Focusing on the control variables, C_1, the coefficient on the *interest-bearing debt ratio*, is estimated to be positive and significant if the regression does not include the *zero-leverage dummy*, suggesting the possible involvement of supply factors in the lending market, the disciplinary effects of debt, and tax-saving effects; this result is consistent with that of Tonogi et al. (2010). When the *zero-leverage dummy* is added to the explanatory variables, its coefficient, C_0, is negative and significant, and the *interest-bearing debt ratio* loses its explanatory power. These results still suggest the involvement of supply factors in the lending market, the disciplinary effects of debt, and tax-saving effects, but many of the positive effects of the *interest-bearing debt ratio* prove to be attributable to the differences between zero-leverage enterprises and enterprises with debt.

The estimates of the *tangibility* coefficient C_2 and the *enterprise asset size* coefficient C_3 are stable both with and without the *zero-leverage dummy*, with the former being negative and significant and the latter being positive and significant. The fact that the coefficient on *tangibility* is negative and significant suggests that the role played by correcting of the distortion of q due to the existence of intangible assets is stronger than the effects of pledgeability are. The fact that *enterprise asset size* has a positive and significant effect may reflect the easing of borrowing constraints from the effects of corporate size.

5.3.2 Test of the Heterogeneity of Capital Goods

Following Asako et al. (1989, 1997) and the analyses in the previous chapters, this subsection tests the heterogeneity of capital goods by conducting estimations of three models: (A) a Single q model that does not include land, (B) a Single q model that includes land, and (C) a Multiple q model. We compare and contrast these models' respective performances. Note that these models, Model A, Model B, and Model C, can be mutually compared based on the results of previous studies described in Sect. 2.2. When all capital goods are homogeneous, the expression of the Multiple q model in Eq. (5.1) or, originally, in Eq. (2.9) reduces to

$$(q-1)P = \gamma(Z-a). \tag{5.8}$$

Thus, as in the Single q model, the investment function that rewrites Eq. (5.8),

$$Z = a + \frac{1}{\gamma}(q-1)P, \tag{5.9}$$

is estimated from the Z, q, P data that are consistent with the capital goods concepts used in each model. The variable Z represents the investment rate, calculated as the ratio of total investment to total capital stock obtained by aggregating the multiple capital goods. To focus on the comparison with Asako et al. (1989, 1997),[4] we exclude the control variables used in Sect. 5.2 from the estimations of all models, and standard OLS estimations are conducted using cross-section data for each year. Tables 5.4, 5.5 and 5.6 show the estimation results not only for the full sample but also for major manufacturing firms, as Asako et al. (1989, 1997) which focus only on listed manufacturing firms.

To interpret the estimation results, the Single q model that does not include land (see Table 5.4) is first compared to the Single q model that includes land (see Table 5.5). Focusing on the $1/\gamma$ estimates for the full sample, only the result for 2004 for cases that exclude land is not significant. The results for all other years are significant in both cases, but the parameter estimates are larger and more plausible, if only slightly, in the cases that include land.

For major manufacturing enterprises, cases that include land differ more clearly from those that do not. In the latter cases, $1/\gamma$ is not estimated to be significant from 2004 to 2005 and in 2011, whereas, in the former cases, it is estimated to be positive and significant in all years. Even when $1/\gamma$ is estimated as significant in both cases, the estimates in the cases that include land are greater and more theoretically plausible. Thus, the results strongly suggest that, within the Single q framework, capital stock should include land. This conclusion is also reached by Asako et al. (1997), who analyze listed enterprises in the manufacturing industry from 1977 to 1992. In a more detailed comparison, Asako et al. (1997), estimate that $1/\gamma$ is nearly

[4]However, unlike the analysis in this chapter, Asako et al. (1989, 1997) employ the average q concept.

Table 5.4 Single q model results of $1/\gamma$ (year by year), not including land

	Full sample	Manufacturing, major enterprises
2004	−0.0143	0.0012
2005	0.0080**	0.0009
2006	0.0085**	0.0075**
2007	0.0072**	0.0113**
2008	0.0090**	0.0100**
2009	0.0081**	0.0058*
2010	0.0073**	0.0057**
2011	0.0085**	0.0035
2012	0.0076**	0.0089**
2013	0.0071**	0.0074**

Notes
1. Standard errors are heteroscedasticity robust (Huber–White estimator), with * and ** denoting significance at the 10% and 5% levels, respectively
2. The results of the industry dummies and capital size dummies are omitted from the table

Table 5.5 Single q model results of $1/\gamma$ (year by year), including land

	Full sample	Manufacturing, major enterprises
2004	0.0080**	0.0159**
2005	0.0100**	0.0175**
2006	0.0099**	0.0169**
2007	0.0113**	0.0215**
2008	0.0139**	0.0249**
2009	0.0103**	0.0122*
2010	0.0104**	0.0129**
2011	0.0125**	0.0222**
2012	0.0117**	0.0183**
2013	0.0098**	0.0155**

Notes
1. Standard errors are heteroscedasticity robust (Huber–White estimator), with * and ** denoting significance at the 10% and 5% levels, respectively
2. The results of the industry dummies and capital size dummies are omitted from the table

ten times larger in cases that include land than in those that do not, and they calculate a much larger deviation than the corresponding deviation derived in this chapter.

However, in Asako et al. (1997), for the $1/\gamma$ estimates in cases that include land, its average when it is estimated to be significant is 0.023, which is only slightly larger than our estimate of 0.018 for major manufacturing enterprises. In other words, a

Table 5.6 Multiple q model results (year by year)

	Full sample				Manufacturing, major enterprises			
	γ_K	γ_L	$-\gamma_K a_K$	$-\gamma_L a_L$	γ_K	γ_L	$-\gamma_K a_K$	$-\gamma_L a_L$
2004	3.083**	−2.288**	2.096**	2.168**	3.433**	−4.330**	0.499**	0.768**
2005	2.660**	−1.711**	2.448**	2.408**	2.797**	−2.013**	1.073**	1.387**
2006	2.485**	−1.464**	1.835**	1.865**	3.155**	−0.690	0.961*	1.282**
2007	3.350**	−1.469**	1.169**	1.450**	2.669**	−0.592	0.148	0.354
2008	2.488**	−0.127	0.953**	0.976**	3.565**	−0.720	−0.576	−0.402
2009	2.935**	−1.587**	0.607**	0.560**	1.902**	−1.842	−0.273	−0.427
2010	3.305**	−2.357**	1.038**	1.085**	1.535**	−2.051	0.590**	0.314
2011	3.142**	−1.742**	1.079**	1.188**	3.253**	1.783	0.485	0.680**
2012	4.024**	−1.407	0.855**	1.117**	2.917**	−1.553	0.907*	1.092**
2013	3.573**	−2.273**	1.385**	1.709**	4.943**	−3.254*	0.031	0.137

Notes
1. Standard errors are heteroscedasticity robust (Huber–White estimator), with * and ** denoting significance at the 10% and 5% levels, respectively
2. The results of the industry dummies and capital size dummies are omitted from the table

large part of the extreme difference between cases that include land and those that do not in Asako et al. (1997) occurs because the $1/\gamma$ estimates for the cases that do not include land are too small. At the very least, the estimation results from the Single q model that includes land obtained by Asako et al. (1997) and in this study are quite similar overall considering that the estimation periods and the methods for constructing q are totally different.

Now, we examine the results of the estimations for the Multiple q model (Table 5.6). In the estimations for all of the sample enterprises, all of the variables are estimated to be significant except for γ_L in 2008 and 2012. We find that $\gamma_K, -\gamma_K a_K, -\gamma_L a_L$ are positive and that γ_L is negative, which is generally consistent with the baseline model estimation results over the entire sample period of 2004–2013 obtained in Table 5.3 in the case of no control variables. In the sample limited to major manufacturing firms, the estimates of γ_K and their year-by-year variations differ slightly from those of the entire sample, whereas they are positive and significant in all years. As for the other three parameters, their signs when they are estimated as having a significant effect are consistent with those for the baseline model using the full sample, whereas the significance declines considerably overall. However, the facts that γ_L is not estimated to be significantly negative and that the parameters $-\gamma_K a_K, -\gamma_L a_L$ are not significant (suggesting that $a_K = 0$ and $a_L = 0$) are not necessarily inconsistent with the assumption of a smooth, convex adjustment cost function.

The estimate of γ_K, which is equivalent to the slope of the marginal adjustment cost curve for non-land tangible fixed assets, reaches its maximum of 4.0 in 2012 for the estimation over the full sample and its maximum of 4.9 in 2013 for the estimation over major manufacturing enterprises. This result is theoretically far more plausible than the value of γ suggested by the estimation result of the Single q model including

Table 5.7 Estimated Partial Q values (year by year)

	Full sample		Manufacturing, major enterprises	
	Partial Q_K	Partial Q_L	Partial Q_K	Partial Q_L
2004	2.250	2.185	0.711	0.779
2005	2.582	2.425	1.273	1.381
2006	1.978	1.871	1.204	1.368
2007	1.376	1.450	0.367	0.412
2008	1.102	0.976	−0.303	−0.448
2009	0.749	0.560	−0.159	−0.433
2010	1.198	1.087	0.662	0.307
2011	1.243	1.190	0.657	0.646
2012	1.092	1.118	1.034	1.044
2013	1.604	1.712	0.367	0.140

land (which exceeds 50 even for relatively smaller figures with major manufacturing firms). Furthermore, an F test for the years in which both γ_K and γ_L are estimated to be significant rejects the null hypothesis of $\gamma_K = \gamma_L$ at a significance level of 1% for all years. Thus, from the three models within the q theory framework, we can conclude that the Multiple q model has the strongest conformity to the data.

Next, based on the results shown in Table 5.6, we calculate the Partial $Q_j(= p_j(q_j - 1))$ corresponding to the explanatory variable of the investment function by capital goods type in Eq. (2.18), and we show the results in Table 5.7.[5] We estimate positive values both for the Partial Q_K imputed for non-land tangible fixed assets and for the Partial Q_L imputed for land for every year in the full sample. For major manufacturing enterprises, which is closer to the sample employed by Asako et al. (1997), both the Partial Q_K and the Partial Q_L are positive in every year except 2008 and 2009. The Partial Q_K is negative in 2008 and 2009 because the $-\gamma_K a_K$ estimation values are negative, but they are not significant. Integrating the results of the estimations of Asako et al. (1989, 1997), Asako and Tonogi (2010), and the Chap. 4 of this book, Partial Q_L is negative from 1977 to 1983, positive from 1984 to 1991, negative from 1992 to 2004, and positive from 2004 onwards, which is the estimation sample period used in this chapter. Thus, the sign changes across time periods, reflect such factors as trends in land prices.[6]

[5]From Eq. (2.17) or (2.18), which estimate $\widehat{\gamma}_j$ and $\widehat{a}_j$, respectively, we obtain Partial $\widehat{Q}_j = \widehat{\gamma}_j(Z_j - \widehat{a}_j)$.

[6]In q theory, it goes without saying that the investment amount and the Partial Q are determined simultaneously, and the estimation of the regression equation should be carried out based on this simultaneity problem. However, consistent with the estimation method employed in previous studies, we use OLS.

5.3.3 Comparison of Estimation Results by Equity Capital Size

Along with differences in investment behavior through the heterogeneity of capital goods, we estimate the investment function according to the size of equity capital to identify the different effects of the imperfect nature of the capital market on major enterprises, small enterprises, and micro enterprises as well as differences in the capital stock adjustment process. This subsection examines the results in Table 5.8, which provides estimations by equity capital size for the basic model of Eq. (5.7).

First, the estimations of the investment adjustment cost function parameters $\gamma_K, \gamma_L, -\gamma_K a_K, -\gamma_L a_L$ indicate that γ_j is positive for non-land tangible fixed assets and negative for land, whereas $-\gamma_j a_j$ is positive for both. These basic features are the same as in the baseline model in Table 5.3, and they are common regardless of the equity capital size. However, the estimates of γ_K relating to non-land tangible fixed assets increases as capital size decreases, suggesting that the smaller an enterprise is, the greater its cost of adjusting its capital stock is.

As for the control variables, the estimation results are also broadly the same as for the full sample baseline model. Regarding the coefficient on the *interest-bearing debt ratio*, C_1, however, when we exclude the *zero-leverage dummy*, its positive coefficients are smaller as the enterprise size decreases. For micro enterprises, this coefficient is even negative and significant. These results occur because, as capital size decreases, the factors that cause the coefficient on the *interest-bearing debt ratio* to be positive (such as supply factors in the lending market, the disciplinary effects of debt, and tax-saving effects) become weaker, whereas the factors that cause the coefficient to be negative (including demand factors of the lending market and risk of bankruptcy) become stronger.

When we add the *zero-leverage dummy* to the explanatory variables, the coefficient C_0 on the *zero-leverage dummy* is significant and negative at every capital size level, as in the results of the baseline model for the full sample, suggesting the involvement of supply factors in the lending market, the disciplinary effects of debt, and tax-saving effects. Conversely, the coefficient on the *interest-bearing debt ratio*, C_1, is negative and significant except for small enterprises, suggesting the involvement of elements such as demand factors in the lending market and the risk of bankruptcy, which is the opposite effect from the one suggested by *zero-leverage dummy*.[7] After removing the differences across the capital size groups and controlling the supply factors in the lending market, the disciplinary effects of debt, and tax-saving effects by the *zero-leverage dummy*, factors such as demand factors in the lending market and the risk of bankruptcy, which are not ascertained in the estimation of the full sample, are ascertained as differences between enterprises within the same capital size group.

[7]For small enterprises, this value is positive and significant, but its magnitude is extremely small.

Table 5.8 Baseline model results by equity capital size (FY 2004–13)

	Major Enterprises			Medium-sized enterprises			Small enterprises			Micro enterprises		
	No control variable	Not Including *zero-leverage dummy*	Including *zero-leverage dummy*	No control variable	Not including *zero-leverage dummy*	Including *zero-leverage dummy*	No control variable	Not including *zero-leverage dummy*	Including *zero-leverage dummy*	No control variable	Not including *zero-leverage dummy*	Including *zero-leverage dummy*
γ_K	2.82**	1.95**	2.06**	2.89**	2.05**	2.10**	3.18**	2.53**	2.56**	3.41**	2.96**	2.85**
γ_L	−1.34**	−1.22**	−1.39**	−1.86**	−1.85**	−1.88**	−1.84**	−2.04**	−2.13**	−1.35**	−1.65**	−1.88**
$-\gamma_K a_K$	1.95**	1.89**	2.75**	1.74**	1.61**	2.48**	0.77**	0.89**	1.37**	1.07**	1.29**	1.81**
$-\gamma_L a_L$	1.88**	1.81**	2.64**	1.78**	1.70**	2.47**	0.95**	1.17**	1.65**	1.19**	1.44**	2.00**
C_0			−1.43**			−1.49**			−1.40**			−1.72**
C_1		0.53**	−0.40**		0.42**	−0.21**		0.15*	0.03**		−0.21**	−0.32**
C_2		−3.06**	−3.26**		−2.82**	−3.12**		−2.15**	−2.47**		−1.01**	−1.31**
C_3		0.11**	0.08**		0.14**	0.11**		0.13**	0.11**		0.11**	0.06*
R-squared	0.346	0.407	0.444	0.305	0.370	0.408	0.215	0.266	0.296	0.106	0.125	0.146
N of obs.	32,965	32,695	32,695	39,807	39,807	39,807	29,168	29,168	29,168	3,800	3,800	3,800

Notes

1. Standard errors are heteroscedasticity robust (Huber–White estimator), with * and ** denoting significance at the 10% and 5% levels, respectively
2. The results of the year dummies and industry dummies are omitted from the table

The extent to which the *tangibility* coefficient C_2 is negative shrinks as equity capital decreases. This result occurs because, as enterprise size decreases, the importance of the factors causing a negative coefficient (i.e., the importance of intangible assets) also decreases, whereas the importance of the factors causing the coefficient to be positive (i.e., the easing of borrowing constraints from pledgeability) strengthens.

When taking the difference between zero-leverage enterprises and enterprises with debt into account, the above results can be interpreted that they reflect the funding constraints facing smaller enterprises in that a higher *interest-bearing debt ratio* or a lower *tangibility* tend to inhibit investment. However, the estimates of the *enterprise asset size* coefficient, C_3, are positive and significant at every capital size level, as in the baseline model estimation results for the full samples, suggesting that asset size tends to ease borrowing constraints, but we do not observe a tendency for the estimated coefficient to increase as equity capital decreases.

The value of the estimation results' coefficient of determination decreases as the size of equity capital decreases, indicating that the explanatory power of the investment function decreases. This tendency does not change even when control variables, such as those relating to funding constraints, are added. As discussed in Sect. 5.2, in estimating the investment function based on q theory according to size, the goodness of fit should be better for smaller enterprises because their business structures are simpler and easier to understand through a single investment function and because perfect competition, an underlying assumption of q theory, is nearly established. However, these possibilities are not supported by the above results. We do find that lumpy investment, which could explain the worse goodness of fit for smaller enterprises, is not contradicted by the results in which the estimate of the parameter γ_K, which relates to non-land tangible fixed assets, increases as the size of capital shrinks.[8] Thus, we verify this issue in detail in the next subsection.

5.3.4 Possibility of Lumpy Investment

The lumpy adjustment of capital stock is efficient if the adjustment cost includes a fixed cost portion that is borne every time an adjustment is made regardless of the scale of adjustment. However, if funding constraints exist, a sufficient investment scale may not be possible. As a result, constrained firms are forced to engage in inefficiently smooth (not lumpy) adjustment processes. If so, when applying the investment function based on q theory, the estimation of the parameter γ_K related to non-land tangible fixed assets becomes smaller for enterprises with funding constraints than for enterprises without such constraints. Thus, as is done in many previous studies, after dividing the sample according to whether the firm paid dividends as an indicator of the existence or non-existence of funding constraints, we make

[8]The large estimate of γ_K may also reflect the fact that, within the framework of the smooth, convex adjustment cost function, adjustment involves more friction for small enterprises. However, if so, no systemic reduction in the coefficient of determination should occur.

estimations using Eq. (5.7). When investment behavior may be distorted owing to insufficient funds from paying dividends, shareholders should not want dividends to be paid for the sake of maximizing enterprise value. Thus, the sample of firms that pay dividends is considered not to have funding constraints, and the sample of firms that do not pay dividends is considered to have such constraints.

Table 5.9 shows the estimation results. In the dividend paying sample, we have only 120 observations for micro enterprises throughout the entire period. Thus, estimations are not conducted for such enterprises, as the degrees of freedom are insufficient. The estimates of the *tangibility* coefficient, C_2, are negative and significant

Table 5.9 Difference between the dividend paying sample and the non-dividend paying sample (FY 2004–13)

Results for the dividend paying sample (i.e., no funding constraint sample), by capital size

	Major enterprises	Medium-sized enterprises	Small enterprises
γ_K	2.56**	2.66**	3.20**
γ_L	−2.73**	−2.81**	−3.35**
$-\gamma_K a_K$	3.93**	4.36**	3.55**
$-\gamma_L a_L$	3.93**	4.45**	3.70**
C_0	−1.56**	−1.76**	−1.89**
C_1	−0.04	−0.15**	0.01
C_2	−4.32**	−4.11**	−3.54**
C_3	−0.01	−0.04**	−0.05**
R-squared	0.564	0.565	0.546
No of obs.	23,153	21,292	7,024

Results for the non-dividend paying sample (i.e., funding constraint sample), by capital size

	Major enterprises	Medium-sized enterprises	Small enterprises	Micro enterprises
γ_K	1.18**	1.66**	2.29**	2.85**
γ_L	−1.00**	−1.65**	−2.00**	−1.91**
$-\gamma_K a_K$	0.76*	1.35**	1.26**	1.67**
$-\gamma_L a_L$	0.51	1.28**	1.56**	1.86**
C_0	−0.84**	−1.13**	−1.32**	−1.67**
C_1	−0.03	0.02	0.07**	−0.30**
C_2	−1.58**	−2.18**	−2.12**	−1.16**
C_3	0.14**	0.13**	0.06**	0.07*
R-squared	0.180	0.230	0.221	0.134
No of obs.	9,542	18,515	22,144	3,680

Notes
1. Standard errors are heteroscedasticity robust (Huber–White estimator), with * and ** denoting significance at the 10% and 5% levels, respectively
2. The results of the year dummies and industry dummies are omitted from the table

both for firms paying dividends and those not paying dividends, but the absolute value of the latter is clearly smaller. The estimates of the *enterprise asset size* coefficient, C_3, are negative and significant or not significant for firms paying dividends but are positive and significant for firms not paying dividends. These results indicate that paying a dividend (or not) functions appropriately as an indicator of funding constraints.

The estimates of the parameter γ_K relating to non-land tangible fixed assets are positive and significant in all cases, and the characteristic that greater capital implies a smaller γ_K is common to both the firms pay dividends and those that do not pay dividends. However, the level is clearly smaller for firms that do not pay (i.e., the funding constraints sample). This does not imply a good fit with a smooth, convex adjustment cost function, however, because the coefficient of determination for the sample of firms not paying dividends is clearly lower than that of the sample of firms paying dividends. These results indicate that, regardless of the size of equity capital, at least some investment behavior is lumpy, and the degree of lumpiness increases as the size of capital decreases, indicating that some of the lumpy investment behavior is constrained by the imperfect nature of the capital market. All of these are consistent with what can be forecast from theory.

Then, in our framework of a smooth adjustment cost function, we ascertain the situation regarding lumpy investment or disinvestment as straightforwardly as possible by dividing the investment rate related to non-land tangible fixed assets into certain categories and estimating the investment function for each of these categories. We divide the sample into eight categories at 5% intervals, from an investment rate of 0% up to a rate of 40%, and, together with the negative sample, estimate Eq. (5.7) and compare the estimation performances. As lumpy behavior is to be constrained when funding constraints exist, only the sample of firms paying dividends is targeted.

As is shown in Table 5.10, in the three investment rate categories of 0–5, 5–10, and 10–15%, the parameter γ_K relating to non-land tangible fixed assets is estimated significantly positive and slightly larger than when the investment rate is not categorized. By contrast, for the categories of 15–20% and above, although the signs are positive, they are not significant, and the estimates are unstable. In addition, when the investment rate is negative, the estimates of parameter γ_K relating to non-land tangible fixed assets are not significant (the sign is negative). In other words, in the case of investment in non-land tangible fixed assets, the smooth, convex adjustment cost function framework may not be applicable to comparatively large positive investment rates of over 15% or to negative investments. This result is generally consistent with studies that empirically analyze lumpy investment, such as that of Power (1998), who regards investment rates of 20% or above as large-scale investments (an investment spike).

Table 5.10 Difference by the level of investment rate for tangible fixed assets other than land (dividend paying samples, FY 2004–13)

	$Z_K < 0$	$0 \leqq Z_K < 0.05$	$0.05 \leqq Z_K < 0.1$	$0.1 \leqq Z_K < 0.15$	$0.15 \leqq Z_K < 0.2$	$0.2 \leqq Z_K < 0.25$	$0.25 \leqq Z_K < 0.3$	$0.3 \leqq Z_K < 0.35$	$0.35 \leqq Z_K < 0.4$
γ_K	−0.478	5.201**	7.261**	5.633**	0.091	0.302	5.224	1.537	5.169
γ_L	−2.140**	−2.913**	−2.970**	−4.411**	−3.043**	−3.989**	−3.421**	−2.932**	−3.972**
$-\gamma_K a_K$	3.204**	3.528**	3.519**	3.635**	4.732**	4.548**	4.150**	5.852**	3.395
$-\gamma_L a_L$	3.337**	3.715**	3.811**	4.096**	4.699**	4.334**	5.661**	5.668**	4.740**
C_0	−1.525**	−1.512**	−1.569**	−1.673**	−1.857**	−1.866**	−2.056**	−2.016**	−2.007**
C_1	0.173	0.068	−0.049	−0.161*	−0.458**	−0.260	−0.104	−0.021	0.717*
C_2	−3.966**	−3.507**	−3.668**	−4.061**	−4.573**	−4.646**	−5.916**	−5.416**	−5.171**
C_3	−0.004	−0.059**	−0.036**	−0.040**	−0.025	−0.015	−0.004	−0.045	0.019
R-squared	0.437	0.479	0.544	0.580	0.605	0.627	0.647	0.672	0.673
N of obs.	3,401	12,203	11,610	8,640	5,568	3,244	2,051	1,366	953

Notes

1. Standard errors are heteroscedasticity robust (Huber–White estimator), with * and ** denoting significance at the 10% and 5% levels, respectively
2. The results of the year dummies, industry dummies, and capital size dummies are omitted from the table

5.4 Concluding Remarks

This chapter used survey data from the Financial Statements Statistics of Corporations by Industry (FSSCI) released by Ministry of Finance, Japan from fiscal year 2004 to fiscal year 2013 and considered the heterogeneity of two types of capital goods, non-land tangible fixed assets and land, to verify the extent to which the investment behavior of enterprises of various sizes, ranging from large major enterprises to small and micro enterprises, could be explained within the q theory framework. To this end, considering the imperfect nature of the capital market, we estimated the investment function using the Multiple q model under various settings. The results of the analysis can be summarized as follows.

First, in contrast to prior studies that use data from the financial statements of listed enterprises, our dataset was mostly comprised of data from non-listed enterprises, including small enterprises and much smaller micro enterprises. Therefore, our analyses were innovative in terms of the diversity of enterprise sizes even though various restrictions were placed on the data, mainly because of the sampling survey and limitations on surveyed items. However, the main results of the analysis were generally consistent with those of the prior studies: (i) within the Single q framework that does not consider the heterogeneity of capital goods, a model that considers land to be a capital good with a specific adjustment cost is preferable to a model that excludes land; (ii) for investment behavior that includes land in capital goods, significant heterogeneity was found between land and non-land tangible fixed assets, and a Multiple q model that explicitly considers this distinction was found to be preferable to the Single q model; (iii) however, control variables that are inherently redundant in q theory, such as the imperfect nature of the capital market, had significant explanatory power even in the Multiple q model, indicating that much of enterprises' investment behavior is left unexplained by q theory even after considering the heterogeneity of capital goods.

Second, regarding the control variables, much of the interest-bearing debt ratio's apparent impact on investment behavior is due to differences in investment behaviors between zero leverage enterprises and enterprises with debt, and the apparent impact of tangibility on investment behavior is due to measurement error in q ratio given the growing importance of intangible assets as a quasi-fixed production factor. These findings offer new topics for future research on capital investment.

Third, regarding the differences in investment behavior according to equity capital size, one of the main concerns of this analysis, examinations of the coefficient of determination found that the smaller the company, the worse the fit with the investment function. Furthermore, in the case of non-land tangible fixed assets, the value of this coefficient was significantly higher than for major enterprises (in other words, smaller enterprises experience more friction in the adjustment of capital stock). These findings suggest the existence of lumpy investments that cannot be handled by the q theory framework. In fact, the estimation results after dividing the sample into two subsamples according to the payment or non-payment of dividends as an indicator of funding constraints showed that, regardless of equity capital size, at least some part of investment behavior is lumpy, and the degree of lumpiness increases as the size of equity capital decreases. Thus, for smaller enterprises, some lumpy investment behavior may be constrained by the imperfect nature of the capital market.

Fourth, to ascertain the lumpy investment conditions, the sample was restricted to enterprises paying dividends (enterprises without funding constraints), and this sample was then divided into investment rate levels related to non-land tangible fixed assets. The estimation results indicated that a smooth, convex adjustment cost function can be applied for investment rates in the range of 0–15%.

Finally, we discuss potential issues for future research. Regarding funding constraints, the variables and estimation methods adopted in this study do not provide clear evidence to support the intuition that funding constraints are more serious as equity capital size decreases. However, it is still unclear whether this finding could mean that equity capital size and funding constraints have no relationship, or it could mean that there is a relationship that cannot be ascertained due to problems with the analytical methods. In addition to the issue of funding constraints, it is also necessary to verify the relationship between a zero-leverage and investment behavior using a more appropriate analytical framework.

As suggested by the coefficient of tangibility, the importance of explicitly handling intangible assets as capital goods is something that many researchers are already focusing on, but a considerable divergence separates the economic concept of intangible assets and the intangible assets that are recorded on enterprises' balance sheets. It is not likely to be easy to overcome this problem using data in the FSSCI, but it is an issue worth addressing. Elucidating lumpy investment is a feasible task that extends from the current framework, and it is also the most important research issue. Studies that have already extended the linear investment function based on the Multiple q model to a non-linear framework, including lumpy investment, include those of Asako and Tonogi (2010), Asako, Nakamura, and Tonogi (2016), and Chap. 4 of this book, which analyze listed enterprises. Applying this framework to the FSSCI after dealing appropriately with the data constraints is a promising research task.

References

Abel, A. B., & Blanchard, O. J. (1986). The present value of profits and cyclical movements in investment. *Econometrica, 54,* 249–273.

Asako, K., Kuninori, M., Inoue, T., & Murase H. (1989). Land evaluation and measurement of Tobin's q theory/estimation of Multiple q. *Economics Today, 10*(3). (In Japanese).

Asako, K., Kuninori, M., Inoue, T., & Murase H. (1997). Capital investment and land investment: 1977–1994. In K. Asako & M. Otaki (Eds.), *Dynamics of modern macroeconomics* (pp. 323–349). University of Tokyo Press. (In Japanese).

Asako, K., Nakamura, J., & Tonogi, K. (2016). The development of investment research and Multiple q in Japan. *International Journal of Finance and Accounting 5*(5A), 1–29.

Asako, K., & Tonogi, K. (2010). Heterogeneity of capital stock and Multiple q. *The Economic Review, 61,* 325–341. (In Japanese).

Doms, M., & Dunne, T. (1998). Capital adjustment patterns in manufacturing plants. *Review of Economic Dynamics, 1,* 409–429.

Hulten, C., & Wykoff, F. (1977). *Economic depreciation of the US capital stock*. Report submitted to US Department of Treasury, Office of Tax Analysis. Washington, DC.
Hulten, C., & Wykoff, F. (1981). The measurement of economic depreciation. In C. Hulten (Ed.), *Depreciation inflation and the taxation of income from capital* (pp. 81–125). Washington, DC: Urban Institute.
Nakamura, J., Tonogi, K., & Asako, K. (2017). Investment behaviors by capital good and enterprise size: testing capital goods heterogeneity and capital market imperfection with the FSSCI. *Public Policy Review, 13,* 71–102.
Otaki, M., & Suzuki, K. (1986). Tobin's q theory and fluctuations in profit rate-discount rate. *Kokumin Keizai, 152,* 23–39. (In Japanese).
Power, L. (1998). The missing link: technology, investment, and productivity. *Review of Economics and Statistics, 80,* 300–313.
Suzuki, K. (2001), *Capital investment and money market: information asymmetry and uncertainty*. University of Tokyo Press. (In Japanese).
Tonogi, K., Nakamura, J., & Asako K. (2010). Estimation of Multiple q models of investment: Investment behavior over heterogeneous capital goods during the period of excess capacity reduction. *Economics Today, 31*(2). (In Japanese).

Chapter 6
Extensions of the Multiple q Model: (II) Heterogeneity by Mode of Acquisition

Abstract This chapter evaluates the heterogeneity of capital stock and investment behavior by focusing on and contrasting between heterogeneity across capital goods categories and heterogeneity across acquisition modes. Four categories of capital goods (buildings and structures, machinery and equipment, vessels and vehicles, and land) and three modes of acquisition (new construction, second-hand acquisitions, and large-scale repairs) are mutually matched using microdata from the Cabinet Office and the Development Bank of Japan. Based on the investment rate data by resulting segment (capital good × acquisition mode), we conduct analyses using two approaches: an estimation using the Multiple q investment function that presupposes a convex adjustment cost function, as is assumed in Tobin's q theory, and a factor analysis that allows for a non-convex adjustment cost function. The results of the factor analysis show that regardless of the type of capital good, the factor loadings are similar in segments with common acquisition modes. Furthermore, the parameter values for the investment adjustment costs are more affected by the acquisition mode than they are by the type of capital good. These results, along with those for the Multiple q investment function, reveal that the investment behavior around new construction can be explained (to some extent) by the convex adjustment cost function assumed by Tobin's q theory. However, the results also suggest the existence of a non-convex adjustment cost function for second-hand acquisition and large-scale repair modes. In addition, the results suggest that new construction has the strongest relationship with the replacement investment ratio (or corporate growth).

Keywords Heterogeneity in capital goods · Heterogeneity in acquisition modes · Multiple q model · Factor analysis

6.1 Introduction

The analysis results of the previous chapters show as a whole that a framework based on the Multiple q model is preferable to a framework using the Single q model.

This chapter is a shortened and reorganized version of Tonogi, Nakamura, and Asako (2017). The content of and opinions in this chapter are solely attributable to the authors and are unrelated to any organizations with which the authors are affiliated.

K. Asako et al., *Multiple q and Investment in Japan*,
https://doi.org/10.1007/978-981-15-2981-8_6

However, although these analyses consider the heterogeneity of capital goods, the performance of investment functions based on Tobin's q theory has not dramatically improved. This result may occur for several reasons, but, from the perspective of advancing the research on capital heterogeneity, we must consider the possibility of variance in the adjustment costs due to the acquisition mode, as opposed to heterogeneity being caused only by the physical characteristics of capital goods, such as buildings and structures, machinery and equipment, and land. Prior studies including the earlier chapters of this book have regarded increases in the value of tangible fixed assets (obtained from the company's financial statements) as new acquisitions, but, in fact these figures include acquired second-hand goods and large-scale repairs and renovations. However, these previous studies have not verified whether their analysis results may have been affected by disregarding the heterogeneity between these acquisition modes.

The concept of adjustment costs in investment functions is based on the idea that a type of inefficiency gradually increases as the investment rate increases. This inefficiency arises because the operational resources (e.g., organizational capital, skills of workers) that can be invested in the corporate growth that accompanies capital accumulation are scarce. Thus, for a given value of capital expenditure in mechanical equipment, investments in new or second-hand items are highly likely to lead to corporate growth (e.g., the enhancement of a production line), whereas repairs have a low likelihood of leading to growth and are likely to generate small adjustment costs.

In addition, adjustment costs may differ depending on whether the invested item is new or second-hand because investing in new machines frequently implies introducing new models, which incur costs in terms of training employees to master operational methods. However, second-hand items may generate smaller adjustment costs because they can continue to use the familiar conventional model. Until now, the heterogeneity driven by the capital acquisition mode could be assumed in theory, but it has not been analyzed empirically owing to the difficulty in obtaining the relevant data. However, the Cabinet Office's "Survey on Capital Expenditures and Disposals of Private Enterprises" (hereinafter, the investment/retirement survey), which began in FY 2006, surveys investment amounts by acquisition mode and physical capital classification in a matrix. The survey allows us to simultaneously analyze the heterogeneity of physical goods and the heterogeneity caused by the acquisition mode.

In this analysis, we utilize survey data from the investment/retirement surveys from FY 2009–2013, which we link to the financial data of Japanese listed companies. In this way, we perform a comprehensive analysis of heterogeneity that includes both the heterogeneity of physical goods and the heterogeneity caused by the acquisition mode. However, the investment/retirement survey focuses on companies with capital of over 30 million yen, which are random sampled except for those with capital of over 1 billion yen, which are exhaustively surveyed. Thus, in principle, it is difficult to construct panel data. In addition, the number of valid observations shrinks considerably after matching the financial data. Thus, we follow the procedure proposed by Tonogi, Nakamura, and Asako (2014) and carry out a factor analysis on the fluctuations of each company's investment rates by "capital good × acquisition mode" (hereinafter, we use the term "segment"), and we focus on assessing the basic characteristics of the data.

Specifically, we decompose the data into various categories of shocks common to all segments (factor scores) and sensitivities common to all firms that differ by segment (factor loadings). Furthermore, we utilize the results to decompose the correlation coefficients of the intersegment investment rates in terms of the contribution to the variance of each investment rate into a common factor contribution ratio (communality) and a unique factor contribution ratio (uniqueness).

Through these analyses, we consider problems such as where we can identify homogeneity or heterogeneity out of various combinations of physical goods and acquisition modes. Furthermore, we examine whether the heterogeneity of physical goods or the heterogeneity driven by different acquisition modes is more important. In addition, we report the estimation results using the Multiple q investment function, which we combine with the factor analysis results in considering possible interpretations. If heterogeneity in adjustment costs across acquisition modes exists, then the depth of the relationship between the acquisition mode and corporate growth, as described above, is key. Thus, we also attempt to obtain deeper implications by comparing the factor analysis results to changes in the composition of "investment motive" (i.e., expansion of production capacity, product development and upgrading, efficiency-oriented streamlining and labor saving, research and development, maintenance and repair, or other), as listed in the "Survey on Planned Capital Spending" conducted annually by the Development Bank of Japan.

The remainder of this chapter is organized as follows. Section 6.2 describes the framework for the analysis based on Multiple q investment functions and factor analysis. Section 6.3 outlines the method used for data construction and the statistical characteristics, and Sect. 6.4 reports and interprets the analysis results. Section 6.5 concludes.

6.2 Multiple q Investment Functions and Factor Analysis

In this section, we outline the model used to assess investment behavior by acquisition mode within the framework of the Multiple q investment function. Then, we consider the relationship between the Multiple q investment function and the factor analysis on the investment rates of each investment good. Subsequently, we explain our analytical methodology using factor analysis with respect to capital heterogeneity and homogeneity.

6.2.1 Investment Behavior by Mode of Acquisition within a Multiple q Framework

We assume that there are n categories of capital goods and denote the capital stock of the j-th ($j = 1, 2, \ldots, n$) capital good at the end of the previous period after depreciation as $(1-\delta_j)K_j$, where δ_j is the physical depreciation rate and $K_j^{'}$ is the capital stock after investment. Then, we should obtain capital investment I_j at the beginning of the current period by

$$I_j = K_j^{'} - (1-\delta_j)K_j. \tag{6.1}$$

In each period, there are three modes of acquisition when a firm conducts capital investments: namely, new construction, second-hand acquisitions, and large-scale repairs. The total amount of capital investment is represented by the sum of these three acquisition modes:

$$I_j = I_j^c + I_j^o + I_j^l \tag{6.2}$$

The superscripts c, o, and l represent new construction, second-hand acquisitions, and large-scale repairs, respectively.

Assuming the firm's gross profit function takes a Cobb–Douglas form and has constant returns to scale (homogeneous of degree one), we can express it as follows:

$$\Pi\left(A, K_1^{'}, \ldots, K_n^{'}\right) = AK_1^{'\alpha_1} \cdots K_n^{'\alpha_n}, \quad \sum_{j=1}^{n} \alpha_j = 1, \tag{6.3}$$

where α_j is a parameter that measures each capital good's contribution to the gross profit. If we assume that firms maximize profits, this parameter gives the share of capital good j. The exogenously given parameter A represents the total factor productivity (TFP) or the coefficient of Hicks neutral technological progress.

The adjustment cost function of investment can be separated according to the capital good and the mode of acquisition of the capital good. In addition, we assume that this function can be expressed as a product of the part expressed as a quadratic function of the investment rate based on the capital stock at the end of the period and the part representing the magnitude of the capital stock at the end of the period. In other words, we can express the adjustment cost function as follows:

$$C\left(I_1^c, \ldots, I_n^c, I_1^o, \ldots, I_n^o, I_1^l, \ldots, I_n^l, K_1^{'}, \ldots, K_n^{'}\right)$$
$$= \sum_{j=1}^{n} \left\{ \frac{\gamma_j^c}{2} \left(\frac{I_j^c}{(1-\delta_j)K_j^{'}} - a_j^c \right)^2 (1-\delta_j)K_j^{'} \right.$$

$$+\frac{\gamma_j^o}{2}\left(\frac{I_j^o}{(1-\delta_j)K_j^{'}}-a_j^o\right)^2(1-\delta_j)K_j^{'}$$

$$+\frac{\gamma_j^l}{2}\left(\frac{I_j^l}{(1-\delta_j)K_j^{'}}-a_j^l\right)^2(1-\delta_j)K_j^{'}\Bigg\}, \tag{6.4}$$

where $\gamma_j^h > 0\,(h = c, o, l)$ is a parameter that determines the magnitude of the adjustment cost of investment for each capital good j with acquisition mode h and fulfills an important role in characterizing the investment function according to Tobin's q theory, as clarified below. Here, a_j^h $(h = c, o, l)$ is the parameter corresponding to the investment rate when the adjustment cost for each capital good j with acquisition mode h and takes its minimum value. The adjustment cost increases in an accelerated way as each investment rate deviates from a_j^h.[1]

As explained in detail in Chap. 2, we apply the Bellman equation to the maximization of firm value V under the adjustment cost function given by Eq. (6.4) together with a set of standard assumptions introduced in Chap. 2 but not necessarily precisely referred to here, and we obtain the investment equation as follows:

$$(q-1)P = \sum_{j=1}^{n}\{\gamma_j^c Z_j^c s_j + \gamma_j^o Z_j^o s_j + \gamma_j^l Z_j^l s_j\}$$

$$-\sum_{j=1}^{n}\{\gamma_j^c a_j^c s_j + \gamma_j^o a_j^o s_j + \gamma_j^l a_j^l s_j\}, \tag{6.5}$$

where

$$Z_j^h = \frac{I_j^h}{(1-\delta_j)K_j^{'}}; \quad (h = c, o, l) \tag{6.6}$$

is the investment rate of capital good j with acquisition mode h, and

$$q = \frac{V}{\sum_{j=1}^{n} p_j(1-\delta_j)K_j} \tag{6.7}$$

$$P = \frac{\sum_{j=1}^{n} p_j(1-\delta_j)K_j}{\sum_{j=1}^{n}(1-\delta_j)K_j} = \sum_{j=1}^{n} p_j s_j \tag{6.8}$$

$$s_j = \frac{(1-\delta_j)K_j}{\sum_{j=1}^{n}(1-\delta_j)K_j}. \tag{6.9}$$

[1]In Eq. (6.4), in theory, similarly to the investment rate, this parameter can take a value in the range $a_j^h \leq 1/(1-\delta_j)$, inclusive of negative values.

Here, q refers to the average q based on the capital stock that aggregates n categories of capital goods; P is the implicit deflator of the aggregated capital stock, with p_j representing the price of the j-th capital good;[2] and s_j represents the composition ratio of the j-th capital good in the aggregated capital stock as well as its weighting when aggregating investment rates by capital stock.

In the case in which $\gamma_j^h = \gamma_j, a_j^h = \frac{1}{3}a_j$, the adjustment cost parameters for new construction, second-hand acquisitions, and large-scale repairs are all equivalent, and Eq. (6.5) can be rewritten as follows:

$$(q-1)P = \sum_{j=1}^{n} \gamma_j Z_j s_j - \sum_{j=1}^{n} \gamma_j a_j s_j. \tag{6.10}$$

Here, Z_j is the investment rate related to total investment in the j-th capital good across acquisition modes,

$$Z_j = \frac{I_j}{(1-\delta_j)K_j'} \tag{6.11}$$

and it is defined as the sum of the investment rates by acquisition mode, as given by Eq. (6.6). Within this framework, ordinary Multiple q investment functions can be thought of as special cases that assume an adjustment cost function in which new construction, second-hand acquisitions, and large-scale repairs have the same parameters for each capital good. In this study, we use the system in Eq. (6.5) in our estimation, and we examine whether investment behaviors by acquisition mode can be assessed within the framework of Multiple q investment functions.

6.2.2 Basic Factor Model

We set up our basic factor model in two steps. First, we formulate

$$z_{ij} = b_{j1} f_{i1} + b_{j2} f_{i2} + \cdots + b_{jm} f_{im} + d_j u_{ij}, \tag{6.12}$$

where z_{ij} is the investment rate for the i-th firm ($i = 1, 2, \cdots, N$) and the j-th capital good ($j = 1, 2, \cdots, n$), which is standardized without loss of generality to have zero

[2]The transaction price of equipment is likely to be higher in the case of new construction than the second-hand acquisitions. However, note that this price difference only reflect a real factor, namely, the difference in remaining life. In other words, considering the relationship between the price of capital goods and the rental cost, we should use a capital goods price (price per unit of service) that is common to new construction and second-hand acquisitions in deflating the capital amount. By using the same capital goods price to compute the real amount of equipment for the case of new construction (with higher transaction prices) and second-hand acquisitions (with lower transaction prices), we find a smaller result for the second-hand case reflecting its shorter remaining life. For further details, see Appendix 1 of Tonogi et al. (2017).

mean and unit variance. $f_{i1}, f_{i2}, \cdots, f_{im}$ are m factors scores, such as components of TFP shocks and the cost of capital, and they are also called common factors, as they stimulate all of the investment rates z_{ij} of firm i, whereas u_{ij} represents the individual factors for investment in the j-th capital good of firm i. The coefficients $b_{jw}(w = 1, 2, \cdots, m)$ are referred to as factor loadings, and they indicate the reaction of investment in the j-th capital good to the common factor w, and d_j is the weight of the individual factor loading of the investment rate for the j-th capital good. b_{jw} and d_j are common among all firms, as they are independent of the index i.

In the second step, we introduce three modes of acquisition into Eq. (6.12). By simply replacing z_{ij} and b_{jw} with those decomposed by each acquisition mode h (= c,o,l), the equation is rewritten as

$$z_{ij}^h = b_{j1}^h f_{i1} + b_{j2}^h f_{i2} + \cdots + b_{jm}^h f_{im} + d_j^h u_{ij}^h, \tag{6.13}$$

where the m common factors (factor scores) remain the same as in Eq. (6.12) and are independent of h. This independence arises because common factors embody the characteristics of firm i but are the same regardless of the acquisition mode and the capital good. In contrast, factor loading b_{jw}^h is common among all firms but depends on the index of the acquisition mode h as well as that of the m common factors and the category of capital good j. In other words, differences in investment rates across firms stem from differences in the common factors, whereas differences across capital goods or differences across acquisition modes stem from differences across factor loadings.

If we apply factor analysis with only one common factor to investment rates whose dynamics are driven by the Multiple q framework, the common factor corresponds to the Partial q driven by the TFP shock A, which is common among various capital goods, and each factor loading corresponds to a parameter of the convex adjustment cost for each capital good. If some of the investment rates have the same parameter values for the adjustment costs, their reactions to the Partial q and, equivalently, their factor loadings should also be the same. No matter which adjustment costs other than convex costs are introduced, factor loadings correspond to parameters of the adjustment costs.[3] In this analysis, we classify capital goods into groups using their factor loadings.

6.2.3 *Factor Analysis*

Equation (6.13) can be rewritten in a matrix form:

[3]For the derivation of the precise relationship between Eqs. (6.5) and (6.12) and for the case of non-linear adjustment costs, see Appendix of Tonogi et al. (2014).

$$\begin{array}{ccccc} \boldsymbol{Z} & = & \boldsymbol{FB'} & + & \boldsymbol{UD}, \\ (N \times \{n \times 3\}) & = & (N \times m) \cdot (\{n \times 3\} \times m)' & + & (N \times \{n \times 3\}) \cdot (\{n \times 3\} \times \{n \times 3\}) \end{array} \tag{6.14}$$

where

$$\boldsymbol{Z} = \begin{bmatrix} z_{11}^c & z_{12}^o & \cdots & z_{1n}^l \\ z_{21}^c & z_{22}^o & \cdots & z_{2n}^l \\ \vdots & \vdots & & \vdots \\ z_{N1}^c & z_{N2}^o & \cdots & z_{Nn}^l \end{bmatrix}, \boldsymbol{F} = \begin{bmatrix} f_{11} & f_{12} & \cdots & f_{1m} \\ f_{21} & f_{22} & \cdots & f_{2m} \\ \vdots & \vdots & & \vdots \\ f_{N1} & f_{N2} & \cdots & f_{Nm} \end{bmatrix}, \boldsymbol{B} = \begin{bmatrix} b_{11}^c & b_{12}^o & \cdots & b_{1m}^l \\ b_{21}^c & b_{22}^o & \cdots & b_{2m}^l \\ \vdots & \vdots & & \vdots \\ b_{n1}^c & b_{n2}^o & \cdots & b_{nm}^l \end{bmatrix},$$

$$\boldsymbol{U} = \begin{bmatrix} u_{11}^c & u_{12}^o & \cdots & u_{1n}^l \\ u_{21}^c & u_{22}^o & \cdots & u_{2n}^l \\ \vdots & \vdots & & \vdots \\ u_{N1}^c & u_{N2}^o & \cdots & u_{Nn}^l \end{bmatrix}, \boldsymbol{D} = \begin{bmatrix} d_1^c & 0 & \cdots & 0 \\ 0 & d_2^o & \cdots & 0 \\ \vdots & \vdots & & \vdots \\ 0 & 0 & \cdots & d_n^l \end{bmatrix}.$$

We introduce the following three standard assumptions in conducting the factor analysis in this chapter. First, the averages of the common and individual factors are assumed to be zero. Namely, letting **1** denote the column vector consisting of ones, we obtain

$$\boldsymbol{F'1} = \boldsymbol{0}, \quad \boldsymbol{U'1} = \boldsymbol{0}. \tag{6.15}$$

Second, assuming that common factors are independent of each other, the correlation matrix among common factors can be written as a diagonal matrix to obtain

$$\frac{1}{N}\boldsymbol{F'F} = \boldsymbol{I_m}, \tag{6.16}$$

where $\boldsymbol{I_m}$ is an $(m \times m)$ identity matrix whose diagonal elements are all equal to one and non-diagonal elements are all equal to zero. Third, the common and individual factors are not correlated, and the individual factors are assumed to be orthogonal:

$$\boldsymbol{F'U} = \boldsymbol{0}, \quad \frac{1}{N}\boldsymbol{U'U} = \boldsymbol{I}_{n\times 3}. \tag{6.17}$$

Under these assumptions, the correlation matrix in Eq. (6.13) can be decomposed as follows:

$$\begin{aligned} \boldsymbol{R} &= \frac{1}{N}\boldsymbol{Z'Z} \\ &= \frac{1}{N}\boldsymbol{BF'FB'} + \frac{1}{N}\boldsymbol{BF'UD} + \frac{1}{N}\boldsymbol{DU'FB'} + \frac{1}{N}\boldsymbol{DU'UD} \\ &= \boldsymbol{BB'} + \boldsymbol{D'D}, \end{aligned} \tag{6.18}$$

where the diagonal elements are:

$$\sum_{p=1}^{m}(b_{jp}^{h})^2 + (d_j^h)^2, \tag{6.19}$$

which means that the variance of each investment rate standardized to one can be decomposed into the "communality," which a common factor can explain, and the "uniqueness," which no common factor can explain.[4] If the value of uniqueness is small, then even if the explanatory power of the Multiple q model with convex adjustment costs is weak, non-convex adjustment costs may be able to replicate the dynamics of investment rates.

6.3 Construction of the Data

6.3.1 Total Investment and Total Capital Stock

As in Chap. 4, the data used in the analysis in this chapter are constructed from the Corporate Finance Databank released by the Development Bank of Japan (DBJ), which contains individual firms' financial statement data listed in the First and Second Sections of the Tokyo, Osaka, and Nagoya Stock Exchanges. The data series are extended to FY 2014 in this chapter, whereas it culminated in FY 2004 in the empirical analyses in Chap. 4. Our panel dataset is unbalanced, as it contains delisted and newly listed firms. The capital stock series are constructed by the perpetual inventory method using either 1977 or the first recorded year after 1977 in the Corporate Finance Databank as the benchmark year for each firm. The database contains detailed data of depreciable assets for six items: [1] buildings, [2] structures, [3] machinery and equipment, [4] vessels (including aircrafts), [5] vehicles, and [6] tools, furniture, and fixtures. We compute investment rates for each of these six items as well as those for [7] land.

As was discussed in Chap. 3, two concepts are relevant for investments and capital stock statistics. One is the "progress-based" concept, under which an investment is acknowledged at the time of capitalization as construction work in progress, and the other is the "installation-based" concept, under which an investment is acknowledged when work starts within a production capacity. The latter installation-based concept is consistent with Tobin's q theory, and thus, in the empirical analyses of Chap. 4 and the following chapters, capital investment value is essentially defined as the new acquisition value of capital goods minus the residual market value of capital goods sold or retired. However, the residual market value of capital goods sold or retired is unobservable, and we must estimate it from other data in the financial statements.

[4]In other words, communality and uniqueness correspond to the contribution rates to the non-standardized variances of common and individual factors, respectively.

As we saw in Chap. 3, in previous studies, researchers handle this issue in three ways. The first is to calculate the book value of sold or retired capital through definitional identity equations in accounting; this value is then multiplied by the market-to-book-value ratios estimated under certain assumptions regarding depreciation schedules. We call this method the Proportional method, which is adopted by Asako, Kuninori, Inoue, and Murase (1989) and Hayashi and Inoue (1991). The second is to use the book value of sold or retired capital as the market value to avoid the tendency toward overestimation inherent in the Proportional method. We call this method the Book-Value method, which is adopted by Suzuki (2001).

The third one is to set the current value of sold or retired capital to zero based on the view that it is impossible to correctly estimate the current values of the sold or retired capital. This idea is only valid when we can assume that sold or retired capital as a percentage of net investments is substantially small and almost negligible. We call this method the Zero method, which is adopted by Hori, Saito, and Ando (2006). In this case, sold or retired capital is assumed to be included as part of the physical depreciation of capital stock. However, non-periodic lumpy disinvestments are never captured. The Zero method tracks the evolution of only new acquisitions, whereas the other two methods track the evolution of net investments, which contain not only new acquisitions but also sales and retirements.

6.3.2 *New Construction, Second-Hand Acquisitions, and Large-Scale Repairs*

Next, to obtain the series of investment rates by acquisition mode (new construction, second-hand acquisitions, and large-scale repairs), we link the data for each company's total investment and total capital stock based on financial data with the individual data from the investment/retirement survey using the company name and capital size information. This survey examines the conditions around investment expenditures (i.e., acquisitions of new or second-hand assets and large-scale repairs), as well as retirements of assets in private enterprises. The survey was started in FY 2006 with the objective of providing a basic resource for the creation of capital stock statistics in national accounting. In this study, we use the data from the FY 2009 survey, when the end date of the accounting period was added as a survey item, through the FY 2013 survey. The investment/retirement survey targets approximately 137,000 companies in the workplace population database list, as regulated by Article 27 of the Statistical Law, and is prepared based on the 2012 "Economic Census for Business Activity" (Ministry of Internal Affairs and Communications). From this target list of companies, approximately 30,000 are selected using stratified random sampling separated by capital size[5] across 37 industries. The effective response rate is around

[5]The survey set five tiers for random sampling based on capital: greater than 30 million yen and less than 50 million yen, greater than 50 million yen and less than 100 million yen, greater than 100 million yen and less than 1 billion yen, greater than 1 billion yen and less than 5 billion yen,

50%. Accordingly, of the companies included in the Corporate Financial Databank, we can link 1,168 (2,851 observations) to the investment/retirement survey data. Thus, the average number of observations for each company is 2.44.

In recognizing not only the type of capital good but also the acquisition mode as subjects of heterogeneity, we need to consider the ease with which the "curse of dimensionality" can escalate. Thus, we consolidate capital goods into four categories according to similarities in factor loadings (i.e., similarities in adjustment cost parameters). Specifically, based on the results of Tonogi et al. (2014), we calculate the investment rate according to following categories and procedure[6]:

(i) [1] Buildings and [2] structures are aggregated as "buildings and structures."
(ii) [3] Machinery and equipment and [6] tools, furniture, and fixtures are aggregated as "machinery and equipment."
(iii) [4] Vessels[7] and [5] vehicles are aggregated as "vessels and vehicles."
(iv) [7] Land is used directly as "land."

First, we consolidate the following investment/retirement survey items, which match the Corporate Financial Databank account items, into four categories, as specified above: "buildings and structures," "machinery and equipment," "vessels and vehicles," and "land." Then, we calculate the ratios for new construction acquisition values, second-hand item acquisition values, and the costs of large-scale repairs by capital good.[8] The investment rate by capital good calculated from the financial data is used as the control total. Multiplying this value by the ratios (calculated from the investment/retirement survey for each capital good) of new construction acquisition values, second-hand item acquisition values, and the cost of large-scale repairs, we obtain the investment rate for each capital good and for each acquisition mode z_{ij}^{h} in Eq. (6.13). In addition, the proportions of new construction, second-hand acquisitions, and large-scale repairs in the investment/retirement survey correspond to the aforementioned new acquisition value of capital goods, or the investment values defined by the Zero method. Thus, we choose the data based on the Zero method

and greater than 5 billion yen. However, all companies with capital over 1 billion yen are included as survey targets.

[6]The classification is almost the same as in Chaps. 3 and 4, in which we did not perform a factor analysis, except, in those analyses, [3] machinery and equipment and [6] tools, furniture, and fixtures are treated as independent categories.

[7]In Tonogi et al. (2014), vessels have a different factor loading than other capital goods but are aggregated with vehicles into one category owing to the very small number of observations with positive values for vessels.

[8]We calculate the composition ratio for each item with respect to the total value of the three items. However, because all land acquisitions relate to existing properties, there are only two survey items for land: second-hand acquisition costs and large-scale repairs (i.e., land conditioning and forming costs).

Table 6.1 Basic statistics of new construction, second-hand acquisition, and large-scale repair ratios (the component ratio) by capital good

	N of obs.	Mean	S.D.	Min	Max
Buildings and structures					
New construction	2,722	0.792	0.319	0	1
Second-hand acquisitions	2,722	0.034	0.140	0	1
Large-scale repairs	2,722	0.174	0.296	0	1
Machinery and equipment					
New construction	2,780	0.908	0.188	0	1
Second-hand acquisitions	2,780	0.016	0.079	0	1
Large-scale repairs	2,780	0.076	0.172	0	1
Vessels and vehicles					
New construction	1,702	0.906	0.250	0	1
Second-hand acquisitions	1,702	0.051	0.197	0	1
Large-scale repairs	1,702	0.043	0.166	0	1
Land					
Second-hand acquisitions	835	0.907	0.273	0	1
Large-scale repairs	835	0.093	0.273	0	1

Note For each capital good, we calculate the basic statistics only when investments in either new construction, second-hand acquisitions, or large-scale repairs exists

as the primary subject for the following analysis. The Book-Value and Proportional methods are used to check the robustness of our findings.[9,10]

6.3.3 Basic Statistics

Table 6.1 shows the basic statistics for the component ratios, in terms of investment values, of new construction acquisitions, second-hand item acquisitions, and large-scale repairs for the observations of each capital good that recognize positive values for one or more acquisition modes. Buildings and structures and machinery and equipment have over 2,700 observations respectively out of the 2,851 total linked data items, signifying positive investments by most of the firms. In contrast, the number

[9]The Book-Value and Proportional methods calculate investment amounts that take retirement and sales values (negative investments) into consideration. For this figure to be multiplied by the ratio of new construction, second-hand acquisitions, and large-scale repairs, in calculating invest amounts for each acquisition mode, we need to make a strong assumption that the residual value of the assets to be retired or sold have the same breakdown in terms of the acquisition mode as that of new acquisitions.

[10]According to this priority order, in all relevant tables in this chapter, the Zero method is referred to first, and the Book-Value and Proportional methods follow, if necessary.

of observations making positive investments is drastically smaller for vessels and vehicles (1,702) and land (835). When we compare the average ratios by acquisition mode for each capital good, we observe the highest ratios for new construction, with 79% for buildings and structures and 91% for both machinery and equipment and vessels and vehicles. For buildings and structures and machinery and equipment, the ratios for large-scale repairs are the second highest, following new construction, at 17% and 8%, respectively, whereas the ratios for second-hand acquisitions are the lowest, at 3% and 2%, respectively. For vessels and vehicles, the ratios for second-hand acquisitions and large-scale repairs are similar, at 5% and 4%, respectively. For land, for which new acquisitions do not exist by definition, the ratio for second-hand acquisitions accounts for 91%, and that for large-scale repairs is 9%.

Next, Table 6.2 displays the basic statistics for each variable required for the Multiple q investment functions and the factor analysis. Observations for which the absolute value of Tobin's $Q = (q - 1)P$ exceeds ten are deemed outliers and are excluded from the analysis.[11] Roughly 40 observations are counted as outliers, accounting for 1.5% of the data. As confirmed by prior studies, the Book-Value and Proportional methods, which take sales and retirements into consideration, have negative minimum values for the investment rate. Moreover, large negative values are observed for the Proportional method, which tends to value sales and retirements as more significant. Finally, Tobin's q values are lower than in prior studies because the analysis period starts in FY 2009, when stagnant share prices after the 2008 global financial crisis had a significant impact.

6.4 Estimation Results

In this section, we first discuss the estimation results obtained by the Multiple q model, which assumes a convex adjustment cost function with respect to the investment rate. We also estimate the Multiple q investment functions that do not consider differences between new construction, second-hand acquisitions, and large-scale repairs for comparability with prior studies, especially those described in Chap. 4. Next, we conduct a factor analysis to examine the possibility of non-convex adjustment costs to provide a comprehensive interpretation together with the estimation

[11] Tonogi, Nakamura, and Asako (2010) report that, since the late 1990s, cases of individual companies' average q values exceeding 100 become more prominent, particularly among ICT-related industries, such as software and computer-related information services, with these values exceeding 1,000 in some cases. ICT-related businesses require few tangible fixed assets, and mostly their corporate values come from intangible assets, such as innovative business models and customer networks. In addition, the values of these intangible assets are often not recognized as assets in corporate accounting. Thus, for these companies, a large numerical value is obtained for the average q when it is calculated based on the conventional definition because the denominator is close to zero and the corporate value in the numerator is inflated by intangible assets. However, our analysis targets investment behaviors for tangible assets. Thus, we do not believe it is problematic to exclude companies with extremely high average q values from our analysis because their main sources of corporate value are derived from intangible assets. See also the discussion in Chap. 7.

Table 6.2 Basic statistics of major variables used for the estimation of Multiple q investment function and the factor analysis

	N of obs.	Mean	S.D.	Min	Max
(c) Zero method					
$Q = (q - 1)\,P$	2,812	−0.531	1.335	−9.681	8.084
Investment rate					
Buildings and structures					
Total	2,812	0.053	0.084	0	0.893
New construction	2,812	0.044	0.078	0	0.893
Second-hand acquisitions	2,812	0.003	0.020	0	0.458
Large-scale repairs	2,812	0.005	0.019	0	0.553
Machinery and equipment					
Total	2,812	0.117	0.099	0	0.869
New construction	2,812	0.106	0.097	0	0.835
Second-hand acquisitions	2,812	0.002	0.015	0	0.569
Large-scale repairs	2,812	0.008	0.023	0	0.402
Vessels and vehicles					
Total	2,812	0.104	0.150	0	1.172
New construction	2,812	0.089	0.140	0	1.172
Second-hand acquisitions	2,812	0.004	0.029	0	0.722
Large-scale repairs	2,812	0.004	0.026	0	0.800
Land					
Total	2,812	0.022	0.075	0	0.910
Second-hand acquisitions	2,812	0.017	0.067	0	0.910
Large-scale repairs	2,812	0.000	0.006	0	0.201
Share					
Buildings and structures	2,812	0.391	0.145	0.034	0.974
Machinery and equipment	2,812	0.297	0.213	0.002	0.943
Vessels and vehicles	2,812	0.009	0.036	0	0.925
Land	2,812	0.304	0.185	0	0.917
(b) Book-Value method					
$Q = (q - 1)\,P$	2,811	−0.524	1.312	−9.202	8.002
Investment rate					
Buildings and structures					
Total	2,811	0.040	0.346	−17.423	0.919
New construction	2,811	0.033	0.342	−17.423	0.919
Second-hand acquisitions	2,811	0.002	0.022	−0.540	0.576
Large-scale repairs	2,811	0.004	0.021	−0.442	0.313
Machinery and equipment					

(continued)

Table 6.2 (continued)

	N of obs.	Mean	S.D.	Min	Max
Total	2,811	0.114	0.150	−4.834	0.884
New construction	2,811	0.103	0.138	−4.028	0.849
Second-hand acquisitions	2,811	0.002	0.014	−0.162	0.347
Large-scale repairs	2,811	0.007	0.030	−0.806	0.483
Vessels and vehicles					
Total	2,811	0.075	0.737	−29.339	1.172
New construction	2,811	0.094	0.159	−1.002	1.172
Second-hand acquisitions	2,811	0.005	0.031	−0.214	0.726
Large-scale repairs	2,811	0.004	0.031	−0.015	1.024
Land					
Total	2,811	−0.050	0.968	−32.766	0.995
Second-hand acquisitions	2,811	0.011	0.144	−4.310	0.981
Large-scale repairs	2,811	−0.001	0.017	−0.444	0.206
Share					
Buildings and structures	2,811	0.417	0.156	0.036	0.988
Machinery and equipment	2,811	0.316	0.216	0.001	0.944
Vessels and vehicles	2,811	0.009	0.036	0	0.921
Land	2,811	0.258	0.176	0	0.917
(a) Proportional method					
$Q = (q - 1)P$	2,811	−0.525	1.317	−9.416	8.181
Investment rate					
Buildings and structures					
Total	2,811	0.030	0.588	−29.775	1.049
New construction	2,811	0.026	0.578	−29.775	1.049
Second-hand acquisitions	2,811	0.002	0.038	−1.680	0.648
Large-scale repairs	2,811	0.003	0.039	−1.668	0.326
Machinery and equipment					
Total	2,811	−0.203	11.136	−581.098	1.097
New construction	2,811	−0.195	11.072	−581.098	0.922
Second-hand acquisitions	2,811	−0.001	0.103	−5.345	0.448
Large-scale repairs	2,811	−0.003	0.527	−27.833	0.509
Vessels and vehicles					

(continued)

Table 6.2 (continued)

	N of obs.	Mean	S.D.	Min	Max
Total	2,811	−0.412	11.620	−574.066	1.172
New construction	2,811	−0.257	11.332	−574.066	1.172
Second-hand acquisitions	2,811	0.002	0.112	−5.229	1.066
Large-scale repairs	2,811	0.004	0.042	−0.971	1.172
Land					
Total	2,811	−0.050	0.968	−32.766	0.995
Second-hand acquisitions	2,811	0.012	0.144	−4.310	0.981
Large-scale repairs	2,811	−0.001	0.017	−0.444	0.206
Share					
Buildings and structures	2,811	0.419	0.162	0.012	0.989
Machinery and equipment	2,811	0.288	0.213	0	0.944
Vessels and vehicles	2,811	0.007	0.035	0	0.923
Land	2,811	0.285	0.192	0	0.921

results of the Multiple q model. Furthermore, as noted in Sect. 6.2, the factors estimated by the factor analysis are firm-specific and affect all capital goods and acquisition modes equally for each firm. They are thought to correspond to the productivity shocks that affect Tobin's q. Thus, we conduct an additional verification of the relationship between a firm's growth opportunity and acquisition modes by regressing the estimated factors on Tobin's q. The results show that the acquisition mode, rather than the type of capital good, is the significant factor that determines the adjustment cost structure (i.e., convex or non-convex) and that the mode of acquisition is strongly related to a firm's growth opportunity. We further examine the validity of these interpretations by comparing the time-series changes in the mean values of factor loadings with the results of the DBJ's "Survey on Planned Capital Spending."

6.4.1 Estimation Results of the Multiple q Model

Table 6.3 shows the estimation results obtained using the standard Multiple q model, ignoring differences in acquisition modes, under almost the same surroundings as those of estimation results in Chap. 4 except for the number of sample firms, the sample periods, and the classification of capital goods. Here, we report only the results of the fixed-effects model because the Hausman test selects this model for both the Zero method (the base case) and the Book-Value and Proportional methods (reference cases). In the estimation results for the Zero method, the adjustment cost parameter γ is significant, with positive values for machinery and equipment and land. In addition, in the Tobin's q theory framework, the cash flow ratio, which is theoretically redundant, is also significant and positive. Keeping certain differences,

Table 6.3 Estimation results of standard Multiple q investment function ignoring differences in acquisition modes

		(c) Zero method		(b) Book-Value method		(a) Proportional method	
γ	Buildings and structures	−0.689	(0.406)*	−0.340	(0.300)	0.019	(0.260)
	Machinery and equipment	1.339	(0.563)**	0.847	(0.414)**	0.024	(0.122)
	Vessels and vehicles	−0.214	(4.883)	1.939	(3.627)	2.425	(4.391)
	Land	1.257	(0.544)**	0.148	(0.338)	0.107	(0.294)
$-\gamma*\alpha$	Buildings and structures	2.337	(0.830)***	0.230	(0.520)	−0.006	(0.437)
	Machinery and equipment	−0.322	(0.868)	−2.251	(0.653)***	−0.970	(0.517)*
	Vessels and vehicles	8.221	(4.934)*	4.922	(4.338)	3.091	(4.287)
Cash flow ratio		3.232	(0.438)***	3.164	(0.436)***	3.171	(0.441)***
Interest-bearing debt ratio		−0.496	(0.367)	−0.482	(0.366)	−0.481	(0.368)
R-squared: within		0.047		0.047		0.040	
R-squared: between		0.002		0.000		0.007	
R-squared: overall		0.003		0.000		0.005	
Number of observations		2,812		2,811		2,811	
Number of firms		1,152		1,151		1,151	

Note The fixed-effects model was selected for all the cases based on the Hausman test. Standard errors are shown in parenthesis
*, **, and *** denote significance at the 10%, 5%, and 1% level, respectively

such as the decrease in the number of observations owing to matching with the investment/retirement survey, in mind, our results are very similar to those of prior studies that only utilize data from the Corporate Financial Databank.

Table 6.4 shows the estimation results using the extended Multiple q model, which takes into consideration the heterogeneity among acquisition modes. In this case, we also report only the results of the fixed-effects model because the Hausman test selects this model across all methods. In the estimation results obtained by the Zero method, the adjustment cost parameter γ is significant and positive only for new construction in machinery and equipment. Thus, we can say that significant

Table 6.4 Estimation results of extended Multiple q investment function taking into consideration differences in acquisition modes

		(c) Zero method		(b) Book-Value method		(a) Proportional method	
γ	*Buildings and structures*						
	New construction	−0.601	(0.437)	−0.197	(0.316)	0.197	(0.289)
	Second-hand acquisitions	−0.189	(1.745)	−1.178	(1.460)	−0.830	(1.003)
	Large-scale repairs	0.023	(1.374)	−0.997	(1.412)	−1.296	(1.297)
	Machinery and equipment						
	New construction	1.440	(0.584)**	0.992	(0.444)**	0.074	(0.193)
	Second-hand acquisitions	1.802	(2.042)	5.655	(3.329)*	−0.166	(0.513)
	Large-scale repairs	−1.656	(2.771)	−1.387	(1.996)	0.474	(0.565)
	Vessels and vehicles						
	New construction	−0.279	(5.640)	0.133	(5.110)	1.828	(4.800)
	Second-hand acquisitions	0.987	(21.867)	−2.882	(23.717)	−16.204	(26.333)
	Large-scale repairs	−1.406	(21.929)	−91.059	(98.650)	−115.539	(76.703)
	Land						
	Second-hand acquisitions	0.167	(0.605)	−0.595	(0.450)	−0.397	(0.414)
	Large-scale repairs	12.730	(10.927)	−0.884	(2.579)	0.004	(2.207)
$-\gamma*\alpha$	Buildings and structures	1.486	(0.813)*	−0.185	(0.501)	−0.225	(0.425)
	Machinery and equipment	−0.922	(0.849)	−2.713	(0.644)***	−1.252	(0.501)**
	Vessels and vehicles	8.385	(5.019)*	5.138	(4.527)	4.513	(4.369)
Cash flow ratio		3.243	(0.441)***	3.199	(0.438)***	3.213	(0.441)***
Interest-bearing debt ratio		−0.473	(0.369)	−0.504	(0.366)	−0.487	(0.369)
R-squared: within		0.045		0.051		0.044	
R-squared: between		0.001		0.000		0.007	
R-squared: overall		0.001		0.000		0.004	
Number of observations		2,812		2,811		2,811	
Number of firms		1,152		1,151		1,151	

Note
The fixed-effects model was selected for all the cases based on the Hausman test. Standard errors are shown in parenthesis
*, **, and ***denote significance at the 10%, 5%, and 1% level, respectively

and positive γ of machinery and equipment that is observed when ignoring differences between the three modes (see Table 6.3) captures the adjustment costs of new construction. From the above results, we can see that only the investment behavior around new construction in machinery and equipment is consistent with Tobin's q theory framework, which assumes a convex adjustment cost function.

6.4.2 Estimation Results of Factor Analysis

Next, we analyze investment behavior using factor analysis, which can also assume a non-convex adjustment cost function. Here, we apply the methods of factor determination and factor rotation following Tonogi et al. (2014). We adopt Thurstone (1947) in determining the number of common factors to set. In general, for $m \times n$ factor loadings, which are hypothetical parameters, to sufficiently explain ${}_nC_2 = n(n-1)/2$ correlation coefficient elements (or the number of off-diagonal elements constituting the correlation matrix between n variables), the number of the latter must exceed that of the former. However, because the number of independent variables decreases by $m(m-1)/2$ (the number of uncorrelated conditions imposed by the mutual independence of m factors), the following relationship must be satisfied:

$$\frac{n(n-1)}{2} \geq nm - \frac{m(m-1)}{2}, \tag{6.20}$$

from which we obtain

$$m \leq \frac{(2n+1) - \sqrt{8n+1}}{2} \tag{6.21}$$

as, among the two opposing inequalities, the more appropriate solution is surely the one with the upper and maximum limit rather than the one with the lower and minimum limit.[12]

In this study, $n = 11 (= 3 \times 3 + 2 \times 1)$, because we have data for new construction, second-hand acquisitions, and large-scale repairs for three of the capital goods (buildings and structures, machinery and equipment, and vessels and vehicles), whereas we only have data for second-hand acquisitions and large-scale repairs for land. Thus, from (6.21), we have $m \leq 6.78$, and thereby the maximum factor count is six. However, we estimate only up to the fifth factor, because the eigenvalue of the sixth factor is negative if we estimate up to the sixth factor.[13] We use an orthogonal rotation (varimax rotation) to convert this estimation into a simple structure in which the factor loadings of both variables have high values for one factor only and values close to zero for the other factor.

---

[12] Meanwhile, the corresponding opposing inequality turns out to be: $m \geq \{2n + 1 + \sqrt{8n+1}\}/2$, which implies $m \geq 16.2$ for $n = 11$.

[13] The eigenvalue represents each factor's level of dominance with respect to all items and signifies the number of dependent variables in the analysis that can be explained by the factor. In this study, we exclude factors with negative eigenvalues.

Table 6.5 Results of the factor analysis

	Factor 1	Factor 2	Factor 3	Factor 4	Factor 5	Uniqueness
(c) Zero method						
Buildings and structures						
New construction	0.006	0.578	−0.006	0.035	0.012	0.665
Second-hand acquisitions	0.561	0.019	0.008	0.262	−0.014	0.616
Large-scale repairs	0.018	0.020	0.476	0.017	−0.009	0.772
Machinery and equipment						
New construction	0.023	0.589	−0.025	0.029	−0.007	0.652
Second-hand acquisitions	0.587	0.035	0.012	−0.030	0.005	0.653
Large-scale repairs	0.017	−0.042	0.528	−0.009	0.006	0.719
Vessels and vehicles						
New construction	0.012	0.272	0.025	0.001	−0.063	0.921
Second-hand acquisitions	0.507	−0.029	0.007	−0.088	0.012	0.735
Large-scale repairs	−0.019	−0.048	0.295	−0.010	0.006	0.910
Land						
Second-hand acquisitions	0.172	0.115	0.000	0.406	0.006	0.792
Large-scale repairs	−0.011	0.095	0.012	0.145	0.101	0.960
(b) Book-Value method						
Buildings and structures						
New construction	0.248	−0.013	0.063	−0.022	0.108	0.922
Second-hand acquisitions	0.045	−0.007	0.388	0.130	−0.051	0.828
Large-scale repairs	−0.045	0.423	0.155	−0.006	0.081	0.788
Machinery and equipment						
New construction	0.511	0.020	0.076	0.016	0.004	0.732
Second-hand acquisitions	0.044	0.012	0.122	0.307	0.002	0.889
Large-scale repairs	0.326	0.388	0.006	0.019	−0.062	0.739
Vessels and vehicles						
New construction	−0.045	0.020	0.006	0.009	−0.015	0.997
Second-hand acquisitions	0.013	0.002	0.059	0.302	−0.009	0.905
Large-scale repairs	0.007	0.283	−0.061	−0.003	−0.086	0.909
Land						
Second-hand acquisitions	0.117	0.140	0.417	−0.008	0.047	0.791
Large-scale repairs	−0.035	0.117	−0.011	−0.011	0.175	0.954
(a) Proportional method						
Buildings and structures						
New construction	0.982	0.005	0.072	0.006	−0.001	0.030
Second-hand acquisitions	0.026	0.121	0.064	0.392	−0.018	0.826

(continued)

Table 6.5 (continued)

	Factor 1	Factor 2	Factor 3	Factor 4	Factor 5	Uniqueness
Large-scale repairs	0.057	0.017	0.854	0.004	0.051	0.265
Machinery and equipment						
New construction	0.985	0.001	0.021	0.004	0.001	0.030
Second-hand acquisitions	0.006	0.899	0.045	0.042	−0.005	0.189
Large-scale repairs	0.070	0.019	0.856	0.044	−0.046	0.258
Vessels and vehicles						
New construction	0.024	0.003	0.007	0.015	−0.015	0.999
Second-hand acquisitions	0.002	0.895	−0.014	−0.023	0.005	0.198
Large-scale repairs	0.000	0.002	0.040	−0.039	0.057	0.994
Land						
Second-hand acquisitions	0.039	−0.011	0.342	0.376	0.011	0.740
Large-scale repairs	−0.004	−0.002	0.052	−0.028	0.188	0.961

Note Estimated using the same samples as in Table 6.4

Table 6.5 shows the results of the factor analysis performed on the same data as in the last subsection. The results for the Zero method in Table 6.5 (c) show that, except for land, the factor loadings are the largest for second-hand acquisitions in the first factor, for new construction in the second factor, and for large-scale repairs in the third factor. Land has large factor loadings in the fourth and fifth factors. Second-hand acquisitions have the lowest values for uniqueness except in the case of machinery and equipment.[14]

For reference purposes, we also consider the results obtained using the Book-Value and Proportional methods. These methods calculate the investment rates by assuming that the composition ratio by acquisition mode of sold or retired capital is consistent with that of new acquisitions. Therefore, it should be noted that the estimation accuracy decreases with higher ratios of negative investments to new acquisitions because measurement error can easily occur in the residual market prices of sold or retired capital.

First, we consider Table 6.5 (b), which shows the results obtained using the Book-Value method. Large factor loadings are observed as follows: in the first factor for the new construction of buildings and structures and machinery and equipment, in the second factor for large-scale repairs of capital goods other than land, in the third factor for second-hand acquisitions of buildings and structures and land, and in the fourth factor for second-hand acquisitions of machinery and equipment and vessels and vehicles. No particular tendencies are observed with regard to uniqueness, as observed for the Zero method. These results are not as clear as those for the Zero method, but we do find results that differ from those for the Zero method. That is,

[14]The factor analysis results do not vary greatly even when excluding observations with 100% new construction in the investment/retirement survey.

we observe a relationship between the first factor and new construction, the second factor and large-scale repairs, and the third factor and second-hand acquisitions.

Next, we consider Table 6.5 (a), which shows the results obtained using the Proportional method. Large factor loadings are observed as follows: in the first factor for the new construction of buildings and structures and machinery and equipment, in the second factor for second-hand acquisitions of machinery and equipment and vessels and vehicles, in the third factor for large-scale repairs of buildings and structures and machinery and equipment, and in the fourth factor for second-hand acquisitions of buildings and structures and land. No tendencies are observed in terms of uniqueness, in contrast to the results for the Zero method. Similar to the Book-Value method case, these results are not as clear as those of the Zero method. However, we find a relationship between the first factor and new construction, the second factor and second-hand acquisitions, and the third factor and large-scale repairs.

6.4.3 Overall Interpretation of the Multiple q Model and Factor Analysis

In this section, we consider an interpretation consistent with both the estimation results from the extended Multiple q investment function described in Sect. 6.4.1 and the factor analysis described in Sect. 6.4.2. In the Multiple q investment function, the adjustment cost parameter γ is estimated as significant and positive only for new construction of machinery and equipment. That is, this parameter is not significant for new construction of other capital goods. Together with the results of the factor analysis in which the investment behavior around new construction is mostly explained by a common factor regardless of the type of capital good, we can say that the influence of γ for capital goods other than machinery and equipment is absorbed by the γ of machinery and equipment owing to its proximity. Thus, we can interpret the investment behavior around new construction consistently if we assume that it follows a convex adjustment cost function regardless of the capital good type.

For second-hand acquisitions and large-scale repairs, no capital goods have a significant and positive adjustment cost parameter γ when using the Multiple q model. However, in the factor analysis, as in the case of new construction, the respective specific common factors for second-hand acquisitions and large-scale repairs can capture their movement, regardless of the capital good type in the factor analysis. Thus, we can interpret these results consistently if we assume that the investment behaviors of second-hand acquisitions and large-scale repairs follow a non-convex adjustment cost function regardless of the capital good type. In particular, it is natural for large-scale repairs to follow a non-convex adjustment cost, as the name suggests.

Asako and Tonogi (2010) and the analyses in Chap. 4 estimate the investment function using a standard Multiple q model. They consider the possibility of partial homogeneity by assuming the existence of five categories of capital goods, and they test the homogeneity between "a certain capital good" and "four other capital goods deemed (supposedly) mutually homogeneous." They also perform pairwise tests of the homogeneity of two arbitrary capital goods. As a result, in some cases, partial homogeneity is not rejected depending on the analysis period and the definition of the investment rate, but the combinations of capital goods are not uniform. Thus, if we interpret this finding along with the factor analysis results of this study, given that the total investment activity aggregates activities in new construction, second-hand acquisitions, and large-scale repairs, we find that the major cause of the inconsistency in the results of the homogeneity test conducted by Asako and Tonogi (2010) across the sample periods is that changes in the ratios of new construction, second-hand acquisitions, and large-scale repairs to total investment affect which acquisition mode's factors are dominant in the dynamics of the total investment.

Thus, we verify the above interpretation by regressing $(q - 1)P$ on the investment factors estimated by the factor analysis. We predict that the factors for new construction, which are consistent with the convex adjustment cost function, are estimated as significant and positive, whereas the factors for second-hand acquisitions and large-scale repairs of capital goods are not estimated as significant and positive. We use the fixed-effects model in this estimation, as in the estimation using the Multiple q investment function. We also include the interest-bearing debt and cash flow ratios as control variables.

Table 6.6 shows the estimation results. In the factor analysis estimation results described in Sect. 6.4.2, we observe the following. Using the Zero method, the first factor is mainly related to the investment behavior of second-hand acquisitions, the second factor is related to the investment behavior of new construction, and the third factor is related to the investment behavior of large-scale repairs. Using the Book-Value method, the first factor is mainly related to the investment behavior of new construction, the second factor to the investment behavior of large-scale repairs, and the third factor to the investment behavior of second-hand acquisitions. Then, using

Table 6.6 Results of the regression of Tobin's q on investment factors

	(c) Zero method		(b) Book-Value method		(a) Proportional method	
Factor 1	0.019	(0.095)	1.111	(0.130)***	2.050	(0.060)***
Factor 2	0.221	(0.130)*	−0.622	(0.145)***	−0.028	(0.051)
Factor 3	−0.167	(0.140)	0.205	(0.129)	−0.178	(0.065)***
R-squared: within	0.027		0.072		0.430	
R-squared: between	0.004		0.009		0.000	
R-squared: overall	0.004		0.006		0.001	

Notes
1. The dependent variable $(q - 1)P$ is regressed on the factors estimated in Table 6.5
2. We perform the estimation based on the fixed-effects model with the same set of control variables as in the estimation of Multiple q investment function
3. Standard errors are shown in parenthesis. *, **, and *** denote significance at the 10%, 5%, and 1% level, respectively

the Proportional method, the first factor is mainly related to the investment behavior of new construction, the second factor to the investment behavior of second-hand acquisitions, and the third factor to the investment behavior of large-scale repairs. Thus, we verify whether the factor of new construction (i.e., the second factor of the Zero method and the first factors of the Book-Value and Proportional methods) is estimated as significant and positive. Table 6.6 shows that the new construction factor is significant and positive for all three methods. However, none of the remaining factors are significant and positive.

From the above results, we confirm that capital investment for new construction is consistent with the convex adjustment cost function, whereas that for second-hand acquisitions and large-scale repairs is not. Rather, we observe that the latter two investment behaviors may follow non-convex adjustment cost functions. With convex adjustment costs, the marginal adjustment cost gradually increases as the investment rate increases. Thus, it is optimal to make investments smoothly in small increments rather than making a single large investment. However, it is not unusual for large-scale repairs to follow a non-convex adjustment cost function, as the name itself suggests lumpy investment behavior. In contrast, second-hand acquisitions invoke increases in ordinary production capacity rather than lumpy investments. Thus, it is not clear which aspects are captured by the factor analysis results. In the next section, we explore the acquisition mode selection for capital goods based on their relation to investment motives for corporate growth.

6.5 Acquisition Modes of Investment and Corporate Growth

This section considers the relationship between capital acquisition modes and corporate growth. The analysis thus far has considered three methods (the Proportional, Book-Value, and Zero methods) to construct the capital stock and capital investment data for each capital good. However, we confirm that analysis results under the three methods do not necessarily yield large inconsistencies. Thus, we proceed here using only the Zero method.

6.5.1 Relationship between the Acquisition Modes and Replacement Investment

The adjustment cost of investment is thought to correspond to mainly company organizational changes and re-education costs for workers, which accompany firm growth and the introduction of new technology. However, it is unlikely that these costs are incurred for replacement investments, that is, investments that do not entail increases in production capacity or changes in product lines. Thus, investment mechanisms may vary in such cases. Unfortunately, no data accurately distinguish between replacement and new investments. However, we nevertheless carry out the factor analysis after dividing the sample into two parts by assuming that the ratio of replacement investments relatively small if the total investment rate is greater than or equal to the total capital depreciation rate[15] and is relatively large otherwise. If the explanatory power decreases for any of the factors for new construction, second-hand acquisitions, or large-scale repairs as a result of splitting the sample, we consider this result to be evidence of a relationship between the factor and the replacement investment ratio (or, otherwise, corporate growth).

Tables 6.7 and 6.8 show the results of the factor analysis and the regression analysis of Tobin's q on each factor for the sample of 1,297 observations for which the total investment rate exceeds or is equal to the total capital depreciation rate (Table 6.7) and for the sample of 1,554 cases for which the total investment rate is below the total capital depreciation rate (Table 6.8). First, Table 6.7 shows that the first factor is second-hand acquisitions, the second factor is large-scale repairs, and the third factor is new construction. Table 6.8 shows that the first factor is large-scale repairs, the second factor is second-hand acquisitions, and the third factor is new construction. Comparing these results to those in Table 6.5 (factor analysis results under the Zero method across all samples), we find that, for the full sample, the first factor is second-hand acquisitions, the second factor is new construction, and the third factor is large-scale repairs. That is, the factor ranking of new construction decreases for both groups when we split the sample. Furthermore, Table 6.6 (results of regression of Tobin's q on the factors for the full sample using the Zero method) shows that the factor for new construction is significant and positive, whereas Tables 6.7 and 6.8 indicate positive but insignificant values.

From the above results, we observe that dividing the sample using the replacement investment ratio makes it difficult to extract the new construction factor in factor analysis. In other words, the factor for new construction has a deep relationship with the replacement investment ratio (or corporate growth). When viewed across the full sample, this interpretation is consistent with the results shown in Table 6.6, which indicates a positive linear correlation between the factor for new construction and the average q.

6.5.2 Acquisition Mode of Capital Goods and Capital Investment Motives

Thus far, the results suggest that the new construction factor is related to corporate growth opportunities. Therefore, in this section, we reference the Development Bank

[15]Here, the total capital depreciation rate refers to physical depreciation (not tax depreciation). It is calculated as the weighted average of the capital depreciation rates for each capital good, using the real capital stock values as weight. We refer to Hulten and Wykoff (1977, 1981) for the values of the capital depreciation rate for each capital good. The total investment rate used for comparison is calculated based on the total investment figure, including land.

Table 6.7 Results of the factor analysis and the regression of Tobin's q on investment factors based on (c) Zero method using the samples with the total investment rate greater than or equal to the total capital depreciation rate

Basic statistics of new construction, second-hand acquisition, and large-scale repair ratios (the component ratio) by capital good

	N of obs.	Mean	S.D.	Min	Max
Buildings and structures					
New construction	1,266	0.820	0.292	0	1
Second-hand acquisitions	1,266	0.056	0.180	0	1
Large-scale repairs	1,266	0.124	0.240	0	1
Machinery and equipment					
New construction	1,272	0.914	0.176	0	1
Second-hand acquisitions	1,272	0.016	0.073	0	1
Large-scale repairs	1,272	0.070	0.160	0	1
Vessels and vehicles					
New construction	851	0.921	0.223	0	1
Second-hand acquisitions	851	0.039	0.167	0	1
Large-scale repairs	851	0.040	0.157	0	1
Land					
Second-hand acquisitions	532	0.920	0.252	0	1
Large-scale repairs	532	0.080	0.252	0	1

Results of the factor analysis

	Factor 1	Factor 2	Factor 3	Factor 4	Factor 5	Uniqueness
Buildings and structures						
New construction	−0.028	−0.072	0.495	−0.002	0.013	0.749
Second-hand acquisitions	0.551	−0.026	−0.080	0.291	−0.025	0.604
Large-scale repairs	0.007	0.456	−0.047	−0.004	−0.023	0.789
Machinery and equipment						
New construction	−0.006	−0.108	0.503	−0.025	−0.012	0.735
Second-hand acquisitions	0.656	0.007	0.022	−0.008	0.005	0.569
Large-scale repairs	0.010	0.534	−0.102	−0.029	0.013	0.703
Vessels and vehicles						
New construction	0.010	−0.012	0.206	−0.036	−0.084	0.949
Second-hand acquisitions	0.652	0.014	0.000	−0.041	0.006	0.573
Large-scale repairs	−0.021	0.306	−0.085	−0.029	0.024	0.898
Land						

(continued)

Table 6.7 (continued)

Results of the factor analysis						
	Factor 1	Factor 2	Factor 3	Factor 4	Factor 5	Uniqueness
Second-hand acquisitions	0.106	−0.048	−0.027	0.446	0.002	0.787
Large-scale repairs	−0.019	0.033	0.190	0.228	0.081	0.904

Results of the regression of Tobin's q on investment factors		
Factor 1	0.004	(0.159)
Factor 2	−0.253	(0.259)
Factor 3	0.279	(0.288)
R-squared: within	0.084	
R-squared: between	0.003	
R-squared: overall	0.004	

Notes
1. The number of samples with the total investment rate greater than or equal to the total capital depreciation rate is 1,297
2. For each capital good, we calculate the basic statistics only when investments in either new construction, second-hand acquisitions, or large-scale repairs exists
3. In the regression analysis, the dependent variable $(q-1)P$ is regressed on the factors estimated in the factor analysis. We perform the estimation based on the fixed-effects model with the same set of control variables as in the estimation of Multiple q investment function
4. Standard errors are shown in parenthesis. *, **, and *** denote significance at the 10%, 5%, and 1% level, respectively

of Japan's annual "Survey on Planned Capital Spending" (hereinafter, the "capital spending survey") to directly observe the relationship between investment activities broken down by "investment motive" (i.e, expansion of production capacity, product development and upgrading, streamlining and labor saving, research and development, maintenance and repair, and other) and the activities in each factor. Because the capital spending survey only publishes macro results and results aggregated by industry,[16] a time-series comparison requires calculating aggregate values of the factors for each fiscal year. For consistency with the aggregation method of the capital spending survey, we use a weighted average such that each company's total actual investment is used as the weighting.

Figure 6.1 shows the movement in aggregated values obtained by taking a weighted average of the estimation results for each factor in Table 6.5 (c) (where

[16]The capital spending survey aggregates data using the following steps:

(i) Each company returns a survey response of their composition ratios on investment motives.

(ii) The investment amount by investment motive is calculated by multiplying the composition ratios of the investment motives by the total investment amounts (including land) for each company.

(iii) The overall ratios for investment motives are calculated by dividing the investment amount totaled for each investment motive by the total investment amount (including land).

That is, the value is congruent to the weighted average of each company's response on the component ratios of investment motives calculated over the total investment amount (including land).

Table 6.8 Results of the factor analysis and the regression of Tobin's q on investment factors based on (c) Zero method using the samples with the investment rate below the depreciation rate

Basic statistics of the investment rate

	N of obs.	Mean	S.D.	Min	Max
Buildings and structures					
New construction	1,456	0.768	0.340	0	1
Second-hand acquisitions	1,456	0.014	0.087	0	1
Large-scale repair	1,456	0.217	0.332	0	1
Machinery and equipment					
New construction	1,508	0.903	0.198	0	1
Second-hand acquisitions	1,508	0.016	0.084	0	1
Large-scale repair	1,508	0.081	0.181	0	1
Vessels and vehicles					
New construction	851	0.891	0.274	0	1
Second-hand acquisitions	851	0.063	0.222	0	1
Large-scale repair	851	0.046	0.175	0	1
Land					
Second-hand acquisitions	303	0.884	0.304	0	1
Large-scale repair	303	0.116	0.304	0	1

Results of the factor analysis

	Factor 1	Factor 2	Factor 3	Factor 4	Factor 5	Uniqueness
Buildings and structures						
New construction	−0.139	−0.011	0.207	0.063	−0.011	0.934
Second-hand acquisitions	−0.002	0.317	−0.005	0.033	0.000	0.898
Large-scale repair	0.485	−0.012	0.004	−0.009	0.001	0.764
Machinery and equipment						
New construction	−0.152	−0.048	0.161	−0.108	0.038	0.936
Second-hand acquisitions	−0.013	0.221	−0.075	−0.097	0.010	0.936
Large-scale repair	0.512	0.010	−0.040	0.022	−0.003	0.736
Vessels and vehicles						
New construction	−0.002	0.003	0.244	0.011	0.003	0.940
Second-hand acquisitions	0.028	0.062	−0.094	0.103	0.057	0.973
Large-scale repair	0.335	−0.003	0.028	−0.043	0.001	0.885
Land						
Second-hand acquisitions	0.004	0.199	0.081	0.178	−0.005	0.922
Large-scale repair	0.022	−0.009	−0.050	0.029	−0.091	0.988

Results of the regression of Tobin's q on investment factors

Factor 1	−0.042	(0.243)

(continued)

Table 6.8 (continued)

Results of the regression of Tobin's q on investment factors		
Factor 2	−0.007	(0.262)
Factor 3	0.176	(0.380)
R-squared: within	0.001	
R-squared: between	0.000	
R-squared: overall	0.000	

Notes
1. The number of samples with the total investment rate below the total capital depreciation rate is 1,554
2. For each capital good, we calculate the basic statistics only when investments in either new construction, second-hand acquisitions, or large-scale repairs exists
3. In the regression analysis, the dependent variable $(q - 1)P$ is regressed on the factors estimated in the factor analysis. We perform the estimation based on the fixed-effects model with the same set of control variables as in the estimation of Multiple q investment function
4. Standard errors are shown in parenthesis. *, **, and *** denote significance at the 10%, 5%, and 1% level, respectively

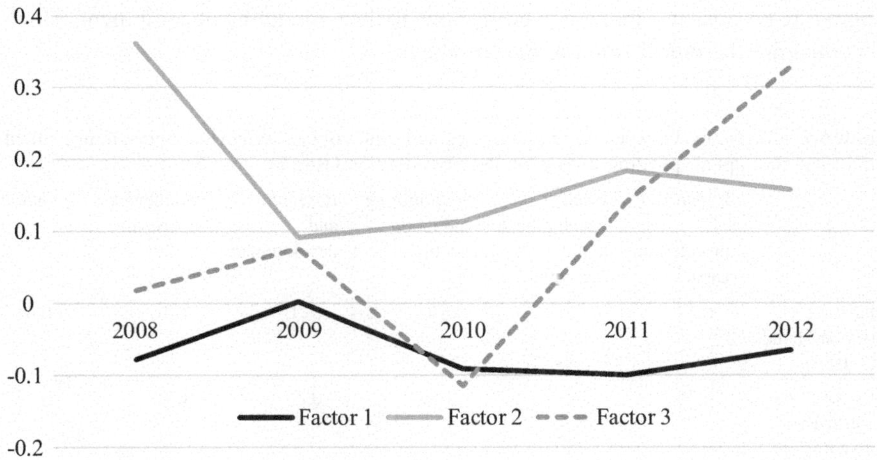

Fig. 6.1 Time series change in macro-aggregated values of investment factors *Notes* 1. The macro-aggregated values of factors use the weighted averages of factors estimated using (c) Zero method in Table 6.5 using the real capital spending figures of each company as the weight. 2. The factor 1 is mainly related to second-hand acquisitions, the factor 2 to new construction, and the factor 3 to large-scale repairs

factor analysis is carried out for the full sample using the Zero method) using the real investment values as weights by fiscal year. In 2009, the first factor (that for second-hand acquisitions) temporarily increases to reflect the economic downturn from the global financial crisis, whereas the second factor (that for new construction) decreases. Subsequently, the second factor bottoms out in 2010 and then recover.

We believe that the capital goods for which capital investment is possible using second-hand acquisitions have low levels of irreversibility owing to the existence of secondary markets. Recalling the uncertainty and risk of liquidity exhaustion immediately following the global financial crisis, we can say that the temporary increase in the second-hand factor is consistent with the theory that irreversible investment is suppressed under the umbrella of uncertainty.

Table 6.9 gives the results of using the sample across FY 2008 and 2012 to show the correlation between the macro aggregated value of the aforementioned factors and the ratios of each investment motive (for all industries) in the capital spending survey. First, we verify the investment motives with which each factor is highly correlated. The factor for new construction is correlated with various motives for capital investment, but, in particular, it has high positive correlations with expansion of production capacity and research and development, which are consistent with the previous regression result that the factor for new construction has significantly positive explanatory power for Tobin's q. Second-hand acquisitions of equipment also have a positive correlation with expansion of production capacity, but they are most highly correlated with efficiency-oriented streamlining and labor saving. The factor for large-scale repairs is highly correlated with product development and upgrading because it is thought to correspond to the remodeling of equipment, which accompanies the introduction of new products.

Table 6.9 Correlation between the macro-aggregated values of factors and the shares of investment motives in the capital spending survey (on the basis of all industries)

	Expansion of production capacity	Product development and upgrading	Streamlining and labor saving	Research and development	Maintenance and repair	Other
Factor 1 (second-hand, ex-land)	0.23	−0.23	0.30	−0.20	0.16	−0.64
Factor 2 (new construction, ex-land)	0.76	0.44	0.60	0.86	0.70	−0.27
Factor 3 (large-scale repair, ex-land)	−0.31	0.79	−0.15	0.46	−0.53	0.21
Factor 4 (second-hand, land)	0.41	−0.22	0.29	0.13	0.56	0.06
Factor 5 (large-scale repair, land)	−0.33	−0.87	−0.35	−0.92	−0.10	0.15

Note The macro-aggregated values of factors use the weighted averages of factors estimated using (c) Zero method in Table 6.5 using the real capital spending figures of each company as the weight. The shares of investment motives in the capital spending survey use the values of all industries

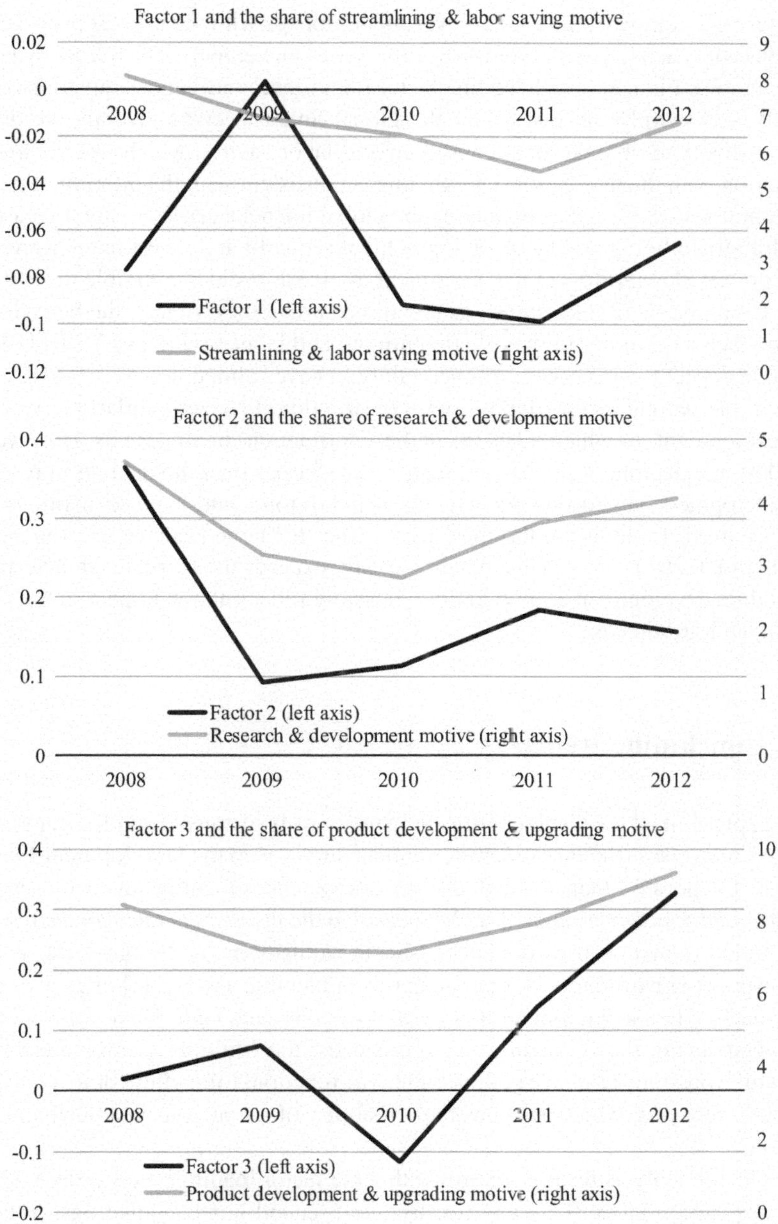

Fig. 6.2 Time series change in highly-correlated combinations of the macro-aggregated values of factors and the share of investment motives in the capital spending survey (on the basis of all industries) *Notes* 1. The macro-aggregated values of factors use the weighted averages of factors estimated using (c) Zero method in Table 6.5 using the real capital spending figures of each company as the weight. The shares of investment motives in the capital spending survey use the values of all industries. 2. The factor 1 is mainly related to second-hand acquisitions, the factor 2 to new construction, and the factor 3 to large-scale repairs

Figure 6.2 compares the capital investment motives with the highest positive correlations with each factor and shows the time-series movements. The following points are of interest. First, although the first factor (that for second-hand acquisitions) temporarily and sharply increases after the global financial crisis, overall, we do not observe this type of spike in streamlining and labor saving, which has the highest correlation with the first factor. This finding is consistent with the interpretation that the economic downturn accompanying the global financial crisis did not increase the need for streamlining and labor saving but that second-hand investments were relatively preferred regardless of the investment motive to avoid irreversible investments under the umbrella of uncertainty, as mentioned previously. In fact, the behavior for the first factor is similar to that of streamlining and labor saving in FY 2011–2012, when we expect the influences of uncertainty to have calmed down.

Next, the second factor (that for new construction) behaves similarly to research and development (to which it has the highest correlation) in all periods. However, in FY 2009, the decline in the second factor was sharper than the decline in research and development, suggesting that a temporary shift to second-hand acquisitions may have occurred. In addition, the third factor (that for large-scale repairs) increased sharply in FY 2011–2012. This increase greatly exceeds the increases in investment for product development and upgrading, possibly reflecting the impact of the Great East Japan Earthquake.

6.6 Concluding Remarks

This chapter linked the Cabinet Office's "Survey of Investments and Retirements of Private Enterprises (the investment/retirement survey)" to the Development Bank of Japan's "Corporate Finance Databank" to analyze investment behavior by segment (capital good × acquisition mode). We measured the investment rates for each acquisition mode (new construction, second-hand acquisitions, and large-scale repairs) with respect to investments in four categories of tangible assets: buildings and structures, machinery and equipment, vessels and vehicles, and land. Then, we conducted an analysis using the following two approaches: the Multiple q investment function, which presumes a convex adjustment cost function, following Tobin's q theory, and factor analysis, which assumes the possibility of a non-convex adjustment cost function.

The factor analysis results confirmed that the factor loadings are similar within a given acquisition mode (i.e., new construction, second-hand acquisitions, or large-scale repairs), regardless of the type of capital good. In other words, differences in acquisition modes are thought to have a greater influence on the adjustment cost parameter values for investment than the type of capital good has. When we combine the estimation results from the Multiple q model with the factor analysis results, we find that the investment behavior around new construction can be explained (to some extent) by the convex adjustment cost function assumed by Tobin's q theory. At the same time, the results suggest the existence of a non-convex adjustment cost function regarding second-hand acquisitions and large-scale repairs. In addition, the results suggest that the factor for new construction has a strong relationship with the replacement investment ratio (or corporate growth).

Based on these results, when we compare the movements of the macro aggregated values of factors and the "investment motive" composition of the DBJ's "Survey on Planned Capital Spending," the factor for new construction has a high correlation with investment motives closely tied to growth opportunities, such as research and development and the expansion of production capacity. We also find that investment in second-hand goods spiked immediately after the global financial crisis, which we interpret as the influence of investment behavior taken to avoid irreversibility. Moreover, large-scale repairs are said to be lumpy in nature, but this characteristic is likely to have been more strongly expressed given our chosen sample period, which includes the Great East Japan Earthquake. Thus, the reasons for the inconsistency with the convex adjustment cost function differ for second-hand and large-scale repairs.

To date, various models have been employed to explain companies' capital investment behavior, starting with the Tobin's *q* model, which is based on a convex adjustment cost function, and including the irreversibility of investment (adjustment costs that are asymmetric for positive and negative investments) and lumpy investments (adjustment costs that entail fixed costs), among others. Our results show that at least some of the heterogeneous aspects of investment behavior are attributable to differences in investment behaviors by acquisition mode. Thus, the overall investment dynamics that encompass these heterogeneous investments can vary depending on the relative proportions of acquisition modes within a given period, and they can be smooth (i.e., consistent with the convex adjustment cost function) or lumpy (i.e., inconsistent with the convex adjustment cost function). However, our results may be strongly influenced by the analysis period, which includes the global financial crisis and the Great East Japan Earthquake. Future research topics include conducting a longer-term analysis following the accumulation of additional data from the investment/retirement survey and checking the robustness of the results by matching financial data that includes unlisted companies.

References

Asako, K., Kuninori, M., Inoue, T., & Murase, H. (1989). Land evaluation and measurement of Tobin's *q* theory/estimation of Multiple *q*. *Economics Today, 10*(3). (In Japanese).

Asako, K., & Tonogi, K. (2010). Heterogeneity of capital stock and Multiple *q*. *The Economic Review, 61,* 325–341. (In Japanese).

Hayashi, F., & Inoue, T. (1991). The Relation between firm growth and *Q* with multiple capital goods: Theory and evidence from panel data on Japanese firms. *Econometrica, 59,* 731–753.

Hori, K., Saito, M., & Ando, K. (2006). What caused fixed investment to stagnate during the 1990s in Japan? Evidence from panel data of listed companies. *Japanese Economic Review, 57,* 283–306.

Hulten, C., & Wykoff, F. (1977), *Economic Depreciation of the US Capital Stock.* Report submitted to US Department of Treasury, Office of Tax Analysis, Washington, D.C.

Hulten, C., & Wykoff, F. (1981). The measurement of economic depreciation. In C. Hulten (ed.), *Depreciation inflation and the taxation of income from capital* (pp. 81–125). Washington, D.C.: Urban Institute.

Thurstone, L. L. (1947). *Multiple factor analysis,* University of Chicago Press.

Tonogi, K., Nakamura, J., & Asako, K. (2010). Estimation of Multiple q models of investment: Investment behavior over heterogeneous capital goods during the period of excess capacity reduction. *Economics Today*, *31*(2). (In Japanese).

Tonogi, K., Nakamura, J., & Asako, K. (2014). Heterogeneity of capital stocks in Japan: Classification by factor analysis. *Journal of Knowledge Management, Economics and Information Technology, 4*(2), 1–34.

Tonogi, K., Nakamura, J., & Asako, K. (2017). Heterogeneity of capital and investment behavior by acquisition mode—new construction, second-hand, and large-scale repair. *Rissho University, Economics Quarterly, 67*(2&3), 29–71. (In Japanese).

Chapter 7
Heterogeneity of Capital: Concluding Remarks

Abstract This chapter summarizes the research results obtained by the studies discussed in this book by applying the Multiple q model of capital investment. We conclude that the characteristics and features of capital stocks are considerably different enough that we can affirm that they are heterogeneous with respect to either their physical attributes or the qualitative classifications to which they belong. In modeling a firm's investment behavior reflecting the costs and benefits of adjusting each heterogeneous capital stock, we emphasize that costs do not necessarily exhibit the linearity and convexity on which the standard neoclassical investment theory is based, and from these deviations, the irreversibility and lumpiness of investments may emerge. We also point out that investment behavior is constrained by capital market imperfections, implying that scrutinizing the Multiple q model is not sufficient to eliminate the discrepancy between the theory and empirical performance of Tobin's q models.

Keywords Multiple q model · Heterogeneity of capital · Non-linear adjustment cost · Lumpy investment · Capital market imperfection

In this book, we first reviewed the development of capital investment research and clarified the present state-of-the-art understanding in this field from both theoretical and empirical viewpoints with a focus that emphasized but was not limited to developments in Japan. The starting point for line of analysis is that Tobin's q theory, although profoundly rooted in the microeconomic foundations of firms, has not been able to live up to expectations in empirical research. We then attempted to improve the empirical performance of Tobin's q theory of capital investment by incorporating the heterogeneity of capital goods and non-linear adjustment costs in investment. In doing so, we constructed a tractable Multiple q model and cultivated the available data by either creating data under alternative settings when data were missing or excavating unutilized micro survey data. Taken together, the empirical investigations described throughout this book strongly support our supposition that capital stocks

The content of and opinions in this chapter are solely attributable to the authors and are unrelated to any organizations with which the authors are affiliated.

K. Asako et al., *Multiple q and Investment in Japan*,
https://doi.org/10.1007/978-981-15-2981-8_7

are heterogeneous with respect to categories of capital goods, sizes of enterprises, and modes of capital acquisition.

7.1 The Multiple *q* Model: What Is Now Known

Asako, Kuninori, Inoue, and Murase (1989, 1997) analyzed the manufacturing industry and obtain estimates of the investment function (or the adjustment cost parameters) using two categories of capital goods, land and non-land capital stock, that is, all capital stock other than land. Their calculation of non-land capital stock followed the Proportional method, which is explained in Chap. 3 of this book. They created capital stock and gross investment series for multiple capital goods that considered differences in the price-change and capital deprecation rates for five categories of capital assets, including buildings, structures, and machinery, and totaled them together with inventory. That is, they focused on land within capital goods and carry out their analysis using two capital goods because, in those days, investments in land were very active in Japan alongside a rapid increase in asset prices; it was thought that treating land as a capital good (a quasi-fixed production factor) that incurs a unique adjustment cost at the time of investment might improve the goodness of fit of the q model.

For this reason, great care was taken in constructing the land data, and precise calculations were made for elements such as differences in the rates of increase of land values according to the purpose of use and location. Using cross-section data from each year, the validity of the following three models was tested: a Single q model that assumes away land as capital stock and excludes it; a Single q model that identifies land as capital and includes it; and a Multiple q model. In the Single q model that excludes land, land is not included in capital stock, reflecting the presupposition that investment in land incurs no adjustment costs and, thus, the Partial q of land is always equal to one, whereas, in the Single q model that does include land, land is homogeneous with other capital goods and can be added as is. In the Multiple q model, investments in land and investments in non-land capital stocks have different adjustment costs and, thus, land and non-land capital goods each have a different Partial q.

Asako et al. (1989), analyzing fiscal year 1977 to fiscal year 1987, show that, within the Single q framework, cases in which land is included in capital stock are more compatible with q theory than are cases in which it is not. In addition, the results of the estimations from the Multiple q model indicate clear differences in the estimated values of the adjustment cost parameters for land and non-land capital stock, indicating that the Single q model is not suitable. However, in some years, the estimated Partial Q of the Multiple q model takes a negative value (or the Partial q is less than one). Although the trend in the investment rate for non-land capital stock is more or less consistent with its estimated Partial Q, the investment rate for land is persistently positive even in years in which a negative Partial Q is obtained. Asako et al. (1989) argue that the Partial Q of land is negative because of a bubble in land prices and an excessively high price of land as a capital good.

Asako et al. (1997), who extend the analysis period to fiscal year 1994, in sequence with their previous study, try to answer the questions left unanswered by Asako et al. (1989) by making modifications, such as excluding the increase in the value of land due to the increase in real land prices from land investments by individual firms and using the concept of gross investment rather than that of net investment for non-land capital stock. As a result, whereas Asako et al. (1989) identify several years in which the Partial Q of non-land capital stock is negative, Asako et al. (1997) find that this value is positive every year with a stable and positive correlation with the gross investment rate, which is consistent with the theory. However, they find that the Partial Q of land, which is positive for several years in the analysis of Asako et al. (1989), is negative every year, and the result is once again inconsistent with the gross investment rate of land. Although land is a production factor with its own unique adjustment costs, according to their interpretation, this result might still have been caused by a bubble in land prices and the overestimation of its contribution as a production factor.

In Chap. 4 of this book, which originated from Tonogi, Nakamura, and Asako (2010), Asako and Tonogi (2010), and Asako, Nakamura and Tonogi (2016), we analyzed the Multiple q model based on unbalanced panel data from approximately 2,500 listed firms, including the non-manufacturing industry, covering fiscal year 1982 to fiscal year 2004 (divided into four periods in accordance with business cycle phases dated by the Cabinet Office). After subdividing non-land capital stock into four categories (i.e., buildings and structures; machinery and equipment; vessels and vehicles; and tools, furniture, and fixtures), we constructed a time series for gross investment and capital stock using three data construction methods with regard to the evaluation of the sale and retirement amounts for existing facilities, as was explained in detail in Chap. 3. We also added the cash flow and interest-bearing debt ratios as additional control variables, and we estimated the Multiple q investment function to obtain the following results.

First, the null hypothesis that the parameters relating to the adjustment costs of the five categories of capital goods, including land, are all equal was rejected for all four sample periods. Based on this result, considering the possibility of partial homogeneity, we tested the homogeneity between a certain capital good and the other four capital goods, which were regarded (tentatively) as homogeneous, and we conducted pairwise tests in which any two of the capital goods were homogeneous. We confirmed that, although partial homogeneity was not rejected in some cases, these combinations were not uniform across sample periods and the data construction methods for gross investment and capital stock, and we concluded that the Multiple q model should be used based on the assumption that these five capital goods are fundamentally heterogeneous.

However, the significance and robustness of the parameters of the adjustment cost function were not high. Even in cases with relatively high explanatory power using the Zero method, for which sales and retirements of existing facilities are uniformly considered to be zero, the cash flow and interest-bearing debt ratios, which should be inherently redundant in the framework of q theory, were estimated to have significant effects. Thus, we confirmed that factors remained that could not be explained by simply considering the heterogeneity of capital goods while still maintaining the same convex-type adjustment cost framework.

The parameter of the adjustment cost function was often estimated to be insignificant, perhaps owing to the influence of additional control variables. In addition, as was pointed out in Chap. 2, we also found major differences in the Partial q estimates of Asako and Tonogi (2010) depending on the analysis period and the data construction method. In contrast, the land Partial q (and not Partial Q) estimates were comparatively stable, and, regardless of the data construction method, they were significantly positive in the estimation periods up to bubble economy (1982–86, 1987–91) and significantly negative after the collapse of the bubble economy (1992–97, 1998–2004).

7.2 Non-linear Adjustment Costs and Lumpy Investment

The estimation results for the Multiple q model in Chap. 4, which were extended to include the possibility that the adjustment cost function contains a non-convex portion, further highlight the variety of forms of investment functions depending on the capital goods category, the estimation period, and whether new acquisition behavior is considered alone or integrated with sale and retirement behavior. That is, although we observed some cases that fit purely-convex adjustment cost functions, we confirmed that, overall, a majority of cases include non-convex portions, and even in these cases, the non-convex areas of the investment rate distribution varied considerably depending on the categories of capital goods and the estimation period. However, we have tested only a small portion of the possible adjustment processes created by various forms of heterogeneity.

As such, we present an overview of a future research agenda for the empirical analysis of capital investment using the Multiple q framework, excluding the extensions discussed in Chaps. 5 and 6. First, we should perform an estimation that more explicitly incorporates non-linearity by easing the so-called "curse of dimension" problem. As we have seen so far, the financial data for Japan's listed firms include detailed information pertaining to capital stock broken down by type of goods. These data present an ideal platform for analyzing the heterogeneity of capital goods, but they also poses a serious challenge to computational resources when trying to analyze goods-based information while preserving its integrity as much as possible. For this reason, the non-linearity of investment functions referenced in the present study is simply incorporated as forms that do not fit a linear relationship with q. As in Cooper and Haltiwanger's (2006) comprehensive adjustment cost function introduced in Chap. 1, a multiple-capital goods model that more explicitly includes several types of non-linearity could potentially be estimated by conducting a factor analysis in advance to consolidate the capital goods dimensions without losing essential information.[1]

A second agenda for further research is analyzing the adjustment process for sale and retirement behavior on its own. In the past, we have analyzed the heterogeneity of new acquisition behavior and sale and retirement behavior through data comparisons for only new acquisitions and for integrated data of new acquisitions and sales and retirements. This method is currently unavoidable for obtaining stable estimation results, as the sample of sales and retirements is small and the possibility of measurement error is considerably larger than in the case of new acquisitions. However, this method is an expediency and creates challenges in that it only indirectly analyzes sale and retirement behavior. By using micro data included in official statistics as well as the financial data that have accumulated since 2005, which have previously been excluded from the data sets used since Tonogi et al. (2010), we should look for opportunities to construct data that can withstand the analysis of sale and retirement behavior on its own.

Third, an important research agenda is exploring the possibility of extending the scope of capital stock as a quasi-fixed factor of production. Conventionally, for example, it was not uncommon to estimate the investment function by considering inventory as part of capital stock. In the future, given the growing importance of intangible assets amid economic growth and corporate management and the spread of leases for tangible fixed assets, they should perhaps also be considered part of the capital stock. This point is not limited to the Multiple q model but is a fundamental question posed for all of capital investment research, and broad consideration from the field is anticipated.

7.3 Heterogeneity of Capital by Enterprise Size and by Mode of Acquisition

In Chaps. 5 and 6, respectively, we extended the empirical analysis of the basic Multiple q model in several directions, mainly to test the heterogeneity of capital goods by enterprise size and by mode of acquiring capital goods. These investigations were made possible by newly mined datasets, namely, individual survey slip data from the Financial Statements Statistics of Corporations by Industry (FSSCI) released by Ministry of Finance in Chap. 5 and an original matching of microdata from the Cabinet Office and the Development Bank of Japan in Chap. 6.

In Chap. 5, we extended the Multiple q model to individual firm data that include small and medium-sized enterprises as well as large ones. To do so in a feasible way, we simply divided capital goods into land and non-land tangible fixed assets. The analysis period was set as ten years, from fiscal year 2004 to fiscal year 2013, to continue sequentially from the period covered in the previous chapters. Analyzing

[1] Examples include Chap. 6 of this book and Tonogi, Nakamura, and Asako (2014).

this period enabled us to see whether changes had occurred in the effects of the heterogeneity of capital goods since fiscal year 2004 for major enterprises. Our estimation results showed that, irrespective of enterprise size, land should be treated as an independent capital good that incurs unique adjustment costs. However, we also found that variables such as the debt ratio and tangibility, which are considered redundant under the standard Tobin's q theory, have significant explanatory power and that there are lumpy investment behaviors that cannot be handled by a smooth investment adjustment cost function. The lumpiness of investment behavior is higher for smaller firms, suggesting that capital market imperfections would constrain some lumpy investments.

In Chap. 6, we evaluated the heterogeneity of capital stock and investment behavior by focusing on and contrasting between the heterogeneity by type of capital good and the heterogeneity by capital acquisition mode. We mutually matched four categories of capital goods (buildings and structures, machinery and equipment, vessels and vehicles, and land) and three modes of acquisition (new construction, second-hand acquisitions, and large-scale repairs) using microdata from Cabinet Office and the Development Bank of Japan. We conducted analyses using two approaches: an estimation of the Multiple q investment function presupposing a convex adjustment cost function, as assumed in the q theory, and a factor analysis that assumed the possibility of a non-convex adjustment cost function.

The factor analysis confirmed that the factor loadings are similar within a given acquisition mode (i.e., new construction, second-hand acquisitions, and large-scale repairs) regardless of the capital good type. In other words, differences in acquisition mode are thought to have a greater influence on the adjustment cost parameter values for investment than the category of capital good has. When we combined the estimation results from the Multiple q model with those from the factor analysis, we found that the investment behavior around new construction can be explained (to some extent) by the convex adjustment cost function assumed by Tobin's q theory. At the same time, the results suggested the existence of non-convex adjustment cost functions for second-hand acquisitions and large-scale repairs. In addition, the results suggested that the factor for new construction has a strong relationship with the replacement investment ratio (or corporate growth).

Based on the above results, when we compared movements in the macro aggregated values of factors and the "investment motive" composition of the DBJ's "Survey on Planned Capital Spending," the factor for new construction was highly in correlation with investment motives closely tied to growth opportunities, such as research and development and the expansion of production capacity. Investment in second-hand goods spiked immediately after the global financial crisis of the late 2000s, which we interpret as the influence of investment behavior intended to avoid irreversibility. Moreover, large-scale repairs are said to be lumpy in nature, but this characteristic is likely to have been more strongly expressed given our chosen sample period, which includes the Great East Japan Earthquake. Thus, the reasons for inconsistency with the convex adjustment cost function differ for second-hand acquisitions and large-scale repairs.

To date, various models have been employed to explain firms' capital investment behavior, starting with Tobin's q model, based on the convex adjustment cost function, as well as the irreversibility of investment (adjustment costs that are asymmetric for positive and negative investments) and lumpy investment (adjustment costs that include fixed costs), among others. Our results in Chap. 6 showed that at least some of the heterogeneous activity in investment behavior is attributable to differences in investment behaviors by capital acquisition mode. Thus, the overall investment dynamics that encompass these heterogeneous investments can vary depending on the relative proportions of acquisition modes within a given period, and they can be smooth (consistent with the convex adjustment cost function) or lumpy (inconsistent with the convex adjustment cost function). However, our results may be strongly influenced by the analysis period, which includes the global financial crisis and the Great East Japan Earthquake. Future research topics therefore include conducting a longer-term analysis and checking the robustness of the results by extending the data to smaller, unlisted firms.

7.4 Epilogue

In concluding this book, we admit that works remains to be done to fill the gap between the theory and empirical practice of Tobin's q theory of investment. However, with respect to our main theme of the heterogeneity of capital goods, we have established the validity of the Multiple q model of investment when differentiating capital goods on the basis of both physical attributes and selected qualitative characteristics. We are therefore determined to further scrutinize our research surrounding the Multiple q model so as to both deepen and widen our understanding of investment behavior, especially in Japan.

Examples of such research agenda include evaluating the qualitative differences in capitals belonging to diversified industries within the same firm, as well as statistically testing the homogeneity between historically accumulated capital and newly acquired capitals through M&A (merger and acquisition), between domestic capital and those accumulated through FDI (foreign direct investment), and so on. Intangible capitals *vis-à-vis* tangible ones may also be a source of causing heterogeneity of capital on every stage from individual firm to industry and national economy. Differences in the ratio of intangible capital to tangible capital yield, *ceteris paribus*, differences in firm's TFP (total factor productivity) and thereby differences in respective equity prices in the financial market. The framework of the Multiple q model can identify the source of these differences with the estimated parameters of the respective investment adjustment cost functions.

References

Asako, K., Kuninori, M., Inoue, T., & Murase, H. (1989). Land evaluation and measurement of tobin's q theory/estimation of Multiple q. *Economics Today, 10*(3). (In Japanese).

Asako, K., Kuninori, M., Inoue, T., & Murase, H. (1997). Capital investment and land investment: 1977-1994. In K. Asako, & M. Otaki (Eds.), *Dynamics of modern macroeconomics* (pp. 323–349). University of Tokyo Press. (In Japanese).

Asako, K., Nakamura, J., & Tonogi, K. (2016). The Development of investment research and Multiple q in Japan. *International Journal of Finance and Accounting, 5*(5A) 1–29.

Asako, K., & Tonogi, K. (2010). Heterogeneity of capital stock and Multiple q. *The Economic Review, 61,* 325–341. (In Japanese).

Cooper, R., & Haltiwanger, J. C. (2006). On the nature of capital adjustment costs. *Review of Economic Studies, 73,* 611–633.

Tonogi, K., Nakamura, J., & Asako, K. (2010). Estimation of Multiple q models of investment: investment behavior over heterogeneous capital goods during the period of excess capacity reduction. *Economics Today, 31*(2). (In Japanese).

Tonogi, K., Nakamura, J., & Asako, K. (2014). Heterogeneity of capital stocks in Japan: Classification by factor analysis. *Journal of Knowledge Management, Economics and Information Technology, 4*(2), 1–34.

The manufacturer's authorised representative in the EU is Springer Nature Customer Service Centre GmbH, Europaplatz 3, 69115 Heidelberg, Germany. If you have any concerns regarding our products, please contact ProductSafety@springernature.com

Printed and bound by CPI Group (UK) Ltd, Croydon, CR0 4YY

30/09/2026

02225559-0001